MOBILIZING

AN ASIAN AMERICAN
COMMUNITY

In the series

Asian American History and Culture

edited by Sucheng Chan, David Palumbo-Liu, and Michael Omi

A list of additional titles in this series appears at the back of this book.

MOBILIZING

AN ASIAN AMERICAN

COMMUNITY

Linda Trinh Võ

Temple University Press
PHILADELPHIA

Temple University Press
1601 North Broad Street
Philadelphia PA 19122
www.temple.edu/tempress

Copyright © 2004 by Temple University
All rights reserved
Published 2004
Printed in the United States of America

⊖ The paper used in this publication meets the requirements of the American National
Standard for Information Sciences—Permanence of Paper for Printed Library Materials,
ANSI Z39.48-1992

Library of Congress Cataloging-in-Publication Data

Võ, Linda Trinh, 1964–
    Mobilizing an Asian American community / Linda Trinh Võ.
        p.   cm. — (Asian American history and culture)
    Includes bibliographical references (p.) and index.
    ISBN 1-59213-261-8 (cloth : alk. paper) — ISBN 1-59213-262-6 (pbk. : alk. paper)
    1. Asian Americans—California—San Diego—Social conditions—20th century.
2. Asian Americans—California—San Diego—Ethnic identity.   3. Asian Americans—
California—San Diego—Politics and government—20th century.   4. Asian Americans—Social conditions—Case studies.   5. San Diego (Calif.)—Social conditions—
20th century.   6. San Diego (Calif.)—Ethnic relations.   I. Title.   II. Series.

F869.S22V6 2004
305.895'0794985–dc22   2003068669

2   4   6   8   9   7   5   3   1

For my loving partner, Bill Ross,
and our children, Aisha and Kian—
who remind me always of what is important

and

For the San Diego Asian American community—
who taught me the meaning of having a voice

Contents

Acknowledgments

I must thank first and foremost the many individuals I met during my ethnographic fieldwork in the San Diego Asian community. They welcomed me so warmly and allowed me to observe and participate in their community. My deepest gratitude goes to those I interviewed for generously giving me their time and sharing with me the richness of their lives (their names are listed at the end of the manuscript). I have tried to present their stories from their perspectives so their voices may be heard, although I take full responsibility for the interpretations. My appreciation to the individuals who shared invaluable personal documents with me, especially Gil Ontai and Mary Ann Salaber, and to Margaret Iwanaga-Penrose for giving me access to the Union of Pan Asian Communities documents at San Diego State University library. I owe Amber Matthew a debt of thanks for helping me transcribe endless hours of taped interviews. My appreciation also to the artists and activists who allowed me to use the mural that graces the cover of this book—their struggles for social justice are not forgotten.

At the University of California, San Diego, I acknowledge the encouragement and guidance of Steve Cornell, Jeff Haydu, Yen Le Espiritu, Lisa Lowe, and David G. Gutiérrez, who as my dissertation committee members saw an earlier version of this project. They helped me sharpen my analytical skills and challenged me with their insightful comments. My deepest gratitude goes to Wendy Ng, Judith Liu, and Don Kelly for introducing me to the possibility of studying Asian Americans. I thank the faculty in the Department of

Ethnic Studies at UC San Diego for providing me with an intellectual home, especially Yen Espiritu, Ross Frank, Ramon Gutiérrez, Leland Saito, Paule Cruz Takash, and George Lipsitz, who has been especially encouraging. I was fortunate enough to participate in a graduate study group that provided me with camaraderie over many meals: Cindy Bauer, Berit Dencker, Ana Devic, Cristina Escobar, Laura Miller, Mary Rose Mueller, Margaret Ovenden, and Anna Szemere.

Many thanks to the colleagues who have enriched my life personally and intellectually over the years: Margaret Abraham, Jose Calderon, Sucheng Chan, KarenMary Davalos, Shilpa Davé, Pawan Dhingra, Hien Do, Augusto Espiritu, Tim Fong, Evelyn Nakano Glenn, Evelyn Hu-DeHart, Shirley Hune, Emily Ignacio, Victor Jew, Peter Kiang, Nazli Kibria, Becky King, Russell Leong, Nhi Lieu, Antoinette Charfauros McDaniel, Ken Maffitt, Martin Manalansan, Gina Masequesmay, Gail Nomura, Franklin Odo, Gary Okihiro, Edward Park, Lisa Sun-Hee Park, Isabelle Pelaud, Kristie Peterson, Vu Pham, Chandan Reddy, Dylan Rodriguez, Curtiss Takada Rooks, Marian Sciachitano, Jiannbin "J" Shiao, Paul Spickard, Brett Stockdill, Steve Sumida, Dana Takagi, David Takeuchi, Hung Thai, Charlene Tung, Kieu Linh Caroline Valverde, Brandy Liên Worrall, David Yoo, Henry Yu, and Helen Zia. I appreciate the warm support of my friends Susan Amick, Steve Amick, Andi Ricker, and Collin Tong. LeLy Hayslip and Shirley Cameron touched my life in ways they will never know. I thank Benson Tong for his sustaining support and friendship. Rick Bonus, an exceptional collaborator and friend, has been generous in all respects. Mary Yu Danico has enriched my life professionally and is an extraordinary friend.

At Oberlin College, where I was a visiting assistant professor, I wish to thank David Kamitsuka and other faculty, staff, and students for teaching me important lessons about the struggle for Asian American studies. I also learned much from my colleagues in the Department of Comparative American Cultures at Washington State University, especially Jose Alamillo, Kelly Ervin, Shelli Fowler, Yolanda Flores-Niemann, Rory Ong, Marcos Pizarro, and Theresa Schenck. My appreciation for the support of my colleagues in the Department of Asian American Studies at UC Irvine: Yong Chen, Dorothy Fujita-Rony, Ketu Katrak, Claire Jean Kim, Karen Leonard, John Liu, Glen Mimura, and Mary Ann Takemoto. June Kurata, Danielle McClellan, Tammy Sung, and Debbie Chu deserve thanks for their assistance. While at UCI, I have benefited greatly from knowing Victor Becerra, Jackie Dooley,

Raul Fernandez, Anne Frank, Tiana Johnson, Gil Gonzalez, Anna Gonzalez, Inderpal Grewal, Doug Haynes, Val Jenness, Laura Kang, Bill Landis, Sunny Lee, Nancy Naples, Vivian Price, Rowena Robles, Vicki Ruiz, David Smith, Prany Sananikone, and Rudy Torres. Sincere thanks to my talented research assistants Chris Cameron, Chiayu Chang, Nicole Chiu, Rosie Rimando, Jessica Shim, and especially Quan Tran, who has been so resourceful. Over the years at all the campuses with which I have been affiliated, I was fortunate to benefit from intellectual exchanges with numerous undergraduate and graduate students who sharpened my analytical skills and shared my commitment to building a meaningful intellectual community.

Bing Wong, a Chinese American restaurateur in San Bernardino, California, provided me with a scholarship to attend college, and I will always remember this. I thank the University of California Humanities Research Institute for providing me with a fellowship and appreciate the dialogues I had there with colleagues who helped me reshape this project. The University of California, Berkeley Chancellor's Postdoctoral Fellowship for Diversity, during which I was affiliated with Asian American Studies, gave me valuable time to revise this manuscript. The UC Irvine Humanities Center was also instrumental in providing crucial funding for this book project.

My thanks to my exceptional editor, Janet Francendese, at Temple University Press, who supported this project in its early stages and whose wise guidance has been invaluable. I appreciate the support of Michael Omi, the series editor, who has been extraordinarily generous with providing me constructive comments to reorganize and redefine my ideas. Thanks to Bobbe Needham and Lynne Frost for skillful copy editing and project management, as well as to Jennifer French, who moved production along so smoothly.

I thank my mother, Thuy Hanlon, for passing on her energy and determined nature to me. Thanks to my father, Robert Hanlon, for literally showing me much of the world and initially instilling in me an interest in sociology. My sister Christine has given me special support over the years. I am grateful to the Crosson, Cuthbert, Hassan, Langga, and Robinson families for their understanding and encouragement as well.

Since my undergraduate days, I have been extremely fortunate to have an amazing and devoted partner, Bill Ross, who has shared in my every accomplishment. Simple words of thanks cannot express my appreciation for all he has provided me—constant encouragement, editorial skills, wit, sharing of household chores and child-care responsibilities, and gentle reminders to "enjoy" life. Our children, Aisha and Kian, give me wonderful balance in my life and bring me an abundance of joy and laughter. I have learned much from seeing the world through their eyes.

My thanks to the editors and publishers who allowed me to include, in this book, sections of some chapters that have appeared in earlier publications:

Chapter Three includes revised sections from Linda Trinh Võ, "The Politics of Social Services for a 'Model Minority': The Union of Pan Asian Communities." Pages 241–272 in *Asian and Latino Immigrants in a Restructuring Economy: The Metamorphosis of Southern California*, edited by Marta López-Garza and David R. Diaz. Copyright © 2001 by the Board of Trustees of the Leland Stanford Jr. University. Used with the permission of Stanford University Press, www.sup.org.

Chapter Five includes revised sections from Linda Trinh Võ, "Asian Immigrants, Asian Americans, and the Politics of Economic Mobilization in San Diego." *Amerasia Journal* 22, no. 2 (1996): 89–108. Copyright © 1996 by the UCLA Asian American Studies Center. Used with permission of UCLA Asian American Studies Center Press.

MOBILIZING

AN ASIAN AMERICAN
COMMUNITY

1

Introduction

Paths of Resistance and Accommodation for Asian Americans

San Diego calls itself "America's Finest City." It is certainly admired for its ideal weather, miles of beautiful beaches, and manufactured tourist attractions, such as Sea World, the San Diego Zoo, Legoland, and Hotel Del Coronado. It is also known for its proximity to Mexico, as well as for its large military complexes, most notably its navy docks. However, it is not widely identified with having a large community of Asian Americans (more than 200,000), especially one that is engaging in social change.[1] Perhaps few people notice San Diego's Asian American communities because there is no recognizable "Chinatown" or compact Asian ethnic enclave that draws tourists searching for inexpensive trinkets, photo opportunities, or exotic meals. Rather than being concentrated in well-defined and highly visible areas, Asian Americans in San Diego are dispersed in residential pockets, where they blend into multiracial neighborhoods; their commercial clusters, which are located throughout the region, cater mainly to locals. In many ways, Asian residents, like other San Diegans, lead ordinary daily lives that go unnoticed. Nevertheless, they also engage in a wide array of political, cultural, social, and economic activities that are specific to their shared identity as Asian Americans.

In cities across the country, Asian Americans are often viewed as passive, quaint populations that are immune to anti-immigrant policies, civil rights backlash, labor exploitation,

1

glass-ceiling discrimination, hate crimes, and police mistreatment. This view regards Asian Americans as well integrated and accepted on equal terms into mainstream America, evidence that "multiculturalism" has been achieved. In fact, their histories and their lives today show a deep engagement with matters of racial justice. Asian Americans have challenged unjust immigration policies, antimiscegenation laws, prevention from U.S. citizenship, marginalization from educational institutions, exploitation in the workplace, exclusion from labor unions, and enforced residential segregation; when necessary, they have used their fists to defend themselves (Chan 1991; Takaki 1989a). Despite efforts to exclude them from America's borders and to marginalize them from every facet of U.S. life, Asian Americans have survived and persisted, and at times, even thrived.

Asian Americans in San Diego who work for social change are constrained by a shortage of resources, lack of access to elite positions of power, and profound differences within their group. The majority are foreign-born, with a substantial percentage being non-English or limited-English speaking; they have differing immigration histories and trace their ancestry to numerous countries; they are an economically stratified group with varying educations, occupations, and incomes; and they are spatially dispersed throughout urban and suburban areas. What interests could members of this group possibly share? What injustices affect them all? Do they have the ability to form coherent resurgent ideologies, leadership, and organizations? Despite the obstacles, Asian American coalitions have grown in San Diego, with increasing numbers of activists and organizations working to defend and advance their economic, social, cultural, and political interests. In this book, I look to these activists and their organizations to gain a more nuanced understanding of how people and groups negotiate and resist oppression on an everyday basis and to broaden our understanding of how racialized people of color engage in political action, as well as how they build and sustain a community.

This book is a critical analysis of how both the larger sociopolitical changes and the demographic transformations of the Asian American population affect its mobilization and activism and how these, in turn, affect the formation of Asian American organizations, communities, and identities. Marxist scholars, using the functionalist approach, theorized that industrial development and the processes of political and economic modernization are antithetical to ethnic persistence. However, my work supports scholars who have proposed that larger-scale cultural identities have survived, and that, in some cases, ethnic mobilization has been revitalized in modern societies (Nagel 1996; Smith 1981). In the contemporary period, social structures provide both opportunities and constraints for collective action for racialized groups. Asian American demographic shifts simultaneously hinder and enhance the availability of resources and the viability of collective struggle. Rather than seeing mobilization as a smooth, linear process for Asian Americans, I use the *interactive mobilization model* to show that it is a dialectical relationship between social order and human action marked by interplays of resistance and accommodation. This is an analysis of coalition building as much as of internal conflict within the Asian American community and with the greater San Diego community. It is about how Asian Americans have challenged San Diego to live up to its slogan, "America's Finest City." Although it is a story about San Diego, it could as easily describe other sites across the country where Asians reside.

The San Diego Case

My work builds and expands on the overviews of contemporary Asian American activism by Espiritu (1992) and Wei (1993), who focus on national Asian American activities and grassroots organizing in major cities such as San Francisco, New York, or Los Angeles and on selective moments. I focus on perhaps the less dramatic but no less important mobilization efforts that take place from the early 1970s to the mid-1990s in one setting. San Diego represents the type of mobilization that occurred, and continues to occur, in sites where Asians are perhaps fewer in number and do not hold confrontational street protests but are no less vigilant in their efforts to provide for the needs of their communities. What I captured in San Diego reflects myriad Asian American communities throughout the country where people struggle to organize diverse groups, find sufficient resources, create leaders, and define strategies. These daily occurrences may not capture media attention, but collectively and over time, they create social improvements for Asian Americans.

By contextualizing how and why mobilization emerges and evolves in one community over three decades, my study provides an understanding of long-term models of everyday forms of activism. In contrast to earlier studies, it explains the impact of recent demographic transformations on organizational resources and efforts. San Diego provided an ideal site because of the diversity of its Asian American population and the existence of both longstanding and newly formed Asian American organizations. I focus on various social, economic, political, and cultural pan-Asian organizing in San Diego to examine the contradictions and complexities of identity and community formations. In comparison to discussions of mobilization that focus on specific groups of Asian Americans, such as the Chinese and Japanese (Fong 1994; Saito 1998), I focus on organizational processes among a diverse population that includes Filipinos, Koreans, Southeast Asians, and, to some extent, South Asians. My study has broader implications for analyzing the complexity of mobilization at the national level, since nationwide organizations are based on regional and local organizational processes.

Bordered by the Pacific Ocean and Mexico, San Diego is the second-largest city in California and the sixth largest in the nation. In the 1990s, when I began my research, Asians were estimated to compose 8 percent of the San Diego County and 12 percent of the San Diego city population (U.S. Bureau of Census 1990c), and the growth of the latter correlates closely with the increasing percentage of Asians in the state as a whole. The Immigration Act of 1965 brought large-scale immigration from Asia, and the arrival of refugee populations in the post-1975 period added a new generation to a once dwindling Asian American population. San Diego reflects changes in California, where people of color are becoming the numerical majority, making it a prime site to also examine relations among Asian Americans and other racial groups.

Methodology

My research methodology involves both historical and ethnographic approaches. I collected historical data from the local libraries, historical foundations, the downtown redevelopment agency, local organizational archives, governmental institutions, and private individuals to piece together the history of Asian American organizations and mobilization in San Diego. For nearly two years, from 1992 to 1994, I conducted ethnographic fieldwork as both an observer and a participant. My project included attending, and sometimes participating in, primarily Asian American activities, including planning meetings, political events, ethnic festivals, community forums, redevelopment project discussions, business meetings, and informal gatherings. As part of my fieldwork, I was a board member of the San Diego chapter of the Asian Business Association (ABA) and served as its newsletter editor. My involvement in this organization gave me wider entrée into the Asian

American community, because many of the individuals involved in ABA were also involved in various other single-ethnic and pan-Asian organizations and activities. I told all those I regularly interacted with that I was there to study Asian American organizations (Võ 2000). The kind of data I was able to gather differed according to the origin and development of the organization or the processes of organizational activities.

In addition to my fieldwork, I completed thirty formal interviews with Asian American activists and informal interviews with Asians and non-Asians involved with Asian American activities.[2] What I have captured is a glimpse of a lifetime endeavor for many, while for others it consumes only a phase of their life. The individuals I had close contact with and those I chose to interview to some extent reflect the great diversity of the Asian American population in terms of ethnicity, immigration history, class background, political viewpoint, and organizational strategy. However, these organizational leaders do not represent a cross section of the Asian population in San Diego; they are a select group who play key roles in assessing the needs of the community, defining the agenda for the community, and representing the Asian American community to the larger society. There are multiple levels of power, and being a recognized Asian American community leader does not mean one is powerful in the larger society. Such differential distinctions of power are important if we are to understand why Asian American activists continue to mobilize for social justice and racial equality.

Ethnographic fieldwork is an interactive and subjective process. Although I was considered an insider because of my ethnic ancestry as a Vietnamese American, there were also noticeable differences—including ethnic, cultural, political, generational, class, educational, sexual, gender, and linguistic—between my Asian American informants and myself that shaped the process of my research project (Võ 2000). As I immersed myself in the community, I was constantly negotiating these differences while also figuring out how others positioned themselves. I have tried to present the voices and actions of those I studied with respect and sensitivity, even when I did not agree with their ideologies or strategies. However, I am quite aware that the data collected and the analysis of the data are colored by my biases and agendas as a scholar and activist. Given the complex nature of fieldwork, this study is a selective and partial collection of facts, observations, interviews, and interpretations—essentially snapshots of an evolving, dynamic community, with highlights of some of its members.

Racialization, Mobilization, and Resistance

Although we understand that race is not biologically fixed or determined but socially and politically constructed, racialized groups realize, through their individual and institutional interactions, that it has
real implications for their everyday lives (Omi and Winant 1986). Asian
immigrants recognized early on that regardless of their ethnic differences, they were lumped together by the larger society under the terms
"Asiatic," "Mongolian," and "Oriental" (Espiritu 1992; Heizer and
Almquist 1971). They also recognized that this imposed racial categorization determined their subordinate position in the racial hierarchy
and was used as a basis for their economic, social, and political exclusion (Almaguer 1994). Beginning in the 1960s, they rejected the commonly used term "Oriental" because of its negative connotation, renaming themselves "Asian Americans," a term coined by Yuji Ichioka, and
this discursive strategy became a symbol of resistance and opposition
(Espiritu 1992). Rather than using the term "panethnic" to describe this
process, I prefer "pan-Asian," since it emphasizes this process as one of
"racialization," signifying it as dynamic and interactive.

In addition to the perceptions of the larger society, state bureaucra-
cies, unwilling to deal with the intricacies of subgroup difference, initiate new aggregate racial categories that can inadvertently activate
group mobilization (Nagel and Olzak 1982). These classification systems, once institutionalized, become the basis for the distribution of
resources by presenting groups with a particular logic for collective
action (Cornell 1988; Davis 1991; Kasinitz 1992; Nagel 1996; Padilla
1985; Woldemikael 1989). In this instrumental model of group formation, the institutional structures provide the incentive to mobilize for
competitive entitlement programs designated for disadvantaged minority groups, such as the equitable distribution of economic resources, fair
political representation, and access to social services (Glazer and Moynihan 1963; Yancey, Ericksen, and Juliani 1976). All my respondents recognized this process; for example, a Japanese American woman elaborates on the need to organize collectively: "So, I think it makes sense,
if they're lumping us together, we might as well become more cohesive
as a group and at least support each other. Hopefully that will help us
in the long run."

Racialized groups do not merely accept the labels imposed upon
them by dominant group members or institutions; they have some
power to reshape these categories (Gutiérrez 1995). Public and private

institutions have used the racial classification "Asian American" partly because of their own political agendas and partly to accommodate the demands of this group, but the usage has not been uniform, which furthers the ambiguity over the Asian American category. Asians themselves continually reconstruct the boundaries of "Asian America," not necessarily in alignment with the category conceived by the government. Thus, racialized group formation is constructed by external ascription and internal self-definition—it is emergent, malleable, and variable, not an ascribed constant, and is shaped by material interests, as well as by concrete organizational and conceptual possibilities and constraints.

A social movement has been defined as "a type of behavior in which a large number of participants consciously attempt to change existing institutions and establish a new order of life" (Blumberg 1991: 191). Resource-mobilization models emphasize variables for collective action and focus on how groups, through collective protest, manipulate resources and institutions (Zald and McCarthy 1979). Social movements range from spontaneous informal protests to more formal collective actions that include the development of organizations (McCarthy and Zald 1977). Mobilization includes a wide range of tactics, from mass-based protest to lobbying politicians, and the strategies a group adopts depend partly on the resources available to it. Groups may vary in the type of resources they possess, such as numbers, money, organizations, human capital, networks, and leaders. Not all resources are equally important all the time; their value can fluctuate according to circumstances (Jenkins 1983). Furthermore, having organizational resources does not lead to social change unless one can mobilize them (McAdam 1982). These social movement theories apply especially to protest movements (Gamson 1975; Morris 1984), revolutions (Tilly 1978), and state- and nation-building (Young 1976). However, resistance and mobilization have varying operative forms, for, as Comaroff so eloquently puts it, "if we confine our historical scrutiny to the zero-sum heroics of revolution successfully achieved, we discount the vast proportion of human social action which is played out, perforce, on a more humble scale. We also evade, by teleological reasoning, the real questions that remain as to what *are* the transformative motors of history" (1985: 261).

Social structures set the parameters of collective action for oppositional groups (Enloe 1981; Piven and Cloward 1979). As Marx states in an often quoted but appropriate comment: "Men make their own history, but they do not make it just as they please; they do not make it under circumstances chosen by themselves, but under circumstances directly encountered, given and transmitted from the past" (1987: 15). Anti-hegemonic projects are not isolated from the hegemony in which they exist, and groups resist within the constraints placed upon them by the hegemonic structure. Asian Americans employ both conformist and oppositional political strategies, so they practice a *politics of resistance* and a *politics of accommodation* simultaneously (Ortiz and Marin 1989). They use their organizations to challenge the dominant power structure, but their goal is to be incorporated into this structure, namely U.S. society, thereby sustaining the existing social order; I explore this paradox later in my book.

During the 1960s and 1970s, reflecting a period of social upheaval in this country, the political strategies of community activists and racial groups were more confrontational. As sociopolitical circumstances changed, groups began to lean toward tactics that emphasized working with institutions to resolve group concerns. At the time of the Yellow Power movement, Asian American activists were involved in confrontational, radical political struggles against colonialism, imperialism, and capitalism, particularly the Third World Liberation movement (Ho 2000; Louie and Omatsu 2001; Nakanishi 1985–1986). They protested the Vietnam War, created their own media publications, demanded Asian American studies courses on university campuses, and formed community-based organizations (Omatsu 1994; Wei 1993). However, we cannot regard the 1960s and 1970s model of activism as the only one for Asian Americans. In the post–civil rights era, the protest politics of direct confrontation has been replaced or augmented by the politics of incorporation (Browning, Marshall, and Tabb 1984). The earlier era brought new opportunities and resources for communities of color and produced a level of Asian American activism not possible earlier. A new generation of U.S.-born and foreign-born activists have appropriated the term "Asian American," reshaping and reconceptualizing it as a means of incorporation into mainstream society. Although newer activists may not fully grasp the historical context of the term or its connection to those radical power movements, they assert their need to construct their own movement frames in a very different historical moment.

Rapid demographic growth strengthened Asian American clout, because larger numbers give the group more leverage; yet coordinating the ever-increasing population has made mobilization more challenging because of its ethnic, generational, gender, sexual, political, linguistic, and class differences. During the late 1960s and early 1970s, U.S.-born Chinese and Japanese Americans dominated the Asian American movement, but by the 1980s, other ethnic groups rivaled them in dominance. Asian socioeconomic resources changed dramatically by the early 1990s with the influx of new immigrants from Asia who were well educated and skilled, and the economic mobility of the native-born population, which made more human and material capital available to Asian American organizations. While class differences make it difficult for Asian Americans to organize (Espiritu and Ong 1994), I argue that class is only one factor that can lead to fragmentation, and in many instances, it is not the most significant barrier. It is assumed that the U.S.-born population plays an active role in Asian American mobilization, while the crucial role of first-generation immigrants has been neglected (but see Saito and Horton 1994). By the late 1980s in San Diego, first-generation Asian immigrants and migrants had revitalized existing Asian American organizations and were playing a primary role in creating new ones. These examples present some of the factors that divide Asian Americans, but as I argue throughout my book, these same factors are beneficial for community organizing.

Organizations, Communities, and Identities

Mobilization manifests itself most clearly in formal organizations and is one representation of a group's efforts to counter its marginal position in the institutional life of the larger society. More importantly, the continuing existence of race-based organizations whose goal is to create social change indicates that groups feel that racial inequities and injustices persist in our society. They bring to the fore the disjuncture between U.S. ideals of democracy and its practices of racism, personal and institutional, that impact Asian Americans. In the mid-1800s, Alexis de Tocqueville (1969) recognized the crucial role that civic associations play in the democratizing process in U.S. society. In the modern period, these formally structured organizations help bring about legal, legislative, and social reforms for oppressed groups and assist in the strategic coordination of human and material resources (Piven and Cloward 1979; Morris 1984). Organizational development has become the foundation on which racialized groups sustain collective action.

Participating in organizations is not a novel concept for Asian Americans. Since their arrival in the United States, they have formed social, cultural, religious, economic, and political organizations, and this process continues today. The ebb and flow of Asian American organizations I studied depended on the activists, issues, resources, and political climate. Through my research, I was able to contextualize the web of relationships between individuals and organizations, making it possible for me to analyze the varying organizational patterns that developed. Whether created as a defensive response to external actions or as a proactive strategy, whether built within institutionalized frameworks or outside them, whether short-lived or enduring, these organizations provided a forum for interaction among Asian American individuals and groups in a formalized setting, making possible constructions of community and identity.

What constitutes a "community" has been a persistent question among social science researchers. Sociologists have focused on the negative impact of industrialization, urbanization, and bureaucratization on the breakdown of interpersonal contact and communal solidarity, which result in the decline or dissipation of community (Suttles 1972).[3] Modernity is characterized by fragmentation and isolation, yet a sense of community can be derived from participation in associations (Bellah et al. 1985). The persistence of ethnic community is often discussed in a social and spatial sense, as "an aggregate of people who occupy a common and bounded territory within which they establish and participate in common institutions" (Gans 1962: 104). However, individuals can have a wide array of interpersonal networks in neighborhoods, in kinship systems, and in occupational structures within a spatially defined territory; proximity is not an absolute precondition, since close networks can exist in unbounded areas (Tilly 1973; Wellman 1979). Thus, an ethnic boundary is not a geographic or a territorial one; rather it is a social boundary that unites individuals, reflected in the institutions and organizations of the community (Barth 1969). It is no longer assumed that the dissolution of ethnic concentrations and increased occupational mobility will lead to a decline in ethnic connections.

While these theories do not explicitly address Asian Americans, they implicitly allow for the reconceptualization of Asian American communities as spatially unbounded networks. Recent scholarship on Asian Americans has investigated the territorial as well as the discursive spaces where social, cultural, and political manifestations of Asian American identities and communities are constructed (Bonus 2000; Võ and Bonus 2002). In San Diego, Asian Americans occupy separate locales, with only a few concentrated neighborhoods, but despite limited daily interaction on either the individual or group level, they are connected through organizational networks. It is also through organizational components that Asian Americans forge a social sense of community, albeit an evolving one, that participants, and outsiders too, recognize. When members of the mainstream society want to dispense information to the Asian American community or elicit its views, they direct their requests to organizational leaders and members, thereby reinforcing the existence of such a community. Similar to Anderson's (1983) concept of nations, the constructivist approach conceives of a racialized group as an "imagined community" that is capable of reinventing itself. While community studies tend to privilege homogeneity, I focus on the ways in which a community, to survive, must constantly acknowledge its heterogeneity. Although I often employ the term "community," I am cognizant of its internal multiplicity and interchangeably use the plural term "communities" to denote the array of voices.

The boundaries of community and citizenship can be quite porous for Americans of Asian ancestry in an age of globalization, especially with a large immigrant population that is connected to homelands in Asia, in addition to other locations (Hu-DeHart 1999; Ong 1999). They may have transnational links, for example, with relatives who remain in the homeland or as a consequence of entrepreneurial ties or political affinities. Outsiders also remind them that they "belong" over there because of their racial features. At times, Asian Americans distance and disengage themselves from these transnational links and portray themselves as loyal "Americans" who should be treated accordingly. In other cases, using their biculturalism, they position themselves as transnational subjects, essentially the "bridge" between America and Asia and, ironically, attempt to use this affiliation to enhance their status in America. This positioning depends on their lived experiences, material capital, political socialization, and desired goals; most important, it can vary depending on circumstances. I examine how these transnational connections, real or imagined, impact the formation of the local Asian American community, as well as how members maneuver their global connections and disconnections to Asia.

Although the focus of my research is Asian Americans, I examine their relationship and analyze their efforts at collective organizing with other racial communities. Being categorized with other "minority" groups, such as African Americans, Latinos, and Native Americans, has forced them to recognize their shared experiences of discrimination and to consider how they might benefit from coalitions with other racialized communities. Yet, other racial groups are wary of the influx of post-1965

Asian immigrants and refugees, whom they perceive as either competitors for employment, housing, and governmental assistance (Thornton and Taylor 1988) or as members of an "advantaged" population. I show, throughout my book, the incentives and rewards that encourage racial groups to build coalitions, as well as the conditions that make for racial competition and strife between these racial communities.

I have a separate chapter on identity formation, but the social construction of an Asian American identity is central to *each* chapter. I treat identity work as an amorphous, interactive entity that is based less on a common culture than on shared personal, political, and economic experiences and goals. Impersonal structures intersect with personal experiences to encourage a racialized oppositional consciousness and collective action (Kelley 1994; Morris 1984; Takahashi 1997). For racialized populations, a shared perception of grievances and structural inequalities can lead to group affirmation and group assertion in a concerted struggle for racial equity. As George Lipsitz so succinctly puts it: "People exploited as a group logically seek group solutions to their common problems" (1988: 230). The construction of an Asian American identity and a politicized group consciousness is often a response to internal pressures and external structures. Rather than assume that highly race-conscious individuals joined these organizations, I found that organizations played a fundamental role in shaping the community, as well as politicizing its members. Mobilization is more than just an instrumental strategy; organizations can create social networks for mutual support and camaraderie that help produce and sustain an Asian American consciousness.

Overview of the Book

Organized by general chronological periods extending over three decades, from the early 1970s to the mid-1990s, this book analyzes the ways in which the community, as a collective, intervened on issues that mattered to its members and their efforts to find their own voice. The emergence of particular forms of organizations in San Diego is not exclusive to a specific decade; rather there are continuous shifts and overlaps in the mobilization processes of Asian Americans. My intent is to explain the issues that encouraged Asian Americans to organize and the factors that are conducive or unfavorable to mobilizing effectively. Throughout, I focus on how demographic transformations as well as larger political and economic changes shape mobilization efforts. As networks enlarged and resources emerged, the community expanded the possibilities for organizing, adding new complexity to their voices and agendas. Chapter Two presents a historical overview of the pattern of Asian immigration and settlement in San Diego County since the mid-1800s.

In Chapter Three, I analyze the formation of the Union of Pan Asian Communities, a nonprofit social service organization developed in the early 1970s in response to the state's policy on allocating funding. The organization was pivotal in gaining funds and creating programs for impoverished Asian immigrants and refugees, a group literally ignored by mainstream governmental agencies. Chapter Four examines how Asian Americans mobilized to counter anti-Asian racial stereotypes on a local television show and later a radio show. In the fifth chapter, I focus on the formation of an Asian American business organization that has worked on protecting its members' economic interests and on providing new economic opportunities, domestically and internationally. Chapter Six discusses how a group that lacks political clout, strong political leadership, and a clear political agenda manages to strategically mobilize a fragmented community to become involved in the mainstream electoral process.

Chapter Seven documents how and why a spatially dispersed Asian American population attempts to bring together its resources to have a meaningful voice in the redevelopment process of the Asian American historic district in downtown San Diego. In Chapter Eight, I analyze the formation of multilayered, multifaceted, and evolving Asian American identities from the perspective of the activists. They bring to their organizational efforts varying concepts of identity, which are often reshaped while working in the community organizations. The concluding chapter notes what factors continue to shape the character of Asian American identities, organizations, and communities. This is a study as much about collaboration and consensus as about contradictions and controversies, as much about continuities as about disjuncture.

I wanted to find out precisely how, in the post–civil rights era when Asian Americans were given some avenues of entrance into the U.S. mainstream, these individuals and groups altered their strategies and negotiated their differences. The argument I make is that no single tension exists in mobilization or coalition work, and more important, the conflict is not always over racial or ethnic differences, as many people assume. My intent was to understand how various tensions manifest themselves in the mobilization process for Asian Americans—differences in gender, sexuality, class, personality, language, generation, or immigration status, in addition to different ideologies, strategies, or resources that impact the development of various kinds of organizations. I show how these tensions have transformed over time for the community and examine how they change with the circumstances and the issues (economic, political, social, or cultural) in one community. I also pay attention to how Asian Americans construct their relationship with Asia and how they connect with other racialized communities of color.

Conclusion

My study examines the dialectical processes of Asian American mobilization, which is shaped by interactions between Asian Americans and by contestations between Asian Americans and the larger society. Even as they continue to question the racialization of their diverse communities, Asian Americans recognize the efficacy of strategically employing the racial model. Asians in the United States have what can be considered conventional goals and agendas—they want to participate in the social, political, economic, and cultural life of this country. The paths they have chosen are at times rather conventional, at other times pragmatic yet unconventional. Ironically, even with a more diverse Asian American population geographically dispersed throughout the San Diego area, Asian American organizations there have gained momentum.

2

Asian Immigration and Settlement in San Diego

My fieldwork and interviews heightened my awareness of the heterogeneity of the Asian American population. I met individuals whose family members came to the United States as laborers, missionaries, railroad workers, war brides, refugees, military personnel, and professionals, as documented and undocumented immigrants. I interacted with new immigrants who came as children, as college students, and as adults who were twice or even thrice immigrants. They were employed in a diversity of occupations; their proficiency in English varied, as well as their ability to speak additional languages; and they had varying political philosophies. They had grown up in ethnic enclaves, white suburbs, and multiracial neighborhoods and on U.S. military bases. Some were multiethnic or multiracial Asian Americans. There were transnational migrants who made frequent business or social trips to Asia, while others had never left California. The variety even among those born abroad was evident at one of the monthly community meetings, when I discovered that none of the eight individuals dining at my table, myself included, had taken a direct route from Asia to the United States, nor did we fit into the general immigration patterns for our particular ethnic group.

Among the many factors that affect the ebb and flow of immigration of Asians to this country and San Diego are global economic systems, immigration regulations, U.S. foreign relations, sociopolitical events in Asia, and domestic labor policies. Factors in their countries of origin that push them to emigrate include war, natural disaster, conscription, and economic or political instability. The United States offers pull factors, such as educational and economic opportunities or reunion with loved ones (Barringer, Gardner, and Levin 1993). While some leave their homeland and come directly to the United States, others follow the indirect or stepwise migration route by settling in an intermediary country before arriving here (Barkan 1992), so they have been "twice displaced" or even "thrice displaced." In comparison to earlier generations, current immigrants from Asia are more ethnically, culturally, and economically diverse. Tracing the Asian settlement pattern in San Diego shows how this pattern is similar to their settlement in other cities, and also depicts the uniqueness of the San Diego case.

San Diego County, situated in the southwest corner of California, is about the size of the state of Connecticut and stretches sixty-five miles north to south and eighty-six miles west to east. It is 125 miles south of Los Angeles, 500 miles south of San Francisco. In the 1990s when I began my fieldwork, San Diego County's 4,261 square miles had a population of 2.5 million and included eighteen incorporated cities and several unincorporated communities (see Figure 1).[1] The county is bounded on the north by Orange and Riverside Counties, on the east by the agricultural communities of Imperial County, on the west by the Pacific Ocean, and on the south by Tijuana, part of Baja California, Mexico. In 1848, after the Mexican-American War, the Treaty of Guadalupe Hidalgo forced Mexico to cede northern portions of its territory, including the San Diego area, to the United States. The city of San Diego is 324 square miles, with a total population of 1,110,549 in 1990. San Diego proper was incorporated in 1850 just after California became the thirty-first state; it surpassed San Francisco as the second-largest city in California in the mid-1970s.

Early Settlement, 1850s to World War II

Between the mid-1800s and World War II, the Asian population in San Diego was primarily Chinese, Japanese, and Filipino. The first major influx of Chinese to the West Coast came during the Gold Rush period starting in 1848, while others were recruited as unskilled contract laborers to work on the construction of the transnational railroad (Daniels 1988). In California, Chinese male laborers numbered 20,000 in 1852; 56,000 in 1860, when one of every ten individuals in the state was Chinese; and 75,000 by 1880. To discourage the Chinese from settling per-

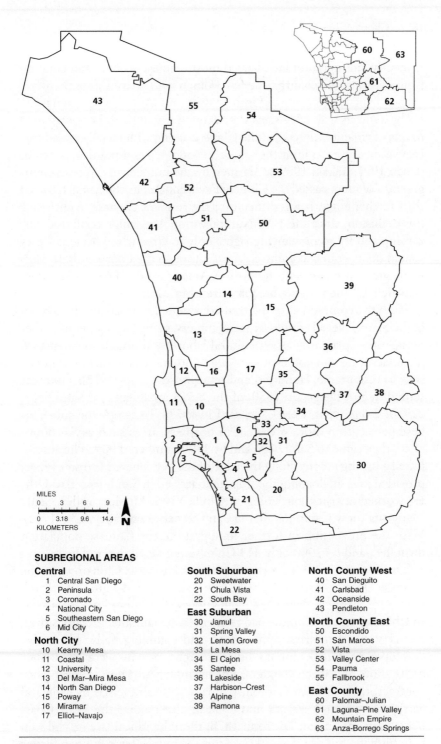

SUBREGIONAL AREAS

Central
1 Central San Diego
2 Peninsula
3 Coronado
4 National City
5 Southeastern San Diego
6 Mid City

North City
10 Kearny Mesa
11 Coastal
12 University
13 Del Mar–Mira Mesa
14 North San Diego
15 Poway
16 Miramar
17 Elliot–Navajo

South Suburban
20 Sweetwater
21 Chula Vista
22 South Bay

East Suburban
30 Jamul
31 Spring Valley
32 Lemon Grove
33 La Mesa
34 El Cajon
35 Santee
36 Lakeside
37 Harbison–Crest
38 Alpine
39 Ramona

North County West
40 San Dieguito
41 Carlsbad
42 Oceanside
43 Pendleton

North County East
50 Escondido
51 San Marcos
52 Vista
53 Valley Center
54 Pauma
55 Fallbrook

East County
60 Palomar–Julian
61 Laguna–Pine Valley
62 Mountain Empire
63 Anza-Borrego Springs

FIGURE 1. San Diego Subregional Areas
Source: SANDAG, The San Diego Association of Governments, March 1991.

manently, immigration laws barred most Chinese women and children from entering the country; the few women who arrived were the wives of merchants or were forced into prostitution. Anti-Chinese agitation, led by nativists who felt Asians were economic competitors, contributed to acts of violence directed at the Chinese, along with racially biased legislative measures to limit their social, economic, and political activities (Chan 1991; Takaki 1989a). Alarmed by the number of Chinese immigrants, Congress passed the Chinese Exclusion Act in 1882, which barred their further entry. It was difficult for the resident Chinese to challenge this exclusion, since the 1790 Naturalization Act, which conferred citizenship and its accompanying rights only to "free white persons," prevented them from becoming citizens. Although the Fourteenth Amendment granted citizenship to African Americans in 1868, Asians were classified as "aliens ineligible for citizenship" until the 1940s.

With the completion of the transcontinental railroad and forced out of the Sierra-Nevada mines by white miners, many Chinese found other occupations, primarily as agricultural laborers, although some entered manufacturing and domestic service and others started small businesses such as restaurants, laundries, and retail stores (Light 1972); a number settled in San Diego. In 1880, of the 8,618 inhabitants of San Diego, 229, or 2.6 percent, were Chinese (Liu 1977). To escape the anti-Chinese persecution more prevalent in northern areas such as San Francisco, they came to San Diego and by 1890 numbered 909. They established a fishing colony along the edge of the bay, where Horton's Wharf provided jobs off-loading the ships that arrived in San Diego Bay. Others worked at truck gardening in Chula Vista, Mission Valley, Santa Margarita (now Camp Pendleton), and Sweetwater Valley (Chu 1982). With the prevention of further immigration, the Chinese population dwindled, and by 1900 only 414 Chinese remained in San Diego.

The Chinese were segregated in an area known as Chinatown or the Chinese Quarter, part of the Stingeree District, a red-light district well known for brothels, dance halls, and saloons that catered to Caucasians. In Chinatown, the Chinese had residences, restaurants, grocery stores, herbal stores, laundries, opium dens, and gambling halls. There also developed an elite group of Chinese merchants, who were often labor contractors and moneylenders. For example, Ah Quin, a local labor contractor, came from Canton, China, to San Francisco in 1868 and worked as a house servant and cook in cities along the West Coast before settling in San Diego in 1878; there he raised twelve children with his wife, Sue (M. Lee 2002). After the railroad was built and labor contracting was no longer profitable, Ah Quin concentrated on his produce store and property-management business and became the unofficial mayor of Chinatown (Novarro 1986). The residential clusters and their shared occupational patterns reinforced a sense of community for those who lived in the Chinatown area, referred to as "bachelor societies" given the predominance of males.

Shortly after immigration from China was suspended, the Japanese were recruited to replace the Chinese as cheap laborers. Like the Chinese, the Japanese, who first arrived in San Diego between 1885 and 1887, worked as railroad laborers, farmers, fishermen, and merchants (Estes 1978). By 1908, there were 55,000 Japanese on the mainland and 150,000 in the Hawaiian Islands (Shinagawa and Jang 1998). With the assistance of a more powerful home government than the Chinese, the Japanese brought wives with them or used the "picture bride" practice, a form of arranged marriage, so they were able to establish families (Ichioka 1988). Under pressure from the U.S. government, the Japanese government agreed to prevent further immigration of Japanese in the Gentlemen's Agreement of 1907–1908.

Like the Chinese, many Japanese came south to escape the anti-Japanese activity in northern California, although they were not entirely free of it in San Diego. Japanese farmers or seasonal laborers grew vegetables or worked in the packing sheds in areas such as Bonita, Chula Vista, La Mesa, Lemon Grove, Mission Valley, Oceanside, Otay Mesa, Pacific Beach, Palm City, San Marcos, Spring Valley, and Vista (Estes 1978). Since Caucasian brokers refused to sell the produce grown by the Japanese, they established their own cooperative, the Vegetable Growers' Market, at 400 Sixth Street. In 1887, Azumagasaki Kikumatsu opened Go Ban to import Japanese goods, the city's first Japanese-owned and -operated business, which was followed by other retail businesses (Estes 1978). Japanese women worked in farming, small businesses, or local canneries. The Japanese were clustered in downtown areas next to Chinatown, where they opened up pool halls, restaurants, barbershops, and boardinghouses. While some lived in the segregated downtown areas, many Japanese farmers and laborers lived in more undeveloped parts of San Diego, but the downtown area remained the center of religious, cultural, and social events.

By the time the Immigration Act of 1924 was passed, limiting immigration of southern and eastern Europeans to the United States and also excluding "aliens ineligible for citizenship," meaning Asians, immigration from China and Japan had slowed to a trickle. A new cheap labor pool was introduced to the country and to San Diego—Filipinos. In 1898 after the Spanish-American War, the Philippines became a U.S. protectorate, and Filipinos were classified as U.S. nationals. While barred from citizenship, they were allowed to travel freely to the United States, and California agriculturists, as well as Hawaiian plantation owners, recruited workers from the Philippines, mainly from Ilocos, Visayan, and Manila, and also tried to use them to quell labor agitation. In the 1920s, Filipinos in the United States as students or *pensionados* were joined by farm laborers, commonly called *manongs*, many of whom hoped to attain education and wealth (Castillo 1976). In 1930, there were 108,260 Filipinos in the country, with 30,470 in California, and this predominantly male population experienced the same harsh exclusions directed at other Asians (Bonus 2000).

It is estimated that 48 Filipinos lived in the city of San Diego in 1920, 394 in 1930, and 800 in 1940; however, these census figures may only be approximate, given the migratory nature of the population at the time (Melendy 1977). During the Depression, restrictionists, attempting to curb what they perceived to be an influx of competitive "foreign" laborers, pushed for the passage of the 1934 Tydings-McDuffie Act, which would make the Philippines an independent commonwealth in ten years. Once the act passed, Filipinos were reclassified as immigrant aliens like other Asians, which subsequently limited their entrance to the United States to 50 persons per year (Shinagawa and Jang 1998). The scant historical records in San Diego indicate that Filipinos had their own businesses, frequented Chinese and Japanese businesses, and congregated in the sections of town "reserved" for Asians. Economic conditions and the prevailing racial segregation, formal and informal, forced this early generation of Asian immigrants together in confined geographic and social spaces.

The Turning Point: World War II, Citizenship, and Suburbanization, 1940s–1950s

After World War II, there were dramatic changes in the Asian population in San Diego. In 1943, to reward China for being an ally, Congress repealed the 1882 Chinese Exclusion Act and allotted a quota of 105 immigrants of Chinese ancestry per year (Reimers 1985). The Naturalization Act of 1790 was amended to include the Chinese, who could become naturalized citizens. Asian Indians, along with Filipinos, were given the right of naturalization in the Luce-Cellar bill of 1946. The

Philippines was granted independence in 1946, and Filipinos, then barred from immigration along with individuals from other countries in the "Eastern Hemisphere," were allotted 100 immigrant slots (Yu 1980). In 1952, the McCarran-Walter Immigration and Nationality Act made minor improvements by abolishing the Asiatic-barred zone established in 1917 but limited immigration to two thousand for those from countries in the Asia-Pacific triangle (Hing 1993). While the act did little to change the level of Asian immigration, it gave naturalization rights to the Japanese and Koreans.

These changes in immigration affected the gender composition of the Asian American population; for the first time a significant number of Asian women entered the country. With China as a U.S. ally during World War II, Congress amended the War Brides Act of 1945, which originally did not include Asian American veterans, to allow these servicemen to bring home Asian wives on a nonquota basis (S. Chan 1991; Yuh 2002). During the war, Chinese American soldiers stationed overseas brought back more than six thousand Chinese wives. The U.S. military presence throughout Asia in later decades, particularly in Japan, Korea, the Philippines, Taiwan, Thailand, and Vietnam, led to marriages between American men and Asian women. Through the 1952 McCarran-Walter Act, these women entered not as war brides but as nonquota immigrants; most were married to Americans of non-Asian ancestry (S. Chan 1991). Because of the large number of military personnel in the San Diego area, there has been a concentration there of Asian wives married to U.S. servicemen, who helped to sponsor immigrating family members in the post-1965 era.

Beginning in the 1950s, Filipinos came to San Diego particularly via the navy (Bonus 2000; Espiritu 2003). During World War II, the United States moved its Pacific naval headquarters base from Pearl Harbor to San Diego. This relocation of the Eleventh Naval District and the Naval Air Command brought numbers of navy personnel to San Diego; some remained after their military service was completed, and others returned after retiring from the service. The U.S. military presence in the Philippines led to the recruitment and enlistment of Filipinos, starting in the 1950s and peaking in the 1970s, as more Filipinos joined the U.S. Navy (Cariño 1987). As a Filipina whose father was in the military and who was raised in San Diego comments: "In fact, at that point in time, when I was growing up, until I was like in my twenties, ... it was very rare that you came across a Filipino male that hadn't been in the military in this part of the city." Although they were given an opportunity to join the military, most enlisted Filipinos were assigned menial positions such as cook, inventory clerk, steward, and messboy (Espiritu 1995).

During the war, the majority of Japanese in San Diego were sent to the internment camp at Poston, Arizona. The downtown Japanese community disappeared with the internment of the Japanese, and those who did return to San Diego moved to parts of the county amenable to their presence. After the war, many Asians left to find better opportunities elsewhere, and the majority of those who remained in San Diego moved to the suburbs, as did most of the population, including most of the estimated two thousand Chinese who resided downtown. In 1947 the Supreme Court invalidated restrictive covenants that prohibited Asians and other minorities from buying real estate or receiving loans in all-white neighborhoods, but anecdotal evidence indicates that de facto housing discrimination against Asian Americans persisted until the mid-1950s in San Diego.

Immigration Reform, Immigrants, and Refugees, 1960s–1970s

The Civil Rights movement led to dramatic changes for people of color in this country, but it also had an indirect impact on those living in Asia. This movement brought attention to the racial bias of the 1924 Immigration Act and other immigration restrictions and led to the abolition of discriminatory immigration quotas. In 1965, Congress passed the Cellar-Hart Immigration Reform Act, which abolished restrictive quotas based on national origin that favored European immigrants. This act substituted hemispheric quotas, giving the Western Hemisphere 120,000 and the Eastern Hemisphere 170,000, and allowed an annual quota of 20,000 per nation, regardless of race. When President Lyndon Johnson signed the legislation, he gave a speech that in hindsight shows how the government miscalculated the bill's impact: "This bill that we will sign today is not a revolutionary bill. It does not affect the lives of millions. It will not reshape the structure of our daily lives, or really add importantly to our wealth or our power" (quoted in Kitano and Daniels 1988: 16). It was supposed to eliminate racial bias, and immigration was expected to reflect existing U.S. racial proportions, with a majority of European immigrants. Neither Johnson nor members of the U.S. Congress thought the bill would affect Asian immigration, since few Asians had applied for entrance at U.S. Embassies or Consulates. But that number reflected the improbability of being

TABLE 1. San Diego County Asian Population 1960 and 1970

	1960	1970
Total population	1,033,011	1,357,854
Japanese	4,778	7,515
Chinese	1,586	3,259
Filipino	5,114	14,721
ASIAN TOTAL	11,478	25,495
Asian percentage of total population	1%	2%
Asian foreign-born	84%	58%

Source: Table 28, U.S. Bureau of Census 1963b.

granted a visa under the previous quota system, not the numbers who wanted to emigrate from Asia.

The Immigration Act of 1965 led to a substantial increase of immigrants from Asia, many of whom would use its family reunification and occupational provisions to enter. The reunification provision gave priority to parent, children, spouses, and siblings of U.S. citizens or permanent residents, who could sponsor their relatives. The immigration of Asian women balanced the gender ratio and led to an increase in the population through the establishment of families. The act's occupational preferences provisions allowed immigration of "members of professions and scientists and artists of exceptional ability" and "skilled and unskilled workers in occupations for which labor is in short supply in the U.S." Between 1960 and 1970 in San Diego, the Asian population—with only three subgroups counted (Chinese, Japanese, and Filipino)—doubled. The foreign-born decreased significantly from 84 percent to 58 percent during this year period but remained the majority (see Table 1).

At the end of the Vietnam War, the United States accepted Southeast Asian refugees as a result of U.S. military involvement in the region and the cold war policy against Communist regimes (Chan 2003). These newcomers contribute to the ethnic and class heterogeneity of the Asian American population. Special U.S. legislation, such as the Indochina Migration and Refugee Assistance Act of 1975 and Refugee Act of 1980, granted the refugees admission and initial assistance (Gordon 1987). From the late 1970s to the 1990s, additional agreements or legislation— such as the Orderly Departure Program, the Humanitarian Operation, and the Amerasian Homecoming Act—allowed for other groups to enter the United States as "immigrants," although they were given assistance

TABLE 2. San Diego County Asian Population, 1980

	Population
Total population	1,861,846
Filipino	48,658
Japanese	12,410
Chinese	7,800
Vietnamese	7,307
Hmong	2,464
Korean	2,394
Asian Indian	1,831
Other	6,997
ASIAN TOTAL	89,861
Asian percentage of total population	4.8%
Asian foreign-born	62%

Source: Table 15, U.S. Bureau of the Census 1983a.

similar to that provided those with refugee status (Rumbaut 1996). Before South Vietnam fell to Communist forces in 1975, the few Vietnamese in the United States were mainly students, diplomats, military trainees, or women married to non-Asians. In the post-war years, there was a mass exodus of refugees from Vietnam, Cambodia, and Laos, including those from a variety of ethnic or tribal groups. Many of the first-wave Southeast Asians were processed at Camp Pendleton, a U.S. marine base not far from San Diego, which accounts for the refugees settling in the vicinity of that city. Persecuted by the new political regimes in their homeland, individuals and whole family units who came in later waves escaped by making dangerous escapes by land or sea to nearby countries of first asylum, where they stayed in temporary refugee camps before being settled permanently in a new host country. There are class differences among the population; for example, the first group of Vietnamese came from better educational and occupational backgrounds than succeeding waves. Subsequent waves of Southeast Asians varied in their socioeconomic background and level of adaptation; for instance, those from rural areas with limited education faced difficulty adjusting and continue to rely on low-wage work or welfare to survive. As involuntary immigrants or refugees affected by the political upheavals of their country, the traumas of war and escape, and psychological distress from languishing in refugee camps, Southeast Asians differ in many respects from the rest of the Asian American population, most of whom are voluntary immigrants.

Contemporary Immigration Trends, 1980s–1990s

During the 1980s in San Diego, Asians surpassed Blacks as the second-largest minority group, their numbers increasing at a rate faster than those of the Latino population. In 1980 in San Diego County, the total population was 1,861,846; Asians made up close to 5 percent of the population, at 89,861 (see Table 2). In the 1980s, approximately 62 percent of the Asian population in San Diego was foreign-born (U.S. Bureau of the Census 1983c) and about 30 percent had emigrated from an Asian country between 1975 and 1980 (U.S. Bureau of the Census 1983b). They came to escape economic, political, and social turmoil at home and also to seek improved economic and educational opportunities for themselves and their children.

In 1990, 60 percent of the total international immigration to San Diego was from Asia (Showley 1992; see Table 3). Asians were the fastest-growing population in the county, numbering 198,311—7.9 percent of the total, up from 4.8 percent a decade earlier (Wilkens 1991). In 1990, San Diego County had a population of over 2.5 million, including 6.4 percent Blacks, 0.8 percent American Indian/Eskimo/Aleut, and 20.4 percent Hispanics (U.S. Bureau of the Census 1990b).[2] According to these statistics, approximately 35 percent of the San Diego population,

TABLE 3. San Diego County Asian Population, 1990

	Population
Filipino	95,945
Vietnamese	21,118
Chinese	19,686
Japanese	17,869
Laotian	7,025
Korean	6,722
Asian Indian	5,039
Cambodian	4,185
Hmong	1,585
Thai	1,109
Other	18,028
ASIAN TOTAL	198,311
Asian percentage of total population	7.9%

Source: San Diego Association of Government Information 1991.

over one-third, is part of the "minority" category, and this has impacted ethnic and race relations.

Asian American residents took note of the rising Asian population. An individual who is half Japanese and half Caucasian and was raised in San Diego explains: "There was almost none [Asians] when I was growing up; . . . if you saw another, it was news. You would walk up and talk to them because you wanted to know where they were from. Now it's much more common to see Asians. I'm not surprised to see another Asian in a particular location." A Filipino who moved to the area for employment reasons comments: "Well, there was a time when if it was an Asian person, you knew them, I mean, then all of a sudden I started seeing faces that I had never seen before and I think it was new people were coming in through the school system and the university system. . . . Gosh, I never knew there was so many Asian professionals in San Diego County." A Chinese who came to the area to attend college and stayed after graduation said: "I think there's been a tremendous explosion in the Asian community here over the last five, six years. When I first moved here the Asian community was very invisible."

Ethnicity

While many assume that an Asian coalition indicates only the coming together of Asian subgroups, this view neglects the distinctions among the multilevel "ethnic subgroups." For example, Vietnamese, Cambodians, Laotians, and ethnic groups from the Southeast Asia region such as the Hmong and Iu Mein are lumped into the Indochinese or Southeast Asian grouping, although the groups exhibit distinct ethnic, linguistic, and cultural differences. Even the term "Chinese" is complex; during my fieldwork I interacted with ethnic Chinese from Canada, Cambodia, mainland China, Cuba, Hong Kong, Indonesia, Malaysia, Mexico, Peru, the Philippines, Singapore, Taiwan, and Vietnam, who all have differing historical and cultural experiences. One interviewee of Chinese ancestry was born in the Philippines, moved to Canada as a youth, and relocated to California as an adult. Although there were Chinese organizations locally, she did not feel comfortable joining those for mainland Chinese, because her experiences were culturally different, so she joined pan-Asian ones.

Skeptics of the possibility of building Asian American coalitions argue that new immigrants may bring with them old world ethnic animosities that will prevent them from forming alliances. While an appropriate observation in some scenarios, this perspective unfairly constructs all immigrants as unable to distinguish between Asian nationals and Asian Americans. An immigrant participant explains how he contends with both generational and ethnic differences:

> You can see that the people who are involved do not have a strong, one-sided Asian ethnic [identity] like, "I'm Korean, I'm not going to do anything with the Japanese because of what happened in World War II." . . . For example, say, take a person like Robert. He's Japanese, right? I'm Chinese. I have no grudge against him because of what the Japanese have done to us. The poor guy had no idea. His parents are Japanese Americans. During the second war, it's not their parents that did all of the stuff. I mean, you can't lump them together. They're Americans.

Ethnocentrism may make it difficult for groups to align themselves with other Asian American groups (Hayano 1981); however, this is not always the case. Additionally, the increasing numbers of those of mixed ethnic and racial ancestry, foreign-born and U.S.-born, said they felt more comfortable with the pan-Asian format, something the ethnocentric perspective overlooks.

In many ways, Asian American organizations can transcend some internal conflict among Chinese or Filipinos or Vietnamese, and herein lies its attraction. In San Diego, at a rough estimate, there were at least a hundred Filipino organizations, close to fifty Vietnamese, twenty Chinese, and fewer for the rest of the groups, based on cultural, economic, linguistic, occupational, political, religious, and social interests. Many of these organizations were created because of internal differences within an ethnic group. Internal conflict does affect Asian American organizations, but members can move beyond homeland rivalries or bypass these internal frictions to some extent. In my interactions with participants, U.S.-born and foreign-born generations would mention that they were not active in single-ethnic organizations because of the infighting. Asian American organizations provide a space for a new generation of leaders, in contrast to single-ethnic organizations that often rely on a predominance of traditional elders who may be more likely to be affected by past animosities.

Generation

The increasing number of foreign-born Asians profoundly affects the Asian American population's ability to mobilize politically. At the height of the Asian American movement during the 1960s and 1970s, the U.S. Asian population reached a turning point—Asians born in this country outnumbered those born abroad. In the 1990s, the Asian population reached another turning point—the foreign-born population outnumbered the U.S. born. In San Diego, the foreign-born population has always predominated, with groups such as the Vietnamese having more first-generation members than the Japanese. Some among the older immigrant generation are able to work with U.S.-born Asians, but the younger generation of foreign-born Asians has an easier time forging alliances with U.S.-born Asians.

However, factors such as age, class, education, and socialization experience complicate generational definitions. An individual born abroad who arrives in the United States at age twenty and one who arrives at age forty are both classified as first generation, although their experiences in their homeland and as immigrants may differ significantly. Additionally, those immigrating as children with their parents, often described as the 1.5 generation, have made the community more diverse. The San Diego County Office of Education in 1993 released data for the 1991–1992 school year that showed Anglo students for the first time in the "minority," 49.6 percent, while non-Anglo students accounted for 51.4 percent (Latinos, 30.3 percent; Asians Pacific Islanders, 10.9 percent; African Americans, 8.3 percent; and American Indians 0.9 percent), which reflects the overall racial trend in California. Other immigrants came as international students to attend high school or college and decided to stay permanently. This growing immigrant population and their children have forced longtimers and their children to consider how they will incorporate new groups.

Gender

One dramatic transformation among the Asian American population in the post-1965 era has been the addition of girls and women. Previously, their immigration was highly restricted and, as a result, there were few families and children. The 1965 act allowed Asian women to enter the United States, creating a gender balance; by the 1990s, Asian Pacific American females comprised 51.2 percent of the Asian population and males 48.8 percent (Shinagawa and Jang 1998). Women immigrated as children with their families or as partners with their spouses who came for educational or employment purposes. In some cases, women have forged the immigration path for their families by arriving first, as international students, war brides, or professionals, and then sponsoring family members. Women from Cambodia, Laos, and Vietnam came as refugees seeking asylum from their war-torn countries.

During my fieldwork, I met individuals whose mothers followed these various migration patterns, as well as women whose own stories fit into these groupings.

Women have been crucial to the formation of many organizations in San Diego and have assumed leadership roles as well. From the early 1970s, women emerged as leaders in San Diego's Asian American organizations, carving out a space for themselves in newly formed organizations that did not have to contend, at least to the same extent, with the conventions of single-ethnic organizations. Many of the major single-ethnic organizations have been led predominantly by men and can be quite exclusionary to women even as members, in contrast to Asian American organizations, which gave women opportunities to participate on many levels. Perhaps this scenario occurred because emerging organizations desperately needed volunteers or services, so they accepted anyone who was willing to assist, regardless of gender; once integrated, women paved the way for other women and their participation became customary. Women who were single, married, divorced, or widowed, some with children, have assumed these leadership roles. For the most part, the primary players have been women who have earned respect because of their professional status. In 1990, 60 percent of Asian American women participated in the labor force compared to 57 percent of all women (U.S. Bureau of the Census 1993), so women working outside the home and involved with organizational activities are not perceived as unusual. This is not to say that everyone accepts women as leaders or that gender inequities are absent in these organizations, but these factors represent one among many conflicts that can arise within the mobilization process.

Class

Early immigrants came from similar class backgrounds; however, the post-1965 flows are socioeconomically heterogeneous. In some instances, their homeland class status is transplanted; in others, displacement allows opportunities for upward mobility not possible in their former homeland; in still others, it leads to downward mobility. The average rate of poverty for Asians is 14 percent, higher than the national average of 13 percent (U.S. Bureau of the Census 1993). Related to the issue of poverty are high rates of unemployment and underemployment among Asian Americans (Dunn 1994). Stories about Asian Americans as "model minority" students overpopulating the most prestigious universities in the country overlook the fact that many Asian Americans never attend college or even graduate from high school (Chao 1997). In 1990 in the United States, 78 percent of Asians were high school graduates, slightly higher than the total graduation rate of 75 percent, and 38 percent of Asians had completed a bachelor's degree, compared to 20 percent of the total population (U.S. Bureau of the Census 1993). These educational statistics are deceiving by themselves, since they fail to reveal that many Asians are not employed in occupations, or pursuing careers, commensurate with their levels of education.

Although the influx of the post-1965 immigrants from Asia included the impoverished, the selective immigration process has also brought well-educated and skilled immigrants (Liu and Cheng 1994; Ong and Liu 1994), part of the "brain drain" or the "brain overflow." Asian Indian professionals started coming to the United States in the 1970s, and even though the population of Asian Indians in San Diego is small, it has more than doubled in the last decade (Minocha 1987; Osborne 1994). Starting in 1970, significant numbers of accountants, physicians, nurses, scientists, and engineers from the Philippines were admitted under the professional provision of the 1965 Immigration Act (Cariño 1987; Keely 1973; McDonnell 1989; Yu 1980). Immigrants from Hong Kong and Taiwan, some originally coming as students, are bringing their human resources and financial capital with them. It is estimated that approximately 68 percent of recent Taiwanese immigrants previously held executive, managerial, and professional positions (Zhou 1992). Many Koreans who were well-educated professionals in their homeland have immigrated, and because of discrimination or their limited English skills, a number have become small business owners; some have been successful and others struggle to eke out a living (Light and Bonancich 1988). The diverse class composition contributes to differences in political viewpoints and priorities; however, it also brings valuable resources for mobilizing.

Language

As their population grows, Asian immigrant and Asian American activists have had to contend with language issues in communicating with one another, and this obstacle is often underestimated in assessing their mobilization efforts. This barrier does not exist for African Americans or Native Americans, and only to a lesser extent for Latinos (who have to deal mainly with English and Spanish). In contrast Asian Americans have literally dozens of languages and dialects that potentially can hinder their mobilization efforts. Having interpreters and material translated can aid; however, having some knowledge of English facilitates communication when working with multiple ethnic groups. An English-only interviewee explains that the language issue poses greater challenges for organizers than the generational issue: "It's the language more than anything. I like to say that it's generational also, but I don't think so because I don't have a problem dealing with other generations if they can communicate with me in my language." It should be pointed out that such individuals are not advocating English-only policies or monolingualism, but are speaking pragmatically—a working knowledge of English helps facilitate basic communication, such as that needed to conduct a meeting.

Unlike gatherings of most of the single-ethnic organizations, which use the native dialect, Asian American meetings and functions are conducted in English, which also allows non-Asians to participate. At all the meetings I attended, there were many levels of English spoken, with varying accents. Although this usually was not a problem, I noticed at times that U.S.-born generations were more impatient with non-native speakers than non-native speakers were with one another. At a meeting of primarily Southeast Asians, Vietnamese, Laotian, and Cambodian leaders struggled to converse with one another, their limited English making it difficult to move beyond rather formal communication. Those who speak only limited English expressed hesitancy about participating in organizations that use primarily English, and if they attended large meetings, they were quiet and reserved. Depending on their language socialization at home and at school, immigrants and U.S.-born Asians have differing levels of comfort with their heritage language. For example, I heard individuals speaking to co-ethnics in casual conversations in their ethnic language, so I assumed they were quite proficient. However, a number told me they are comfortable only in casual conversation but have difficulty in political conversations and are not fluent in reading and writing. So rather than participate in single-ethnic organizations, most of which require verbal and written proficiency in an ethnic language, they opt to participate in English-speaking organizations. A number of immigrants and migrants are educated in Western-style schools abroad or in U.S. schools, and their fluent English enables them to communicate with other Asian Americans, in addition to other racial groups.

Geographic Settlement

In comparison to other cities in the United States, San Diego ranked fourth in terms of intended city of residence selected by Asian immigrants and was especially popular with those coming from the Philippines and Vietnam (Gall and Gall 1993). By the mid-1990s, there were about 200,000 Asians in the San Diego area, accounting for almost 8 percent of the total population in San Diego County and 12 percent of the city of San Diego population (U.S. Bureau of the Census 1990b). As a result of chain migration, many Asians moved to San Diego because they had relatives or friends already settled in the area to assist them with housing and employment; others, through the secondary migration process, have come from other states and nearby metropolitan areas such as Los Angeles or Orange County.

The Asian American population is dispersed throughout the city and county, with some concentrated pockets. Approximately 66 percent of the Asian population lives in San Diego, with some variance among ethnic groups.[3] In the 1990s, of the eighteen incorporated communities of San Diego County, fourteen saw Asian population growth of at least 100 percent, while some saw 300 percent growth (Horstman 1991).[4] Asian Indian, Korean, Chinese, Japanese, and Taiwanese populations tend to be dispersed throughout the county, while Southeast Asians are concentrated in Southeast San Diego, East San Diego, Linda Vista, and Mira Mesa, all more affordable areas. There are concentrations of Filipinos in National City, Chula Vista, and Imperial Beach, and they are also moving to the nearby exclusive Bonita and Paradise Hills neighborhoods. This area is known as South Bay or, affectionately, Little Manila or Filipinotown. Like other upwardly mobile Asians, Filipinos have moved to developing suburban communities in North County, such as Mira Mesa (also referred to as "Manila Mesa"), Rancho Bernardo, Rancho Peñasquitos, Oceanside, Poway, and Scripps Ranch.

Noticeable in the 1980s and even more so in the 1990s was the concentration of Asian businesses. Filipinos have significant business sections in National City, while Vietnamese are established in East San Diego and Linda Vista (Telles 1991). For example, East San Diego has more than 400 Vietnamese businesses, including twenty-two restaurants, ten markets, and many fast-food outlets (Vu 1995). An "Asian" business hub has developed in Kearny Mesa, and as one reporter noted, the "Asianization" or "Orientalization" of this area is "the closest thing the city has to an Asian central business district" (Sheehan 1992). A variety of Chinese, Japanese, Korean, Thai, and Vietnamese ethnic restaurants, supermarkets, bookstores, gift shops, billiard parlors, beauty shops, karaoke clubs, video shops, and other businesses have opened in strip malls that are accessible to multiple freeways. The establishment of key businesses, such as the Pacific Gateway Plaza mini-mall, attracted more Asian businesses to the area (Xiang 1991). In the 1990s, large modern supermarkets, such as Yaohan and 99 Ranch Market, and three Asian American banks, East-West Bank, General Bank, and San Diego First Bank, also opened. The development of Kearny Mesa has made it the center of all types of Asian American organizational events.

Institutional and immigration factors are the main emphases in examining coalitions, but geography and infrastructure, often overlooked, also play a significant role in facilitating or hindering coalitions. Although there are areas where certain subgroups are more predominant, the lack of concentrated ethnic neighborhoods, which prevents the establishment of territorial boundaries, distinguishes San Diego from major cities that have established single-ethnic enclaves. Also, the regional areas of the county are neither distinct from one another nor separated by natural waterways, and the freeway system permits access to different segments of the county. In the 1990s, activists came to meetings, which were located primarily in San Diego, from throughout the county.

Conclusion

Asians have an extensive history in San Diego and, even in the most inhospitable conditions, found strategies to survive and to establish and defend their communities. Over the decades, the changing composition of the Asian population in San Diego has transformed the probabilities, forms, and objectives of Asian American collective action. Starting in the 1960s, and becoming especially noticeable during the 1980s, the Asian population grew extensively, with the arrival of new immigrants, migrants, and refugees. Even though ethnic, generational, gender, class, linguistic, and geographic differences polarize Asian Americans, other circumstantial factors, along with the imposition of the racial category, have encouraged them to build alliances with one another and with other communities of color.

3

The Politics of Social Services for a "Model Minority"

The Union of Pan Asian Communities

During the 1960s, scholars and reporters popularized the "model minority" myth, which praised Asian Americans for having quietly achieved the American dream of success without reliance on social services (S. Lee 1996; Osajima 1988; Petersen 1966). An infamous headline from *U.S. News & World Report* read: "One such minority, the nation's 300,000 Chinese-Americans, is winning wealth and respect by dint of its own hard work. Still being taught in Chinatown is the old idea that people should depend on their own efforts—not a welfare check—in order to reach America's 'promised land'" ("Success Story" 1966). However, during this same period, Asian Americans involved in the Asian American movement were calling attention to a range of social problems that faced their ethnic communities and demanding that the state respond adequately to their social service needs (Wei 1993). Throughout these tumultuous years, many community-based organizations (CBOs) were created in Asian American communities across the country, but few survived through the conservative decades that followed.

In San Diego, the Union of Pan Asian Communities (UPAC), a nonprofit multiethnic social services organization, flourished by employing strategies of both resistance and accommodation. Lacking experience in social service work and financial resources, grassroots activists devised an *interactive model of mobilization*. This community-based organization had to gain access to and maneuver within a political system that historically excluded its members from the power structure and marginalized the needs of their communities. Activists who had once been quite isolated built an organizational infrastructure by creating and recreating multilevel networks among Asians at local and national levels and with other minority groups in San Diego. This process was marked by internal division and dissent that altered the composition of the organization, as well as its programs, leadership, and agendas.

Asian American activists had to contend with contrasting images when asking for social service assistance. On the one hand, they were perceived as an "assimilated minority" that lacked social problems; on the other hand, they were viewed as "inassimilable foreigners" undeserving of services. Both misconceptions were used to justify their being passed over for social services. These constructs continue to be obstacles to obtaining program funds, collecting health data, and providing social services. The persistence of the categories "Black, White, and other" in national health data collection, even in the 1990s, symbolizes how racial formation works to render Americans of Asian ancestry "invisible." Factors such as race, culture, language, religion, citizenship, length of residence in the United States, and immigration status are crucial elements that determine the quality and quantity, if any, of fundamental social services obtained by individuals and groups.

Mobilizing for social services engendered the widest possible base of support, given the lack of resources to act on economic or political agendas—few individuals in the community could disagree with the goal of improving the lives of the poor. By highlighting UPAC's leadership and pivotal moments, this chapter analyzes how UPAC transformed itself from an ad hoc grassroots group into a formal institution between the 1970s and the 1990s. I focus on the activism of the leaders of UPAC, because their decisions and actions had the greatest impact on the structure of the organization. Although I attended a number of UPAC events, I rely mainly on interviews and archival documents that focus on the historical development of the organization.[1]

Asian Americans and Social Services

Before the 1970s, Asian Americans assumed responsibility for the social welfare of their communities, mainly because government-oriented social welfare agencies had been wholly unresponsive to their needs. Since Asian immigrants were not granted citizenship until the 1940s, they were denied basic social services provided by the government. Their noncitizenship status cast them as "perpetual foreigners," which the state used to justify its social service negligence. Those who were citizens did not become public welfare clients because they were unaware of their welfare rights and there were limited outreach programs that provided them access. In the post–World War II era, Asian American groups were granted citizenship; however, given their exclusion from services in the past, they were still not provided with adequate social services.

Segregated in ethnic enclaves, Asian American groups formed their own community organizations or benevolent associations based on lineage, language, or regional ties and relied on private donations (Light 1972; Yung 1999). These single-ethnic associations could not meet the broad spectrum of community needs because they did not have the funding, personnel, or expertise to provide adequate services. In many instances, assistance was highly selective, since it evolved around the associations and their elite leaders, who also controlled the economic and political institutions in these enclaves. Given their exclusion from mainstream society, Chinese Americans, for example, were reluctant to seek outside assistance for housing and welfare needs, fearing that intervention from the outside would interfere with their customs and their internal power structure (B. Wong 1977).

In addition to the discriminatory exclusion from state-run services, cultural barriers also prevented Asian Americans from soliciting external assistance. Chinese Americans and Japanese Americans were hesitant to seek mental health services because of prevailing cultural beliefs that mental illness was shameful to the family (B. Kim 1978). Asian Americans have continued to underuse mental health services based on the stigma associated with psychological problems (Gim 1995). Many newer immigrants came from countries where social services were not provided or where relations between the general public and bureaucratic agencies were quite unfavorable; therefore, they were reluctant to request help from governmental agencies in the United States.

As a result of their ineligibility for and their underuse of mainstream social services, Asian Americans were assumed to have few problems that warranted intervention (B. Kim 1978; Sue and Kitano 1973). Despite signs that many in these ethnic communities were experiencing problems with poverty, unemployment, underemployment, mental health, inadequate housing, and juvenile delinquency, the "model minority" thesis that became popular in the 1960s reinforced the idea that Asian Americans were self-sufficient and lacked problems (B. Kim 1973; Sue,

Sue, and Sue 1975). By the 1970s, many politicized Asian Americans expressed anger toward both ethnic-based community agencies and mainstream social service providers for neglecting the needs of the Asian population, particularly the elderly and the poor in ethnic enclaves (Wei 1993).

In San Diego, faith-based groups provided some assistance, but their resources and experience were limited, and their unwillingness to seek outside funding constrained the level of their service delivery. Asian Christian and Buddhist organizations, for example, identified needs, collected preliminary data, or informed members about UPAC's services but played a secondary role in the development of UPAC. A Filipina who would become one of the leaders of UPAC comments: "In the past, most of us had just stood by and let things happen because we thought it was the will of God" (Lau 1990a). She captures the resignation of many first-generation Asians. It was not until the early 1970s that there was a concerted effort to forge the first Asian American organization.[2]

Organizing a Union of Asian Americans

The formation of the Union of Pan Asian Communities (UPAC) organization began in 1972 at a time of social and political upheaval in the United States.[3] Local activism was sparked by emerging activism at the national level, particularly poor peoples' movements and political movements by people of color, which challenged long-standing economic and racial inequities in U.S. society. In the early 1970s, San Diego college students organized the United Asian American Communities (UAAC), a support group, and realized the need to develop a drug education program, but their outreach was limited and the organization soon dissolved, although some of its members later became involved with UPAC.[4] The decision to form UPAC was partly a reaction to the formation of the Asian Pacific Congress. Those involved obtained some funding for an office and staff, claimed they could provide social services, and contacted leaders of single-ethnic organizations for their support. The group was criticized by those who would later form UPAC for having no skills or training in providing social services and therefore produced "zero outreach and zero results." As one UPAC organizer put it: "They hired each other trying to represent the communities; in fact, we did not know who they were until we got a letter from them saying, 'We would like to represent you.' And that's when we found that we better do something."

In the initial stages, a core group of committed Asian American students, social service professionals, traditional leaders of single-ethnic organizations, and other community activists held ad hoc meetings. For the first time, Asian Americans were entering graduate programs in social work, and this educational setting brought together Chinese, Japanese, Filipinos, and Koreans, enabling them to share their concerns. Students in the master's program at San Diego State University's School of Social Work were collaborating on an investigation of social issues in various single-ethnic communities. One of the students was Beverley Yip, a Chinese American woman born in Canada in the 1930s who was involved in the Asian American movement while a student at the University of California at Berkeley; Yip eventually became the first executive director of UPAC. As an intern at the Chinese Social Service Center, she drafted a needs assessment of the Asian American communities and concluded that "there were a lot of Asian groups, there were a lot of Asian organizations, but because of the numbers, there was really no power, no way to make our voice heard." She suggested the need for an organizational structure that would be inclusive of the existing single-ethnic organizations.

Another crucial individual was Vernon Yoshioka, a fourth-generation Japanese American born in the late 1930s, who was active with the Japanese-based Oceanview United Church of Christ and was the president of the local Japanese American Citizens League. Educated at Massachusetts Institute of Technology, he was working as an aerospace engineer for Teledyne Ryan and was involved in their affirmative action program. Working on company time, he became a "paid ambassador" for the Asian American community and was the first chair of UPAC. Originally from northern California, where his parents owned a nursery before being interned during World War II, Yoshioka moved to San Diego in the early 1960s. Interestingly enough, he is a lifelong Republican and ran unsuccessfully for political office in several local elections.

UPAC organizers designed an organizational structure that incorporated existing single-ethnic organizations and their leaders; UPAC incorporated in 1973. They were able to formally bring together seven Asian and Pacific Islander organizations under this umbrella format: Chinese Social Service Center, Council of Pilipino-American Organizations (COPAO), Guamanian Alliance, Chamorro Nation, Sons and Daughters of Guam Club, Japanese American Citizens League, and Korean Association of San Diego.[5] The Samoan Association of America and the India Association were active organizations but could not seek full membership, because they were not incorporated. Through the years, other organizations became members, such as the House of China, Vietnamese Alliance Association, Vietnamese Community Foundation, Cambodian Association of San Diego, Malaysian American Society, Philippine American Community, Thai Association of San Diego, Hui-O-Hawaii, Laotian Friendship Association, and Samoan Senior Citizens Club. Each group had different resources to contribute to the coalition, as articulated by Vernon Yoshioka, who would later argue for maintaining the pan-Asian format: "The Filipino community is the largest Asian group, while the Chinese have been here the longest, and the Japanese community has the strongest financial base, so it makes sense for the communities to work together."[6]

The Politics of Social Service Funding

In the mid-1960s, President Johnson's Great Society campaign and War on Poverty programs initially led to reforms that provided funding for social programs for Asian Americans (Espiritu 1992). The struggle for civil rights and the power movements by people of color during that period also made the government more "responsive" to Asian American demands. Ironically, it was President Nixon's development of the revenue-sharing program that gave Asian Americans access to funds. The program directed federal funds for community development to local bureaucrats, who, at their discretion, could dispense the monies to local agencies. In actuality, Nixon's policy was a reaction to the economic recession confronting the United States, partly a result of the oil embargo, and was intended to curb social service spending by the federal government. Rather than having to contend with the more complex federal funding structure, Asians in San Diego now had to deal only with the simpler local structure.

Grace Blaszkowski, a Filipina assigned as the San Diego County Asian American Community Affairs officer, realized that monies were available and encouraged the community to apply for them using the larger "Asian American or Asian Pacific American" category. As a Japanese American doctor, formerly a UPAC chair, explained: "If they're to get social service monies from the county, they would need someone who could advocate for them, and the way to do that was to get not just someone advocating for the Japanese American community or the Filipino community or the Chinese community, but get them together and say we're advocating for this larger group." Since the welfare state uses larger racial categories to allocate resources, it is strategically useful for smaller groups to reorganize under a larger umbrella (Enloe 1981; Olzak 1983). By funding an Asian American group rather than particular ethnic subgroups, the state can avoid accusations of favoritism (Espiritu 1992).

Yet local politicians initially denied funds for Asian American social programs, arguing first that UPAC was inexperienced in providing social services and second that they lacked sufficient data to show the need for services. The first chair of UPAC explained in a public statement to city council officials:

> Of all the minority communities, the needs of the Pan Asians have been the most neglected and overlooked by governmental agencies. Even funded projects for minorities have failed to serve our communities. As a result, many of our people have remained isolated from the mainstream of our society and continue to suffer from discrimination, unemployment, poverty, ill-health, as well as social, cultural and educational deprivation.[7]

Before 1970, there was no extensive research collected on Asian health issues on local or national levels, and virtually no articles on Asian Americans appeared in the social welfare literature (B. Kim 1973).

Asian American groups also tried to obtain funds from the private sector, particularly through United Way, without much success. Bok-Lim Kim, a Korean American woman who later became a program director of UPAC, comments on this inadequacy of funding:

> We do not get any United Way funds. Not that we haven't tried. For years, we have patiently complied with their interminable planning process hoping that we get a fair chance. United Way does not have a good record when it comes to funding programs that are relevant for Pan Asians.... Currently, only about $12,000 out their $10 million dollar goal will go to an agency that serves Pan Asians.[8]

Like state institutions, this funding agency justified its case by explaining that UPAC had no track record of working with the Asian American community. The prevalent model minority myth accepted by funders hindered the organization's efforts to lobby for funds for social services; they had to counteract this myth to justify their need (B. Kim 1973). In 1974, after extensive political lobbying, UPAC received a combined grant of $36,000 as seed money from the city and county of San Diego, which set a precedent for future funding from both the local and state level and from private funders. While most Asian activists perceived this outside funding positively, others questioned how it might interfere with the internal power dynamics of the community, particularly its leadership structure, since they were now accountable to the state for their actions.

A Transition of Power: Ethnicities, Generations, and Gender

The funding and formation of UPAC impacted the leadership of the Asian American community in three dramatic ways: the authority of single-ethnic organizations was augmented by the broader pan-Asian power structure; traditional leaders had to share power with a new generation of leaders; and women displaced men in leadership positions. The traditional hierarchy was not eliminated; rather, the power structure was altered. It is difficult to ascertain which change caused the most dissension, for each contributed to multiple tensions within the organization and the community.

Initially, to avoid the predominance of any one ethnic group—particularly one that was well established such as the Japanese or Chinese, or one with large numbers such as the Filipinos—UPAC organizers agreed to parity in decision-making power. All the original directors of UPAC were affiliated with the Filipino, Chinese, Japanese, Korean, and Chamorro (Guamanian) organizations. Since each group had two votes on all major decisions, ethnic groups had to submit to the authority of other Asian American subgroups, many of which historically had been antagonistic toward one another. While the leaders of many of the single-ethnic organizations realized the value of pan-Asian mobilization and were willing to work with other ethnic groups, the membership at large often reacted strongly against this decision-making structure. For example, the first chair of UPAC recalled how uncomfortable it was for him as a fourth-generation Japanese American to attend meetings in the Filipino, Korean, and Guamanian communities, whose members vehemently chastised him personally for the World War II traumas inflicted on their peoples by the Japanese military. His family owned a nursery in Hayward, California, before being interned at Topaz, Utah, during the war. He distinctly recalls the reaction he received from some of the groups: "I went to their meetings and they said, 'We don't trust you. We don't want you here.'. . . And sometimes the shouting matches in some of those meetings, it's hard to believe. . . . It was very uncomfortable there, because some of the guys got up and screamed and hollered, you know, 'We don't want this individual in our building!'" He credits the strong leadership of these groups, even when confronted with intense opposition, for sustaining UPAC's pan-Asian format.

Crucial to the planning of the organization was establishing an agreeable alliance between traditional elites, college students, professionals, and other community activists—a predicament that confronted pan-Asian organizers across the country (Kuramoto 1976). To obtain funding, traditional elites needed individuals with academic credentials and professional training who could write proposals for grants (Espiritu 1992). For example, professionals, unlike traditional elites, developed contacts outside Chinatown that allowed them to advocate for medical care or social services and work with mainstream governmental agencies (B. Wong 1977). Yet traditional leaders and community activists, often longtime residents in the area who had organizational experience working with ethnic populations, resented the interference of college students and professionals who lived outside the ethnic enclaves (Lott 1976; B. Wong 1982).

To resolve the conflicts, at least temporarily, the original planners agreed to an organizational structure that included roles for the various activists. Organizers appointed traditional leaders of single-ethnic organizations as officers and board members, while a staff of professionals, paraprofessionals, and volunteers handled the daily functions of the organization. The executive director delegated responsibility to project directors, who were often professionals, and to coordinators, who were often community activists. They tried to maintain an ethnic balance by hiring individuals from a variety of ethnic groups, many of whom served their own ethnic populations. Even though the officers and board consisted of traditional leaders of single-ethnic organizations, they often had to acquiesce to the expertise of the younger generation of professionals not from their own ethnic group. Forging these alliances and creating these networks was a mutually beneficial process, although maintaining this balance of power was a difficult proposition. Ultimately this structure would change.

UPAC also challenged the traditional male domination of Asian American organizations by hiring a female executive director, and by women playing central roles in multiple aspects of the hierarchy of the organization, particularly in the delivery of social services. Women were able to attain these positions because they took the initiative; in addition, there was an absence of male competition in these "helping" professions. The women's authority challenged single-ethnic organizations that were comprised mainly of male leaders (often boards were all male). It appears that although these women challenged male dominance, they did so within an acceptable domain, since social work or caregiving was framed as traditional "women's work" that was merely an extension of the unpaid labor they performed at home. Yet many women active in UPAC were not social service workers per se, but rather they were the ones lobbying local politicians, writing grants, developing programs, and planning fund-raisers, showing that they had moved beyond the narrow gender roles allotted them by the traditional Asian American community.

Women professionals still confront skepticism when working with elders of their own ethnic group who are accustomed to dealing with male authority figures. The second executive director recognized this: "You know, some of the communities have never been happy that Beverley was a female and I am a female." A senior member of UPAC told of having to resolve a situation in which a young Filipina coordinator for a Filipino youth program was introduced by a male coethnic community leader at a planning meeting as someone "who's getting coffee and tea," rather than as someone who was in charge of the program. With changes in the immigration laws, the arrival of Asian women and of whole families has balanced the gender ratio and subsequently altered gender dynamics in organizing. UPAC is an example of women establishing organizational leadership roles and implementing change in a community once dominated by male leaders. It has had a permanent effect on gender relations in the community by placing women in leadership positions in one of the most powerful Asian American organizations in the county, an experience that has helped women make the transition to forms of mobilization beyond social service concerns.

Southeast Asian Refugees and the Transformation of UPAC

Before 1975, the Southeast Asian population in San Diego was not considered central to the local Asian community or to UPAC, since their numbers were so small. In the aftermath of the Vietnam War, refugee populations from Vietnam, Cambodia (or Kampuchea), and Laos became a vital component of the Asian American community, with over one million resettling in the United States (Rumbaut 1995). The U.S. government gave these newcomers refugee status and provided initial funds for resettlement programs, using the exodus from Southeast Asia as a symbol of the failures of Communism. Literature on Southeast Asian refugees often claims that once they entered this country, evacuees were linked by government officials to already established Asian American agencies, which enabled these agencies to accrue more funds (Hein 1989). This was not the case initially in San Diego. In fact, UPAC immediately incorporated these newcomers into the Asian grouping but had a difficult time obtaining funds to assist them, although resettlement funds were plentiful. After much lobbying, UPAC was granted federal funds to provide some required services, thereby enhancing its status—it had additional financial strength and served more Asian American groups.

One of the largest processing centers for the evacuees was at Camp Pendleton, a marine base immediately north of San Diego that processed over 40,000 refugees. UPAC workers proposed to help resettle them, but some politicians were concerned that the involvement of UPAC would encourage the refugees to settle in the San Diego vicinity, which they felt was already burdened by Mexican immigrants (Bates 1975). Asian American activists saw this not merely as anti-refugee or anti-Vietnamese sentiment, but connected it to anti-Asian sentiment in general; they worked on curbing these attacks. In a public statement to the Human Relations Commission, Vernon Yoshioka, the chair of UPAC whose family had been interned during World War II, explained how the negative sentiments directed at the Vietnamese were connected to the Japanese American experience historically: "We appreciate the concern of some individuals on the impact of this sudden immigration upon our economy and society, but we need to address these concerns from a rational and educated standpoint. The hysterical manner in which potential problems have been portrayed is reminiscent of the racial hysteria which led to the Internment of the Japanese American Citizens in 1942."[9] Prompted by the testimony of the Asian American community, the San Diego Human Relations Commission passed a resolution welcoming the refugees and stating that "the involvement and cooperation of the Asian community should be a principle part of the total community effort during this critical transitional period."[10] The commission contacted political representatives, expressing their "concern about the racial tension and derogatory comments with respect to the Asian heritage of these recent arrivals by some local officials."[11] These activists and groups played a protective role in lessening the racial tension between the refugees and the local San Diego population.

Activists were reconstructing the boundaries of the Asian American community by including these new groups in the pan-Asian category. In the proposal for governmental funds written by a group of Asian

Americans, the leaders tried to counteract the negative sentiments by explaining the link between these refugees and the Asian population already in the United States:

> Despite the mixed feelings about the presence of the Vietnamese Refugees in our midst, the fact is that they are here to stay and will start new lives. . . . The Vietnamese people in the various Refugee Camps now form part of the Asian American Community in America, regardless of where they may eventually be re-settled. It is therefore necessary that Asian Americans and Vietnamese residents in the community be involved in the planning and development of programs and policies for the health and welfare and resettlement of these Asians on all levels of government [sic].[12]

They added: "While it's true the refugees' physical needs like food, clothing and shelter are being met by government and civic organizations, there are social service necessities that only Asians who have lived long in the U.S. could give" (quoted in Lopez 1975). Their concern was that national organizations such as the Catholic Church or the Red Cross did not have bilingual or bicultural staff members.

Lacking adequate funds, UPAC was able to use only a small core of voluntary staff to provide a few orientation services from mid-July to early September 1975, as the first wave of evacuees was settled. For civil service jobs, government bodies still required permanent residency status and certification of the intent to become U.S. citizens. The refugees who were willing and qualified to provide social services were still classified as "parolees," ineligible to hold civil service positions. UPAC failed to convince politicians to enact special legislation granting permanent residency status to these newcomers so that they could go to work, citing the precedent set by special legislation granting this privilege to Cuban refugees. Although they were able to get some money through volunteer programs, it was not enough. In good conscience, UPAC stated that they could not recommend that the "volunteers" work forty hours a week, five days a week, for only $200 a month. They also had problems obtaining consistent admission for the workers to enter Camp Pendleton. With this first wave, UPAC's role was directly limited by the federal government's policy of dispersing these refugees throughout the country to avoid creating an economic burden on any one community and in an attempt to quickly assimilate them.

Although UPAC had only a small role in settling the first wave of evacuees, it received additional funding for later refugees. Of the approximately 200,000 refugees resettled in California from 1975 to 1981, an estimated 30,000 (15 percent), many of whom came through the secondary migration process, settled in San Diego (Strand 1989). Later waves of refugees had difficulty adjusting culturally and linguistically, especially those from rural areas, because they had little formal education and few skills suited for their new homeland (Rumbaut 1995). Others suffered mental health problems caused by the loss of loved ones; homesickness; being victims, witnesses, or perpetrators of violent acts of war; loss of social status; and prolonged stays in refugee camps. The East Wind Socialization Center and the Indochinese Service Center were two programs among many sponsored by UPAC that provided adjustment and supportive services for the Southeast Asian population that settled in San Diego. The social workers provided mental health counseling, orientation sessions, recreational activities, English language lessons, and translation services, and also gathered data about the refugee population.

By the early 1990s, the Southeast Asian population comprised one-fourth of the Asian population in San Diego, and its members continued to come mainly as immigrants and as migrants from other U.S. cities (Trueba, Cheng, and Ima 1993). By that time, there were kin and extended social networks to assist them, so there was less need for initial resettlement services. More important, resettlement funding dried up, and UPAC began focusing on other services such as job-training programs.[13] Activists were also aware that the agency was serving a population that many non-Asians considered "undeserving foreigners" or "welfare cheats," so sponsoring programs for those already here "to learn, earn, and get off welfare" was more acceptable to the general public. For example, one of the former chairs of UPAC of mixed Asian ancestry who was born in Hawai'i comments that although UPAC wanted to raise awareness about the plight of the refugees in order to increase its funds, it has been cautious:

> [When I first joined UPAC] I didn't realize there was a large population in San Diego. So it opened a whole arena which I was not aware of in San Diego.... I remember visiting a couple of sites that had nutrition programs for the Southeast Asian communities, for seniors. There was a large population in San Diego, but what struck me was this: ... it was so invisible, but they're there. They were here, and they were suffering, and there was a need, but all under the table. And I asked her [Executive Director Beverley Yip], "Why?" And she said, "If you publicize it, you might get negative reaction to them."

The U.S. public was not receptive to the presence of Asian refugees in the first place, so more publicity could contribute to negative perceptions of Asian American immigrants and refugees and their children as burdens on the welfare state and drains on federal or state monies paid by taxpaying, law-abiding "Americans."

Southeast Asian Americans have mixed feelings about being included in the Asian American rubric, and some started their own organizations, which they felt could best address the needs of their community. The main provider of social services to this population continues to be UPAC.[14] One Vietnamese American community leader who lent his support to the Asian American community stated it was a symbolic gesture to show outsiders that the community was united, but acknowledged that many do not feel their interests are aligned with other Asian Americans. While the Vietnamese Federation, an umbrella organization for a variety of Vietnamese American organizations, has had amicable relations with UPAC, relations with others such as the Indochinese Mutual Assistance Association (IMAA), a social service organization, have been more adversarial, mostly because they were competing for the same limited funds.[15] One UPAC member comments that this competition is actually "good" for the community, arguing that "the population and the need is so great that I always thought that having all your eggs in one basket is not a good idea anyway; ... whoever delivers the best service, I think, should be rewarded." Southeast Asians have been active in other organizations, such as the San Diego Refugee Coalition, which was established in June 1975 to provide a task force to bring people together who were working with the waves of refugees from Southeast Asia, but later included other non-Asian refugees with whom they shared similar problems.[16]

Other Asian Americans see their own ethnic experiences being repeated with the Southeast Asians; for example, at a UPAC fund-raising dinner I attended, a Japanese American nursery owner discussed how he donated tools and equipment to a work program for Southeast Asians sponsored by UPAC. He described how the Japanese, when they first came to this country, started as gardeners and advanced to owning nurseries, small farms, and eventually other kinds of occupations altogether. He felt that the Southeast Asians could do the same. A Chinese American born in Cuba was empathetic, although reluctantly at first, to the plight of refugees because of his own family experiences:

> I see another problem arising as we had with the aliens coming over from Mexico, as we have with the Vietnamese immigration over to the United States, and now the Chinese [being smuggled into America]. Again, as an American, I see it initially as an economic problem. We get to deal with

another problem. . . . But then there's a lot of empathy as well because I myself
was a refugee coming over from Cuba and I can remember the thoughts of
saying, "Wow, we made it. I have a chance. I have an opportunity to make
something of myself." And that was stressed to us [by my parents] when we
first came over here. . . . But you have to be real sympathetic to these people
because they wouldn't be making sacrifices and the expenses of doing something like this unless their lives were that bad. My life or our family life was
bad enough to take on such a venture when we came over from Cuba and
when my mom went from China to Cuba.

The inclusion of the refugees not only transformed the character of the
Asian American population, since they became the largest group that
UPAC serves, but also unexpectedly changed UPAC by providing
another channel of funding that helped to sustain the agency and promote its legitimacy in the mainstream society.

Contestations over Restructuring Ethnic and Elite Power

Starting in 1976, one of the most controversial decisions by UPAC
leaders was to phase out the old power structure of the board of directors and replace it with prominent Asians and non-Asians from a variety of prestigious professions who had political connections. UPAC was
told, directly and indirectly, by various public funders that the organization needed to show it was financially stable and had a strong board
if it wanted to win additional monetary support. Although the issues
were interrelated, the inclusion of Asian American elites was contested
primarily on the basis of class, while the incorporation of non-Asian
elites was objected to on the basis of both class and race. For an organization that identifies itself as grassroots and community based, making this shift to garner recognition and to survive has been regarded as
one of the "perils of legitimacy" (Kuramoto 1976). This organizational
transformation of UPAC represents a core struggle for many grassroots
ethnic organizations—the autonomy model that needs the support of
internal groups versus the dependency model that relies on external
support. The organizers of UPAC realized that choosing to remain
autonomous could lead to the dissolution of the organization, as evi-
denced by the numerous ethnic self-help organizations created in the
1970s that simply disappeared. Ironically, to expand and improve
UPAC's services, organizers had to distance themselves from those who
started and supported UPAC in its early stages, broadening the definition of a community-based organization.

This new format displaced the power of traditional leaders, since board members did not have to be nominated by single-ethnic community organizations and could be drawn from those who could build networks with the mainstream society. In 1976, in addition to having representatives recommended by single-ethnic organizations, UPAC leaders included at-large representatives who did not have to be members of community-based organizations (Yip 1976). Each ethnic organization involved with UPAC had two delegates and an alternate, regardless of the size of the ethnic group. When there was only a handful of single-ethnic organizations, this policy was feasible, but a growing population and an increasing number of single-ethnic organizations made this format more complicated. UPAC organizers realized that single-ethnic leaders well respected by their own communities might not be so highly regarded by other Asian Americans or by the mainstream society. Some UPAC organizers criticized traditional ethnic leaders whose conduct they considered "unprofessional," particularly at meetings with mainstream groups, and whom they regarded as an embarrassment to the organization itself.

The structural change was also prompted by the actions of the Council of Pilipino-American Organizations (COPAO), an umbrella organization of about twenty Filipino organizations (Yu 1980) and one of the founding members of UPAC. COPAO withdrew from UPAC in 1975, announcing its dissatisfaction with the inequities of the pan-Asian format. In one incident, both organizations applied for county funding that would have allowed them to hire more staff members; the positions were given to UPAC. A group of Filipinos involved with COPAO stated that, as the largest Asian subgroup, they should receive the largest portion of funds and should have more decision-making power.[17] Observing what had occurred to Filipino American groups in other areas, these board members and delegates felt that Filipinos were not receiving adequate representation, given their contributions to UPAC:

> In words and deed COPAO participated and contributed talent, resources and facilities to UPAC organization from its infancy. Now, that UPAC has achieved its viability, it has also grown to establish its own identity either as a umbrella organization or sponsoring agency of member communities capable of subordinating the interest and role of ethnic communities. Just like what happened to Los Angeles and San Francisco Philipino-American community organizations and pretty soon in San Diego, it will be all Asians or UPAC and no more Pilipino identity, much less its right of self-determination. . . . [COPAO] has grown by leaps and bounds since 1971 to serve the cause of Pilipino-Americans and that its influence cannot just be ignored by

policy-makers of the City and County of San Diego. Would you be willing to relegate COPAO role in a secondary or subordinate role? Or would you prefer an equal footing with any other Asian organizations?[18]

Leaders of COPAO felt that they not only were jeopardizing their chances for funding by being a member organization of UPAC, but also risked losing their autonomy. Some UPAC organizers thought COPAO had a leadership credibility problem and was not an effectively run organization compared to UPAC, so the loss would be minimal; others felt that COPAO's large numbers were vital to UPAC.

UPAC activists reconsidered their organizational structure and assessed the potential threat of fragmentation, in which single-ethnic groups could argue for more representation based not only on numbers, but also on factors such as number of active organizers or financial donors. With a new structure, UPAC organizers could coordinate joint projects with single-ethnic groups, and if necessary distance themselves from particularly troublesome single-ethnic leaders and their organizations and develop their own programs.

UPAC began recruiting well-to-do Asian Americans to participate, even those not necessarily well known within their ethnic communities. An architect who had recently moved to the area admits he "did not have a sense of any Asian presence in San Diego" before being contacted to join during this period. He comments: "They were looking for people with more status; ... there is a big transition when you are moving from a community board to one in which they want people who have the ability to raise the money and to mainstream. . . . I was a pawn. I didn't know that at that time, but I realized that the organization had a good clientele and a good mission. Then I became profoundly aware of the plight of Asians in San Diego." Although this man was not connected with the Asian American community beforehand and referred to himself as a "banana" (Yellow outside, White inside), his involvement with UPAC changed his perception of himself and the population. Since then he has had a tremendous impact on local Asian activism in multiple arenas, not just social services.

The decision to include non-Asians in UPAC was controversial because of both the class factor and the racial impact on the organization, since wealthy non-Asian philanthropists connected to corporate sponsors would be able to determine, or interfere with, the agenda for Asian Americans. Although the majority of "outsiders" were European Americans, prominent African Americans and Latinos have also been included on the board. Including non-Asians in order to make UPAC more "legitimate" further removed the organization from its grassroots connection to the Asian American community. In 1980, UPAC firmly established its connection to mainstream society by including non-Asians in its fund-raising efforts to purchase a building so that it could locate all its programs at one site. The first year of operation, activists had worked out of the Chinese Social Service Center, and later they rented office space in the downtown area. Investing in property would legitimize UPAC as a stable organization and enable the leadership to approach prominent individuals, politicians, foundations, and corporations for funds. To spearhead the $200,000 building-fund drive, UPAC formed a finance committee of heavy hitters that included Asian American community representatives, prominent Asian and non-Asian business owners and professionals, local politicians, and a representative from the La Jolla Museum of Contemporary Art. Clarence Pendleton of the San Diego Urban League and Ron Pascua of Wells Fargo Bank cochaired the committee. By establishing itself in a single location, UPAC improved its ability to obtain funds and, as one organizer put it, "UPAC wouldn't come and go at the whim of the federal government."

There was also opposition to the inclusion of elite Asians and non-Asians, since decision-making powers would be redirected to those who had little contact with the clients of UPAC or the Asian American communities they served. UPAC attempted to counter this criticism by having a board of directors and also an advisory board that consisted of a mixture of Asian American community members. The UPAC officers continue to be Asian Americans. While these changes were occurring, Beverley Yip remained the executive director, and the staff members, especially the program directors, were still primarily Asian American; thus the daily functions of the organization were maintained by Asian American social workers, not the elite.

As the agency became more institutionalized, organizers also began adhering to stricter hiring standards for staff members, to improve both UPAC's chances of acquiring grants and contracts and its service delivery. The agency had been hiring employees who had "ethnic credentials," meaning they had connections to the ethnic communities UPAC served; now the agency began giving priority to those with college degrees. The second executive director has continued this pattern and has encouraged employees to further their education, although there has been resistance to this policy since it is biased toward those who can afford to become credentialed. She credits these social service workers for bringing new perspectives and organizational skills to UPAC. Some argued that this accommodationist strategy displaces the role of local community-based activists who, through their lived experience, understand the plight of co-ethnics—skills, they argue, that cannot be acquired in any credentialing system.

Some, particularly Executive Director Beverley Yip and a Chinese American attorney from the state attorney general's office who was the chair at the time, realized that foundations judge organizations in part by the composition of their board and staff members. They realized they needed to increase their leverage to obtain funds to improve the quantity and quality of the services. Those who supported the transformation felt it was justified when the Community Foundation Committee, a local funding group, gave UPAC a $25,000 grant following the change. Previously, UPAC had received on average only $2,000 to $5,000 grants for its programs; this was the largest amount it had ever received for a single program. Members of the foundation had even encouraged UPAC to make the structural change and had contacted prominent Asian Americans to join the board of UPAC. Some twenty years later, in 1997, this repositioning and restructuring was still evident, with the executive director retitled president and CEO, and the twelve-member board comprised of a graphic artist (chair), corporate executives, lawyers, engineers, doctors, and other professionals. The primary "community of givers" lists include government funding sources; private charity foundations; Asian American individuals and businesses; and major communication, financial, construction, health care, and educational corporations or institutions. The consensus of community leaders I interviewed who were present during the organizational transformation and who joined UPAC in later years was support for the changes, since they accomplished UPAC's main goal—to make itself a politically and economically stronger organization.

The Politicization of New Immigrants

The influx of well-to-do immigrants from abroad and migrants from other areas in the United States has revitalized ethnic communities and infused new energy into ethnic mobilization. Their resources, namely human capital, including education and expertise, and material capital, have been particularly beneficial to an organization that serves lower-income native-born and foreign-born populations. UPAC incorporates these Asian newcomers into the organization not just as board members or as paid employees, but also in the areas of volunteerism and philanthropy. Judging from the organization's list of benefactors and from the attendance at UPAC's annual charity dinner, financial support from newcomers, both immigrants and migrants, is crucial to the organization. The reduction of public expenditures on social programs at federal, state, and local levels will increase the burden on UPAC to find alternative sources of funding, and encouraging philanthropy among new Asians becomes a way to sustain the organization. A number of the foreign-born and U.S.-born migrants to the San Diego area have become directly and indirectly active in the pan-Asian organization by donating their time, expertise, and services.

As expected, U.S.-born Asians were active in sustaining UPAC, but it was the participation of first-generation Asians at the leadership level that defied the common assumptions of passivity and apathy associated with new immigrants. The second executive director of UPAC, Margaret Iwanaga-Penrose, a Japanese American born in Japan who came to the United States at age twelve, was hand picked by Beverley Yip, a Chinese immigrant from Canada.[19] The two women were close friends until Yip's death in 1991. Iwanaga-Penrose, whose father served in the Japanese army during World War II, says of the former chair of UPAC, a Filipina who immigrated to the United States with her husband and daughter:

> She's remarkable because she comes from the days when she was a POW [prisoner of war during the Japanese occupation of the Philippines] and she works with me. And it's very surprising to some of the Filipino leadership that she's the chairman. And I can't think of anybody else on the board currently with whom I can work better; .... she's a risk taker and I'm a risk taker. ... In spite of the pressures that she gets from her friends, she has chosen to support UPAC, so I really admire her greatly. She again comes from that generation where there can be a lot of bitterness that could be unfairly displaced, and she and I sometimes talk about it, but she just has that kind of humanity that transcends itself. People like that really are the people who are making the difference in San Diego. Not too many leaders in her generation can do that.

These women leaders from UPAC exemplify the ability of immigrants with different experiences to collaborate with one another. Iwanaga-Penrose identifies with the term "risk-takers," describing this new leadership as outspoken and innovative about providing social services and also willing to cross ethnic, gender, and class boundaries.

The Filipina of whom Iwanaga-Penrose speaks, the former chair of UPAC, was born to a well-established family in the Philippines yet suffered financial hardships after the Japanese occupied her country during World War II. She originally immigrated to New York City to seek medical attention for her daughter. She has worked as an accountant in both the Philippines and the United States and has used these skills in her volunteer work with the African American and Asian American communities. She has tried to convince others in her community to contribute to UPAC rather than commit all their efforts to homeland issues, as she conveys in this statement: "I even told them once, they have to make up their mind, you know, are they Americans or are they Filipinos. I said the criticism against giving to the Filipino charities is all the charity monies are going outside the country and there are so many people here that are having a hard time and what are they doing to help their kind here." Her point is that Filipinos who choose to establish roots in the United States have an obligation to participate in the betterment of the lives of their co-ethnics in this country.

Although she lived in an exclusive gated community in north San Diego, she experienced financial setbacks in the Philippines during World War II and in the United States as an immigrant. She conveyed the personal and professional discrimination she encountered as a minority and as a woman in this country and, in so doing, explained how this has sensitized her to the needs of others. She comments on the personal dilemma she faced in justifying the continuation of $50,000 in funds for a child-abuse program, particularly for Southeast Asians, at a county meeting:

> I remember my first time before the board of supervisors, I actually cried because it was so difficult for me to ask for money. I mean, we [my family] never had to ask for money. We were poor but we never told anyone that we were poor. I mean, you know, my father's side, we just made do. And here I was asking for money for child abuse prevention. . . . It's so difficult to ask for money and it's not even for me. It's for people that I don't even know. And to say that in front of everybody that we have problems, you know, we never do that. It's so shameful to admit that you have a problem. . . . That's the perception too, that we're a perfect model community, we have no problems. We do have problems, but rather than talk about it, we'd rather kill ourselves or kill everybody else.

She speaks to the embarrassment she, as well as other organizers, felt admitting that Asian Americans have social problems. She understood that regardless of her class position, she had experienced discrimination, and this enabled her to publicly request governmental assistance for other Asian Americans, even those who had very different class status and immigration experiences than her own. Although some might regard the participation of the immigrant generation as unique, the San

Diego experience clearly demonstrates that new immigrants are concerned about social issues and are involved in social advocacy work.

Ironically, the presence of these well-to-do arrivals, especially from Asian countries experiencing an economic boom, has made it difficult for Asians to request funding for social services. The publicity about Pacific Rim countries and the wealth being created there, particularly at the expense of the U.S. economy, conveys to the general public and to politicians that Asian immigrants and native-born Asians no longer need assistance. As one UPAC activist notes: "Their perception of Japan is the most powerful nation, richer than America, and why should we be helping them [Asians in America], you know." These assumptions do not distinguish among ethnic groups or sending countries, leading to damaging conclusions. The influx of well-to-do immigrants adds new vigor to the model minority myth and contributes to the skepticism that a substantial number of needy Asian Americans exists.

Pan Asian Social Service Programs and a New Social Welfare Paradigm

One factor that allowed UPAC to survive was its willingness to create innovative programs as the population base changed and as new social needs emerged. Its objective was to provide a "culturally and linguistically responsive approach" to the "underserved and unserved" pan-Asian populations.[20] Previously, there was limited data on Asian Americans, and the passage of the Disadvantaged Minority Health Improvement Act of 1990 was part of a concerted effort to ensure the collection of data on Asian Pacific Americans; since 1993, the National Center for Health Statistics has collected vital data on 75 percent of this population (Mineta 1994). Yet, due to inconsistencies in the act itself and its implementation, Asian Americans still rank last among racial groups in the collection, analysis, interpretation, and publication of health data (Ponce and Guillermo 1994). As a result, Asian American social service organizations "have had to rely on outdated studies, anecdotal material, and research with serious methodological or conceptual flaws to make decisions" on health care services (Zane and Takeuchi 1994).

In the 1970s, UPAC social workers had no needs assessment of the mental and physical health concerns of local Asians to rely on, making it challenging to apply for grants or deliver appropriate services. They tried to lobby for better data collection from mainstream groups. UPAC complained about the omission of "Asians and Pilipinos" in the social needs-assessment study completed by the City Housing and Community Services Department in San Diego.[21] Asian Americans were lumped with Native Americans and Arabic into the "All Other" category, and thirteen of sixteen tables in the assessment contained no data on Asian Americans. The interviews were conducted only in English and Spanish, and the community seminar had one Asian American participant out of more than a hundred participants. As a result of these oversights, UPAC organizers had to collect their own research data by interviewing community leaders and conducting community surveys to determine their needs and how best to service these needs, a task they continue to do with limited funds.

Initially UPAC focused its services in the areas of mental health, health promotion, elder care, translation assistance, and escort/transportation services, but over the years the organizers have created a multitude of programs for varying ethnic groups.[22] They also knew that ethnic groups had needs that warranted different approaches, so they created programs targeting several ethnic groups and others serving specific ethnic groups.[23] An excerpt from a handbook summarizes their sensitivity to ethnic differences: "While it is true that historical, cultural and social similarities between the various groups exist, there are also significant differences between them. Each community should be dealt with as a distinct entity" (Union of Pan Asian Communities 1978: 1). For example, the development of a nutritional program for various Asian American elderly subgroups catered to their differing linguistic abilities, their residential locations, and their dietary habits.[24] As a result, this pan-Asian organization, for the most part, gained support from the varying ethnic communities because of its attentiveness to both ethnic distinctions and commonalties.

Public and private funding for programs also changes, and being attuned to these shifts allows an organization to react accordingly. A board member comments on this theme:

UPAC has kept up with the times and has responded to the emerging needs. Some of the old guard are criticizing us for no longer paying attention to the language translation, to old issues of refugee acculturation; but my point is there's no more money for that. What money is available nowadays is for alcohol and substance abuse, for juvenile delinquency prevention, for AIDS. Very few will admit that there are homosexuals in our community. We've always kept it under wraps. So now we have to go into that. Now, some people feel uncomfortable when we address AIDS. I mean, I guess it's from ignorance or whatever, but that's an emerging need. Delinquency—we have Vietnamese kids that operate like military commando-style holdups. We have Filipino boys shooting at each other. We have guns. . . . And, you know, we need to respond to that.

Some of the fastest-growing programs are based on available funding, such as those on the prevention of domestic violence, child abuse, and alcohol and drug abuse and on job training.[25] Additionally, there has been an expansion of funding for juvenile delinquency, gang prevention, teen suicide, and mentorship programs, targeted primarily at Filipino, Hmong, Laotian, and Vietnamese youths. New immigrant and refugee parents preoccupied with economic survival and generational conflicts with their children are contributing factors to these problems (Vigil and Yun 1990; Lau 1990b, 1992; Trueba, Cheng, and Ima 1993). The increase in police and news reports of young Asian American youths in trouble has led to a heightened awareness of the "at-risk" youth problem (Lau 1992, 1993a).[26] UPAC organizers have been proactive in using general funds to create pilot projects to fit the communities' changing needs, with the expectation that funders would eventually channel additional money toward these specific programs.

Even in the early 1990s, UPAC organizers were forced to justify the need for culturally sensitive programs and their legitimacy in providing such service. A representative from the organization explains the consequences of this skepticism:

> We lost the child abuse program because a bunch of mainstream organizations said, "Oh well, we speak all the Asian languages through volunteers." . . . So the County Board of Supervisors cut our program and gave the money to a mainstream agency. And then about ten months later, we did a collaboration with the Urban League and another program . . . and I got the grant back. And then we got the active caseload back [from the mainstream agency]—I think we had six active Asian cases. And over two and a half years we [UPAC] served over 700 folks. Don't tell me "we" can cover Asian languages. That kind of bullshit goes through, you know, because people are ignorant. They don't check it out, they don't realize that you need to have not only a bilingual person, but a bicultural person. You have to have people who are connected with the community. You have to have people who have done, over time, some incredible jobs delivering services. Our politicians make decisions based on what? Fantasy? It's ridiculous.

Originally the agency was given a three-year program-development grant of $392,000, but due to severe cutbacks in the overall state budget at the end of this period, funding was not renewed, and as part of a trickle-down effect the county's Department of Welfare budget was curtailed and the department refused to fund the program. Additionally, the County Board of Supervisors was unwilling to allocate a portion of its $1 million of discretionary funds set aside for endangered social services for the program. According to a number of UPAC activists, some of these politicians relied on the model minority myth to make decisions and in times of budget constraints used this myth to justify their decision. UPAC directors formed a temporary group, the Pan Asian Coalition for Children's Services, chaired by a fourth-generation Chinese American restaurateur and endorsed by thirty-seven Asian American organizations, to assist in lobbying for funds, which included convincing 1,500 Asians to write letters of support to the board of supervisors (Lau 1990a). Even when the mainstream agency was given the responsibility for providing services to Asian Americans, its efforts were as grossly inadequate as in the early 1970s.

UPAC expanded its programs and increased its funding under the guidance of the second UPAC Executive Director, Margaret Iwanaga-Penrose.[27] After she assumed the post, UPAC's 1990 operating budget of $1.6 million grew to over $2.6 million in 1992. An early 1990s brochure states that each year the agency assists over 13,000 San Diegans from approximately eleven Asian and Pacific Islander cultures.[28] According to a 1997 UPAC newsletter, the number of clients had increased to 21,000; by 2002, clients numbered over 50,000 with a $4.5 million budget. There are more than eighty staff members and numerous volunteers who, combined, speak over a dozen Asian languages and dialects.[29] By 1996, the agency operated thirty-five separate programs under various categories of child abuse and domestic violence, consumer and corporate education, cultural adjustment and language assistance, developmental disabilities, economic development, health education, home school partnerships, mental health, senior services, and youth programs. Iwanaga-Penrose has worked on developing innovative programs such as the building of affordable housing projects for low-income families. Another expanding program is the Multicultural Economic Development Project, an entrepreneurship program funded mainly by the city of San Diego for limited-English speakers that provides training and guidance for those interested in starting businesses for water purification, gardening and landscaping, auto repair, import and export, and building maintenance (*UPAC Union* 1997). The growth of such programs persists, for there are still a substantial number of Asian Americans living in conditions of poverty with dire social problems (Nakao 1996; Sue 1993).[30]

Working in the social service sector for ethnic communities can be extremely frustrating and disheartening for both staffers and volunteers.

During my fieldwork, I met a number of individuals who had moved on to other jobs because they felt their efforts and talents were being wasted. Yet others have remained dedicated to this work, regardless of being underpaid and overworked. One participant of UPAC explains the difference between dealing with the high-profile board members and the acknowledgments she receives from the clients and their family members who use and benefit from the social services provided by UPAC: "This is really different from the leadership who 'talk politics and do politics.' For me, whenever I experience this appreciation from people who are voiceless, who are not visible in the community, that's worth it." I also spoke to longtime board members who wanted to be replaced with "new blood" so they could move on to other projects, because their volunteer work was draining their finances (particularly fund-raisers) and taxing their emotional energy. Sustaining such activism has been dependent on dedicated individuals willing to confront the barriers constantly imposed by the state that attempt to prevent them from providing adequate social services to the community.

Beyond the Pan-Asian Community and the Social Service Model

UPAC encompassed a variety of agendas, although its primary focus was social services. While UPAC was commonly viewed as a health and human service agency, its actions went beyond merely delivering services to its clients to involvement in economic and political justice struggles.[31] The original constitution of the organization defined its goal: "to bring the Pan Asian organizations and individuals up to the maximum level of social functioning and well being."[32] Even though the intent of the organizers may have been to provide "direct" social services to the Asian American community, many felt this could be accomplished only by concentrating their energies on "indirect" services and coordinating their activities with those of other racial groups, believing that there was an "inextricable linkage between indirect and direct services."[33] Indirect services can include jointly participating on research projects such as collecting data on Asian Americans or may encompass working on advocacy agendas, for instance, raising awareness about the paucity of Asian Americans employed in the public sphere. Joint participation also simplified matters for Latinos, African Americans, and Native Americans, who could collaborate with one Asian American organization rather than with each Asian subgroup. It provided these groups with networks to

share organizational and human resources and allowed them to negotiate among themselves before contending with mainstream institutions.

The personal experiences of activists often led them to understand
the intersections of their lives as minorities. A lawyer involved with
UPAC whose father was Chamorro and whose mother was Filipino and
Spanish, raised in communities with large Mexican populations, realized he shared commonalities with his neighbors. This sense of commonality was later reinforced during his college years, when through
mutual friends he became involved in Chicano activism at San Diego
State University; he used these models to advocate for better college
opportunities and social services for Asian Americans and Pacific
Islanders. He worked closely with UPAC in its early stages and moved
on to legal and political advocacy work on behalf of the Asian American and Pacific Islander communities. The second executive director of
UPAC, a Japanese American, was involved in the civil rights movement
and was a staff member of the Southern Christian Leadership Conference in Chicago during the 1960s. She credits this experience with
shaping her ideology and actions. These cases indicate how such experiences are representative of the often invisible foundations used by
Asian Americans to build coalitions with other minority groups.

Often there was an incentive for UPAC to collaborate with other
minority groups, for instance, when revenue-sharing funds were allo-
cated to minority groups only if they participated in indirect programs
like data gathering. An example was the Coalition Research Group
(CRG), composed of planning staff from five coalitions: American Indians for Future and Traditions, Black Federation, Community Congress,
Chicano Federation, and UPAC. CRG was responsible for the development and implementation of research designed to enlarge the Human
Care Services Program (HCSP) database in the area of Individual and
Family Crisis. One of the projects was the Single Parent Family project, in which UPAC cooperated with the four community planning
agencies conducting field surveys and compiling statistics. While UPAC
collected data within a designated geographic area in San Diego, it also
gathered data on single-parent Asian American families countywide.[34]

Communities of color were also proactive in forging these alliances,
rather than competing against one another for limited resources. UPAC,
along with the Chicano Federation and the Black Federation, formed
the Minority Coalition to protest the county's unresponsiveness to their
needs. In its statement, the coalition participants defined issues and
problems that affected all their communities of color:

> The County currently has many programs and services which affect minor-
> ity residents of this County. However, because programs are fragmented,
> uncoordinated, and frequently without effective minority input, these efforts
> have not made an impact commensurate with the amounts of tax dollars
> expended. Affirmative Action has not lived up to its mandates. Programs for
> the poor and minorities have been reduced. There seems to be a decrease in
> commitment to help improve the quality of life within our communities.[35]

Another crucial board was the Coalition of Coalitions, which included members of the Minority Coalition and other social service agencies, such as the Community Congress and the Community Agencies Representing the Poor. They met regularly to discuss current information on funding, programs, and changes in policies that would affect their respective social service agencies.

In the process of forming UPAC, the organizers realized there was a lack of Asian Americans in prominent positions at the city level who could represent their interests. A number of interviewees commented that even with graduate degrees in social work, they could not find employment in the public sector, which they attributed to discriminatory hiring practices. UPAC requested significant increases in the employment of Asian Americans in city offices, particularly on the city manager's staff and in the Department of Human Resources and the Personnel Department.[36] It was publicly acknowledged that employment in city offices increased from 6,072 to 6,368 in the 1972–1973 year, while in the same period, Asian American employees decreased from 35 to 27, even though the City Affirmative Action Plan had been initiated in early February.[37]

UPAC members also wanted increased hiring in county agencies and departments, such as in the Affirmative Action Program and the Personnel Department, since the individuals in these positions made decisions on social services. In 1977, UPAC and the Council of Pilipino-American Organizations (COPAO) joined the Chicano Federation in a lawsuit against San Diego County, which resulted in a Consent Decree. This action originated with members of the Chicano community who wanted corrective measures to remedy what they perceived to be an imbalance in the hiring and promoting of county employees. They developed a successful legal strategy to enforce the provisions of the Civil Rights Act of 1964, stating that the county had violated federal civil rights statutes and was not in compliance with federal law that banned discrimination. In the Consent Decree, the county denied any wrongdoing but agreed to make amendments "to recruit, hire, assign and promote Asians, Mexican-American/Latinos, women and blacks."[38]

Some active in UPAC complained that these activities took time and drained resources from their contractual social service obligations. In contrast, others felt that although collaborative work on indirect services was time consuming and costly, it offered long-term benefits, such as providing funds to operate their direct service programs (Peterson 1976). Coordinating with other minority groups allowed Asian Americans to increase their opportunities to obtain funding, yet these have always been fragile alliances. Some Asian Americans disapproved of forming coalitions with other minority groups, arguing that these groups were too dissimilar. Other minority groups complained that welfare benefits should not be given to recent Asian refugees and immigrants but should be limited to more deserving domestic minority groups. The depiction of Asian Americans as the "model minority," a myth used to quell the demands of African Americans and Latinos by blaming these minorities for their own failures, has only added to this friction. In turn, Asian Americans have complained that African Americans and Latinos have been given a disproportionate share of funds. Despite these criticisms, leaders of color in San Diego have continued to form alliances with one another in the area of direct and indirect services.

Beyond Local Pan-Asian Networks

In addition to the formation of UPAC, local activists worked simultaneously to build networks with social service providers and activists at the national level, thereby allowing them to share organizational resources. As one participant wrote: "We believe a consistent and constant effort must be made to keep local communities in touch with regional and national 'communities' so that we do not become complacent and insular into ourselves" (*San Diego Area PAC Report* 1976). Like grassroots mobilization at the local level, this national organization gave Asian American women vital roles, since many national participants were women. This move required new kinds of leaders—namely those with education credentials willing to extend themselves beyond the local ethnic communities. This networking shows how local activism can contribute to national organizations and how national mobilization can stimulate and reaffirm local activists in their struggle.

At the same time that UPAC was being created, the first National Asian American Mental Health Conference was held in 1972, one of the earliest efforts to form a national pan-Asian coalition.[39] The objective was to bring Asian American mental health workers together to identify key social service concerns and to share data on mental health needs. The outcome was the creation of the Asian American Mental Health Federation (AAMHF), which renamed itself the National Coalition of Asian Americans and Pacific Island Peoples for Human Services and Action but used the abbreviated title Pacific Asian Coalition (PAC). It was formed in 1974 and incorporated in 1975, and the National PAC served as the umbrella organization for nine regional affiliate groups across the country (Ignacio 1976).

Realizing that local concerns were similar to national issues, San Diego Asian social workers and social work students, mainly those affiliated with UPAC, immediately organized an ad hoc steering committee to coordinate with the national organization.[40] They saw that PAC's concern with lack of services for Asian Americans, especially in the areas of aging, children and youth, drug abuse, alcoholism, and immigrant adjustment, was aligned with local efforts. The San Diego PAC eventually became part of UPAC, located its office in the UPAC building, and chose eight delegates and eight alternates. Although there were not more than twenty active participants in San Diego (primarily social workers), their conferences, receptions, and workshops attracted a substantial audience from the community.[41] The existence of PAC was an asset to the survival of UPAC, since many who participated in PAC used their knowledge in transforming UPAC.

Organizing on a national level also made it easier to gain initial funding. In September 1973, organizers received funding from the National Institute of Mental Health to help Asian American communities across the nation assess their mental health needs and services by planning and conducting regional conferences and setting up a research center.[42] In 1974, using these funds, PAC organizers established a research center, then named the Asian American Mental Health Research Center (AAMHRC), at the University of California, San Diego, which brought federal resources to the local community. The diverse ethnic population, the existence of UPAC, and the creation of a local PAC chapter along with a local university strengthened the case for bringing the research center to San Diego.[43] Although there was conflict between the community organizations and the university researchers about the "change in direction from community-based to academic research" during the period the center was based in San Diego, local groups benefited from the data collection.

As Asian American social service agencies in various parts of the country became more autonomous or fragmented and leadership conflicts developed, participation in PAC waned. When the director of AAMHRC moved to a university in Chicago, the research center was relocated and maintained, but without the support of the national PAC network. The task of coordinating the diverse social service needs of the local and regional areas became logistically difficult for the national PAC organizers to administer. In spite of these problems, the coalition was effective in representing their needs to federal institutions such as the Civil Rights Commission, the Census Bureau, and the National Institute of Mental Health. Its "inclusive" policy originally proved an asset; however, this also accounts for its decline, since it was attempting to organize diverse local constituents who themselves were relatively new to the pan-Asian mobilization format at this stage. When support for the national PAC organization diminished, the San Diego PAC chapter was dissolved in 1979. From these modest beginnings, there now exist specialized Asian American healthcare and mental health organizations, regional and national conferences, and collaborative research projects at the state and national level that are a resource for UPAC.

Conclusion

The sociopolitical circumstances of the 1970s when UPAC was first created have changed dramatically. At both the local and national levels, retreats from the Great Society programs of the 1960s and 1970s have been drastic, especially since the Reagan budget cuts of the 1980s (Wilson and Aponte 1985). Public support for programs directed at assisting minorities and alleviating poverty is on the wane, representing a syndrome some have labeled "compassion fatigue." Even more alarming (although not surprising, given this country's history) is how the political discourse surrounding the elimination of antipoverty programs intersects with a call to curb the arrival of immigrants, undocumented and documented, and even to deny welfare benefits and services to legal immigrants. The passing of Propositions 187 and 209 in California and the 1996 Welfare Reform Act at the federal level are indicative of these sentiments. Perhaps symbolic is former Governor Pete Wilson of California, who was supportive of UPAC when he was the mayor of San Diego and was one of the organization's first keynote speakers at their installation dinner; Wilson later became known for his anti-immigrant rhetoric and legislation. Although some of the consequences of these state and federal policies have been postponed, or their impact has yet to be determined, it is obvious that the burden on ethnic social service, nonprofit agencies like UPAC, which cater primarily to foreign-born populations, will only increase.

Originally, organizers thought UPAC would be a temporary endeavor that would eventually be incorporated into mainstream social service structures. As one organizer states: "It was the intent that we would set up and do an interim role until we could place qualified social workers . . . in all of the city and county agencies that existed, then there would be no need for UPAC. That was the original goal—to work ourselves out of a job." Another longtime organizer comments on UPAC's growth: "I'm saddened by the fact that we have to have a UPAC. . . . It means that we have some people who are hurting, suffering or having problems. And if an agency like that has to get bigger, that's too bad." The survival and expansion of UPAC speaks to the ability of Asians in San Diego to mobilize effectively for social services, as well as the ongoing failure of the welfare state to address the needs of marginalized populations.

Even though Asian Americans had used creative strategies to better the lives of their populace, as a social service community they remained outside the economic and electoral political power structure. As the organization became institutionalized, its organizers began recognizing that as a nonprofit social service organization, there are limits to taking a direct political advocacy role, especially if repercussions mean decreased funds. In practicing strategies of resistance and accommodation, organizers had to learn institutional rules and procedures and become skilled at knowing where, when, and how social transformation was possible. As San Diego's only pan-Asian organization in these formative years, it became the de facto political representative for the community when there were few Asian Americans with political connections and economic security that could assist the agency. By the late 1980s and early 1990s, new Asian American organizations were created and new leaders emerged who used the foundation built by UPAC to become the "voice" for the Asian American community.

4

Cultural Images
and the Media
Racialization and Oppositional Practices

n early 1971, Asians formed an ad hoc coalition called the
United Asian Community to protest the San Diego High
School production of *The King and I*, declaring the musical
historically inaccurate and demeaning to Asian Americans.[1]
A flyer passed out during a protest summarizes their position:

> The impression given is that they [Asians and Asian Americans]
> lack intelligence, are crude and half civilized, are pagans, polyg-
> amists, docile, and generally inferior human beings. The use of
> stilted and pidgin English throughout the play; the mockery
> made of bowing and "toadlike" postures which is a part of the
> etiquette of many Asian countries; the portrayal of Buddhism as
> an inferior religion; and the subtle ways in which Western cul-
> ture is portrayed as superior to Asians ways, all reinforce nega-
> tive ideas about Asians and Asian Americans that lead to the per-
> petuation of racism.

The protest caused only minimal disruption of the production, and it seems the coalition disbanded shortly thereafter.
It was a difficult struggle, since the play, many proponents
argued, was an integral part of U.S. culture. This has been
a defense consistently used by opponents to thwart attempts
by minority groups to eliminate harmful depictions of them.
At the time, San Diego's Asian American population numbered around 3 percent and there were few Asian American
organizations, so their willingness to mobilize indicates how
significant cultural images of Asians were (and continue to

be) for them. Although the historical context would change in the next decade, the response to the protests against anti-Asian stereotypes would remain disturbingly similar.

The focus of this chapter is the mid-1980s, when San Diego Asians formed a pan-Asian coalition to protest anti-Asian portrayals on a local television show and later, on a local radio program. Asian Americans did not consider these isolated incidents but symbols of a consistent pattern of U.S. racism and Western imperialism that devalued them. The mass media has the capacity to produce controlling images that become culturally embedded and provide ideological justification for the oppression of women and minorities, thereby legitimizing systems of inequities (Collins 1991; Jewell 1993). These distortions, whether intentional or unintentional, lead not only to their cultural marginalization, but also to their economic and political exclusion from mainstream society (Hamamoto 1994). Those in charge of the television show and the radio show regarded their presentation of Asians as merely a form of entertainment. Asian Americans know that these cultural stereotypes are the backdrop against which verbal and physical assaults, even murders, of Asian Americans have occurred.

Contextualizing these events provides an understanding of why Asian Americans chose to mobilize. At the same time that the Asian American population was increasing dramatically in the 1980s, resentment toward Asian Americans also increased (Jo and Mas 1993). In San Diego, the influx of Southeast Asian refugees that began in the mid-1970s would continue into the 1980s. Immigration from Asia and secondary migration of Asians from other parts of the United States rose in this period as well. In a survey of San Diego County residents in 1982, 36 percent of the respondents believed that Asian immigrants had a negative impact on the area, but only 17 percent felt the same about immigrants from Western Europe (Cornelius 1982). A 1984–1985 survey of San Diego city schools revealed that 30 percent of students had negative feelings toward Asian American students; they made remarks like "I don't like the people from Japan and China and Vietnam, you can send them back," and "Send some of the Chinks out of this school to other schools" (quoted in Lau 1990c).

The demographic changes of the 1980s occurred during a period of national economic downturn that was accompanied by an increase in anti-Asian sentiment and violence. The expansion of global economic competition from Asia and the development of U.S. multinational industries resulted in a loss of industrial jobs in the domestic labor market (Wang 1991). To protect U.S. jobs, a "Buy American" campaign was directed not at European products, but primarily at Japanese and Asian products. Growing anti-Japanese sentiment was marked by such slogans as "Unemployment—Made in Japan" and "Toyota-Datsun-Honda = Pearl Harbor" (Daniels 1988: 342). Media reports of Japanese ownership of businesses and real estate in the United States increased noticeable, despite owners from Western nations being more numerous. The 1980s, also referred to as the post–civil rights era, was a period of Reaganism and political backlash against the rights of people of color. This is not to say that the national socioeconomic climate or local disapproval of the influx of Asians to the area contributed directly to these negative portrayals in the local San Diego media; however, they describe the socioeconomic and political climate in which these incidents occurred and help explain why Asian Americans responded as they did.

My fieldwork began after these affairs unfolded, so I have reconstructed the events primarily from interviews, meeting minutes, newspaper articles, correspondence, and organizational newsletters. I saw episodes of the *San Diego at Large* TV show when it originally aired and was perturbed by the stereotypes presented. Although a small number of participants I met could provide me with intimate details of the events, others who were only tangentially involved remembered them as a turning point for local Asian American activism. They recognized that the racial overtones of these stereotypes implicate all Asians; however, they did not always agree upon strategies, nor is there a consensus on how to define "racism." Asian Americans also used this opportunity to form alliances with other minority groups who share a history of contending with denigrating portrayals and exclusion from decision-making positions in the media.

I began to recognize the significance of these events for the community and the amount of energy minority communities expend to eradicate harmful stereotypes—energy that could be spent on more productive endeavors. They have limited resources, so Asian Americans and other minorities have to make prudent choices as to which struggles deserve their attention. The choices are not clear or easy—the equivalent of deciding which fires are most important to extinguish when one has a limited number of firefighters and fire engines. How relevant is combating negative racial imagery when Asian Americans are struggling for food, shelter, and basic health care? Yet they also know that allowing anti-Asian images to go unchallenged contributes to an environment that continues to allow these pressing needs to be ignored.

While there had been other "unflattering" portrayals of Asians in the local media, none generated the same amount of collective action. Like many instances of mobilization, the protest took on a life of its own and resulted in unintended consequences.

The Spark: The *San Diego at Large* Television Show Controversy

In 1986, the character K. C. Wang began appearing periodically on a locally produced television show, Channel 8 KFMB-TV's *San Diego at Large*, which produced stories on the local scene and included comedy sketches. Finding humor in a local advertisement in which an Asian acupuncturist claimed that acupuncture was a cure-all, Larry Himmel, the host of the show, developed a caricature for one of his sketches. Asian Americans later complained that "Larry Himmel portrays a composite Asian character named 'K. C. Wang.' Mr. Himmel, a Caucasian, is made up with eyeliner to obtain the stereotypical slanted eyes, wears a happi coat and headband, speaks in an atrocious, contrived accent, and rambles on like an idiot while performing acupuncture on inanimate objects."[2] The character had buckteeth and bowed repeatedly, saying "honorable" and "Confucius says." In one episode, the character fails a driving test and is unable to get auto insurance, which many activists perceived to be connected to the stereotype of Asian Americans as incompetent drivers. Although the character was supposed to be Chinese, there was reference to other Asian ethnic cultural practices, particularly Japanese. Himmel wore a Japanese *happi* coat, and there was often Japanese koto music playing in the background as well. In another sketch, in reference to a Caucasian actress, the character replies, "No, she's not really Chinese, she's really a JAP (read: Jewish American Princess)," which is a racist term used to identify someone who is Japanese or Japanese American (Hirahara 1987).

In response to the charges, the comedian would later justify his actions as harmless humor and even try to credit the character with improving race relations. Himmel explained that the character was meant to satirize acupuncture commercials on cable stations, not to slur the Asian American community (Curran-Downey 1987a). He clearly did not make the connection between an Asian-derived medical practice and the Asian people. Furthermore, he justified the character by stating: "It's a comedy-based show. From time to time we will offend somebody. No way would I try to demean a race (or ethnic group). If anything, I try and put something out that will explode the stereotypes. But then again if you put it up, it's going to offend somebody" (quoted in Richardson 1987). Using conventional lines of defense, Himmel, first, denied he was a racist and, second, condemned racism. What he failed to comprehend, however, was that his character was a racist depiction, regardless of his intent or motivation.

After watching some episodes of the show, Mary Ann Salaber, a local resident whose father is Filipino and whose mother is Japanese, wrote a letter of complaint to the station: "This character that you portray has a Chinese last name, wears a Japanese *happi* coat . . . has an atrocious accent, and rambles on like an idiot. As an Asian American, I find this extremely offensive and ask that you discontinue further sketches involving 'K. C. Wang.'"[3] She later explained: "I'm not Chinese, but I found it very offensive. There was no differentiation between Chinese and Japanese. It concerns all Asians" (quoted in Hirahara 1987). She received a brief reply from Himmel: "It is not our intentions [*sic*] to stereotype any ethnic divisions nor offend anyone." She explains: "But I wrote to him to let him know that . . . I found it offensive, and all he did was write me back saying that he didn't mean to offend any groups, you know, that it was all done in parody. So I didn't think it was enough."

To press the station to discontinue airing the character, Salaber decided to garner the support of various Asian American organizations. She contacted UPAC, a pan-Asian social service organization in which she had been a board member. In support, Beverley Yip, UPAC's executive director, who was of Chinese ancestry, sent a letter to KFMB-TV objecting to the caricature of a "composite Asian American," requesting they cease portraying Asians in such a derogatory manner.[4] Like Salaber, she was offended by the racist portrayal that perpetuated a "mishmash of Asian stereotypes."

Salaber, president of the San Diego region Asian Pacific American Coalition (APAC), part of a national civil rights organization, also contacted members of the coalition at the state level.[5] The organization, incorporated in 1981, aimed "to advance and promote the concerns, visibility, and participation of Asian Pacific Americans in a democratic process through education and other charitable means."[6] At that time, they were trying to bring attention to incidents of anti-Asian sentiment and violence, issues they thought the Asian American community and the larger society should address. The national president of APAC sent a letter to the station, expressing his agreement that "K. C. Wang" was defamatory to Chinese and to Asians in general.[7] Additionally, the APAC national newsletter continued to report on events in San Diego and encouraged others to send letters of support to the local APAC.

Mingyew Leung, a San Diego resident who was also the national publications officer of APAC, felt the caricature was offensive to both Americans of Asian ancestry and Asian nationals. In his letter of complaint, he conveyed how this depiction could potentially hurt relations between San Diego and Asia, since San Diego was planning to initiate a sister-city program with Yantai, China, and was opening the Graduate School of International Relations and Pacific Studies at the University of California, San Diego:

> What does the program tell Asians and Americans of Asian descent? That because of their physical and cultural differences, they need to be subjected to negative and demeaning stereotypes. That they are not only different but "less than." What does the program tell visiting business people and foreign officials? That although San Diego engages in international relations, trade and commerce with Asians, Americans act discriminately toward a sub-group of people who may be visitors or contributing citizens and residents."[8]

Leung's approach was to articulate to San Diego elites the potential ramifications for a city attempting to develop educational, commercial, and cultural "partnerships" with Asia. Early on, protesters framed the issue from a variety of angles, local and international, but as the issue unfolded, it became a protest grounded in the concept of Asians as Americans, a perspective the main organizers felt would hold more validity.

The requests by Asian activists to discontinue showing sketches with the character or to meet with station managers and producers of the show were ignored, so they decided to go to outside sources for assistance. Salaber was a member of the Human Relations Commission (HRC) Media/Community Relations Task Force Subcommittee and brought the issue to their attention. In response to testimony given at public hearings, the San Diego County HRC, formed by the County of San Diego Board of Supervisors in 1985, established the Media/Community Relations Task Force Subcommittee in the fall of 1986 to address "the lack of effective dialogue leading to the resolution of problems associated with the perpetuation of stereotypes in the community."[9] Having also received complaints from the Black and Jewish communities about negative stereotypes of their members on the show, the subcommittee was prompted to respond to the request by the Asian American community. In December 1986, the subcommittee wrote a letter of complaint to the station and offered to be a mediator by arranging a meeting with the involved groups and by facilitating a dialogue.

After the station complained about interference by this agency, the task force explained that it intervened when it received unsolicited reports from the minority groups about the content of the show, complaints about the lack of responsiveness and lack of sensitivity, and comments about the unsatisfactory resolution of the issue.[10]

In February 1987, over six months after Salaber had written her original letter of complaint, Salaber, Yip, and Leung met with the executive news director of KFMB and the producer of *San Diego at Large*. The strategies used by the station representatives are indicative of the treatment Asian Americans often receive when contesting cultural misrepresentations: to become defensive about the portrayal and to deflect criticism back upon the victims by claiming they are not "sophisticated" enough to understand the humor. The director and producer defended the character as "an intelligent, creative entrepreneur." In her notes of the meeting, Salaber remarked that the producer of the show kept using the term "Orientals" until asked to use the "appropriate" term, "Asian," which for her was "evidence of the level of social consciousness with which we were dealing."

Both sides connected this issue to other groups that have been portrayed negatively; however, station representatives used this connection to delegitimize the claims against them, while Asian representatives used it to validate their claims. The news director felt that the sketches fell into the category of "broad satire" and justified the character: "If we took off every sketch that offended an Asian person, or a Black person, or a Jewish person, we would be left without a show."[11] When asked by the producer what Asians felt was inappropriate about the character, Salaber replied: "For a white person to put on makeup to look Black is offensive. It is just as offensive for a white person to put on makeup to look 'Asian,' and for him to portray a bumbling idiot is adding insult to injury." In an all too familiar tactic, station executives held that because they offend all groups, they are an "equal opportunity" offender, and the Asian community is unjustified in its complaint. Salaber pointed out that although contemporary U.S. society has been sensitized to the inappropriateness of blackface, similar depictions of Asians are still acceptable, which speaks to the varying levels of public awareness about inappropriate portrayals of different racialized groups.

Furthermore, the producer likened the K. C. Wang character to that played by John Belushi, the samurai character on *Saturday Night Live*, which was being televised nationally at the time. For Salaber, this rationalization only showed how racist caricatures can feed off one another and perpetuate the vicious cycle. Additionally, she explained, the Belushi character was on at 11:30 at night, whereas this program was on at 7:30 in the evening, when children were likely to see it. She states, "My concern was that this was something that kids in San Diego are thinking that this is what Asian people were like. I wanted it to end." The concern was the impact this "imaginary" Asian character would have on individuals who had limited contact, if any, with "real" Asian Americans and also how these images would negatively impact the identity of Asian American children who viewed the program.

Station representatives noted that they received letters of support for the character from Caucasians but received very few letters of complaint from the Asian American community. Their assumption was that the silence of the Asian American community authorized the portrayal, or even made it appropriate. Also implicit in their statement about the letters is the reinforcement of the hegemonic order that allows Whites to monopolize how Asians should be portrayed, while Asian Americans are invalidated when voicing concern about their own representation. Furthermore, individuals from the station were dismissing the voices of the Asian Americans who were filing a complaint. Yip commented: "You will find that many Asians opt not to file a formal complaint. It takes an acculturated person to write a letter. You many not hear of it, but the hurt is there." Her reference is to the fact that the majority of Asians in San Diego at the time were first-generation Asians who were perhaps uncomfortable with filing a complaint.

Those who protest cultural misrepresentations are often not taken seriously or are dismissed outright by the accused offenders, who often envision racism as actions perpetrated by extremists, perhaps with white hoods over shaved heads, tattooed swastikas, and black military-style boots. The defendants argue that since they are not racists, it is impossible for them to be guilty of racist acts or statements. They may apologize but admit no intentional racial bias; furthermore, they may place blame on another entity—often the victims themselves. When Asians protest, they are accused of and ridiculed for being humorless or hypersensitive (Sethi 1994). They are blamed for reading too much into an image and for yelling racism when and where it does not exist.

After the meeting, the producers said that they found the opinions "informative and understandable" and would take into consideration the concerns of the Asian community in any future portrayals of Asian characters.[12] Without further explanation, KFMB agreed to discontinue airing further sketches of the character and, for obvious reasons, had no intention of creating any new "Asian" characters.[13] At this point, the protesters felt relieved that the matter was resolved.

The Flame: The KS-103 Radio Show Controversy

But this was only the beginning. The next morning, an article in the local newspaper reported that some members of the Asian community who were upset with the K. C. Wang character held a meeting with station representatives (Curran-Downey 1987a). Randy Miller, a disc jockey for KS-103, a top-forty radio station, read the story. Known for the "shock radio" format of his daily program, which featured music, news, and comedy, Miller decided the meeting between the television station and the Asian American community would be the topic of discussion on his show. He started by questioning the legitimacy of the Human Rights Commission in monitoring the media. He also complained that the Chinese in San Diego were "overreacting" and "awfully thin-skinned," since they could not take a "harmless joke." After telling some Chinese jokes in which he made reference to the Chinese as "Chinamen" and "Chinks" and to their "slanted eyes," he invited his listeners to call in with their "Chinese" jokes. During his three-hour morning program, listeners complied. The few Asian Americans who called in to complain about the jokes were ridiculed. In compensation, Miller asked Chinese listeners to call the next day to make jokes about "Americans." No one responded to his offer.

Approximately seventeen people, members of the Asian American community and others, called the radio station manager to demand an on-air apology. The next day, Miller was not working but had the substitute disc jockey play a recorded message by Miller stating that, in compliance with the management's request, he was making a public apology. He began by explaining that he understood he had offended some people the previous day and would like to apologize—instead, he turned it into another "joke." With a Japanese koto instrumental accompanying him in the background, he proceeded to mock the incident, using a heavy accent: "In honor of the Chinese people, I would like to say it in their native language. . . . I'm velly solly. Velly solly. Solly, Challie [in reference to the infamous Charlie Chan detective character]. Velly, velly solly. Ancient Chinese seclet. I aporogize. Velly solly. I solly. I so solly. You would not believe how solly. Velly velly solly."[14] Representatives from the station would later define this as a "satirical apology," explaining that "Miller was not ordered to do an apology, rather it was a set-up for what he thought was a joke" (Harrison 1987).

While the protest against the *San Diego at Large* television show mobilized a few individuals representing a few organizations, the Miller incident ignited more organized protest. The representative from UPAC and the two representatives from APAC were still involved, but other individuals and organizations joined the coalition. Salaber sent bulletins through the national APAC newsletter, explaining the media incidents in San Diego and urging people to send letters of protest.[15] A tape of the radio "apology" was played to a general assembly of approximately 530 students from California colleges and universities who were attending the annual Asian Pacific Student Union Confer- ence held that year at the University of California, San Diego, and a number wrote letters to the radio station denouncing the actions of the disc jockey. Salaber was involved with the Pan Asian Lawyers Associa- tion (PALS), so she contacted them; Russell Thrasher, an attorney, vol- unteered to help in the negotiation with the radio station manage- ment.[16] Asian law students who were affiliated with the Pan Asian Lawyers Association and members of the Asian Pacific American Law Students Association at the University of San Diego lent their support as well.[17] A few local single-ethnic organizations, including the Japanese American Citizens League (JACL), the Council of Pilipino-American Organizations, the San Diego Chinese Center, and the House of China provided indirect assistance, since they did not have the resources or ability to contend with this issue.[18]

On 20 March, a joint community meeting was held, involving rep- resentatives from at least eleven Asian community organizations. At the meeting, they agreed to form an umbrella organization, the Asians/ Pacific Islanders for Media Responsibility Coalition, to represent their interests. This ad hoc coalition defined the organization as "a coalition of Asian and Pacific Islander students, individuals, and community organizations formed specifically to address the issue of racism on radio station KS 103/Randy Miller issue." Dennis Kobata, a spokesperson for the coalition, later testified: "As Asians and Pacific Islanders we often don't have the money or political clout to fight the injustices we face. But what we do have is the political power of our people. Our coalition was formed because we felt a united effort was needed to get justice from KS-103."[19]

While there were various demands being considered, the activists agreed upon two action items: Demand a public apology from KS-103 management and draft a policy statement on racist remarks for the station to adopt. In essence, they wanted the radio station to make a public apology on the show, to apologize in mainstream and Asian newspapers, and to allow Asian representatives airtime to discuss the harmful effects of perpetuating stereotypes (Core 1987). They contacted all the advertisers, asking them, "Do you realize that your commercial is supporting a racist radio station?" There was disagreement among individuals as to what strategies to pursue. Some wanted to work with the station, while others wanted to organize a boycott immediately against the station and their sponsors and picket the station. Finally, after some discussion, the coalition decided that more drastic measures should be pursued only if the station would not apologize or meet any of their initial demands.

Additionally, the Asian community solicited the assistance of outsiders again, including local politicians and the Human Relations Commission Media Subcommittee, to put pressure on the radio station (Curran-Downey 1987b). Members of APAC representing the Asian American coalition also solicited the assistance of politicians, asking them to contact the Federal Communications Commission (FCC) on their behalf. Congressman Jim Bates of the 44th District, U.S. House of Representatives, who helped with the television show protest, and Assemblyman Peter Chacon of the 79th District, California Legislature, both asked the FCC to investigate the radio show. There was also discussion of, as one organizer put it, "going for their FCC license," which captured the attention of station executives. Since the radio station was framing this as a censorship issue, the Media/Community Relations Task Force Subcommittee, along with APAC, was careful to make it clear that they were not interested in censorship, but were concerned with the general well-being of the Asian American population.

The HRC subcommittee agreed to intervene as a mediator with the radio station. In its public statement, the subcommittee described Miller's actions as "at best discrimination and at worst racial attacks against our *Chinese-American* community" (emphasis mine) by perpetuating "harmful stereotypes and myths . . . which succeed in increasing their alienation from our society."[20] Worth noting is that the subcommittee in its initial public statements framed this as an issue against the Chinese community. In contrast, pan-Asian organizations continuously framed it in their discussions as an issue that affected *all Asians*, and this was particularly evident in the correspondence sent to the radio station. Prompted by the Asian American activists, the commission would later also frame it as an *Asian American* issue. In addition to Salaber, who was part of the HRC Media/Community Relations Task Force Subcommittee, a Filipina who was the secretary of HRC had been the previous president of PALS and a board member of UPAC. Another Chinese who was involved with UPAC was one of the ten members of the HRC board. Having these Asian Americans experienced in pan-Asian organizations involved in the HRC subcommittee helped to frame this as an Asian American issue. Although there was a broad-based grassroots coalition, APAC members, with experience from the protest with the television show, were still in charge of coordinating correspondence and communication between the radio station, politicians, HRC, and the Asian American community.

In early March, Chris Conway, president and general manager of KS-103, met with the HRC subcommittee and in late March met with the Asian American coalition. Throughout this process, he dismissed the claims of the community. Neither he nor Miller ever officially apologized; instead, they issued a formal response stating that Miller "makes fun" of everybody, so this controversy is "much ado about nothing." In correspondence to the Human Rights Commission and to Asian Americans who complained, the radio-station manager explained that it was not the intent of the disc jockey to pick on Chinese Americans or to single out the Asian community; "instead the comments were made as a result of Mr. Millers' interpretation that there had been over-reaction to Larry Himmel's character on KFMB TV."[21] Conway explained: "We do not feel that the remarks were racist and I can assure you that these comments were not made maliciously, nevertheless, we do regret the fact that members of the community took offense." In public statements to the press, station representatives reiterated that they felt the community was "overly sensitive." The discursive strategies of the representatives remove accountability from the victimizer, exonerating them of any wrongdoing since there was supposedly no malicious intent on their part. They simultaneously invalidate the claims of the victims by blaming them for creating an unnecessary complaint.

The station representatives expressed surprise to learn of the racial victimization of Asians and to learn that Asians considered themselves minorities. Conway commented: "I always figured that with the Asian culture being so advanced, that Asians had assimilated into society. But people I talked with said they haven't, with people calling them names on the street" (quoted in Hirahara 1987). In his letter of explanation to Congressman Jim Bates, Conway stated: "In meeting with representatives of these various groups, I was surprised to learn about the extent of discrimination that they feel exists toward Asians in San Diego."[22] These statements show how Conway had positioned Asians as the "model minority," who were assimilated and "just like Whites," yet he contradicted this by commenting on the cultural distinctiveness, particularly the advanced culture, of this seemingly assimilated group. The question left unanswered is whether this "privileging" of Asians and their culture absolves the radio station employees of any responsibility or somehow justifies their actions.

While the station representatives felt that their "harmless jokes" merely resulted in "hurt feelings," the Asian American community felt that the stereotypes were linked to increasing incidents of anti-Asian violence. At the meeting with the managers of KS-103, Asian representatives discussed the history of anti-Asian acts in California and in the United States. Additionally, they pointed to the recently released reports at the statewide and national levels that concluded there was an escalation of anti-Asian violence.[23] In a letter to the station, an individual described his perspective: "They [racial jokes and remarks] denigrate a history and culture. The inaccuracy and the racial backlash that this fosters cannot be measured, but situations such as these of Mr. Miller and those of Mr. Himmel of *San Diego at Large* do contribute to Asia/Asian bashing and xenophobia."[24]

In particular, the protesters connected the impact that stereotypes can have to two poignant events in Asian American history: the incarceration of Japanese Americans in concentration camps during the early 1940s, and the killing of Vincent Chin, a Chinese American, in the early 1980s. At a public hearing, an Asian American testified: "The racist characterization of the Japanese prior to W.W.II help to set the 'moral environment' to incarcerate 120,000 Japanese Americans. There was no public outcry. The only image the public had of Japanese Americans was the racist, dehumanizing stereotypes perpetuated by the Hearst Press and media." While the stereotypes prevalent in the media cannot solely be blamed for the internment of the Japanese, the media portrayals previous to and during their incarceration have been noted for exacerbating, rather than alleviating, racial animosity directed at Japanese Americans (Ogawa 1971).

Regarding the second issue, physical assaults, the violent murder of Vincent Chin symbolizes for Asian Americans the tragedy of an anti-Asian climate in this country. In 1982, Chin, a Chinese American, was murdered by two White, laid-off auto workers in Detroit who mistook him for a Japanese national and allegedly blamed him for their being out of work (Espiritu 1992; Takaki 1989b). At a hearing, a Japanese American representative from the Asian/Pacific Islander Media Responsibility Coalition explained the consequences of Asian bashing:

> Just because an incident as brutal as the racist murder of Vincent Chin has not happened in San Diego yet, does not mean that there are not direct implications for Asians here. . . . You cannot dehumanize people and blame them for all of society's problems without some people taking action, including violent action against those that are portrayed in that way. The racism promoted on KS-103 is not simply a case of bad jokes or people being offended—it is a question of our lives and survival in this society.[25]

Although not addressed directly, these incidents were even more egregious because of the judicial system's failure to protect Asians' rights and the role of the media in promoting these judicial inequalities—in the former case, they were stripped of their constitutional rights as U.S. citizens; in the latter, although both killers pleaded guilty to Chin's murder, they only served one night in jail (Zia 2000). The internment of Japanese Americans and the Vincent Chin murder symbolize literally the "cost" of cultural production for Asian Americans.

In April, it was reported that the radio station did not offer to renew Miller's contract and that he had accepted an offer at a radio station in Atlanta (Arnold 1987). At that point, some members of the coalition felt that the issue was resolved, yet others felt that the radio station had never officially apologized or admitted any wrongdoing, so the community needed to pursue this issue further. The station manager had offered to pay for an ad in an Asian-oriented publication that would restate the station's regret at having offended them, but the protesters wanted a retraction published in a mainstream paper. The strategy to pursue the issue would become a point of contention that led to conflicts within the coalition. As one participant comments:

> And that's when I realized that [there are] people in the Asian community who approach things different, there are some radicals who want to go till death. I was just ready to resolve the issue when I found out his contract wasn't renewed and they let him go; I wrote them a letter and said thank you. . . . I said thank you for showing sensitivity and there was a group of Asians who thought I was, it was like, "How could you do that, we still want to fight this battle."

Although internal divisions on strategies existed, the protest by the Asian community and the formation of the task force gave Asian American groups a channel for voicing their protest. For example, in April 1987, the Council of Pilipino-American Organizations made a formal complaint against a KSDO radio show in regard to comments made about the "smell, poor taste in clothing, and cheapness when dining out of Filipino Americans."[26] Again, Chris Conway, also the manager of this radio station, assured the complainants that caution would be taken in the future and the issue was dropped, but the Media Task Force recommended further monitoring of the station. The protests against both the television and radio show by the Asian community had a larger impact on San Diego, because they were a catalyst for a public hearing that went beyond addressing the stereotypes in the media and extended to the power structure of the media, a welcome but unintended consequence.

The Fire: The Media Hearing and Its Unintended Consequences

Since the protest by the Asian community had prompted generous media attention, the Human Relations Commission Media/Community Relations Task Force Subcommittee decided to use it as a vehicle to gain some visibility for the role of their organization by holding a public forum. The mobilization by the Asian American community contributed directly to the plan for a hearing, and in the announcement flyer, HRC stated: "We are expecting a high level of media attention due to our activities related to "San Diego at Large" and KS 103."[27] The task force invited the public to provide testimony of their representation, or lack of it, in the local media and their relations with media representatives.

The forum brought together a diversity of groups and brought to the fore viewpoints not only from Asians, but also from Blacks, Latinos, gays, and the disabled. Nineteen people gave testimony as individuals and as representatives from a variety of community organizations, with approximately sixty in attendance. All the Asian Americans who testified represented pan-Asian community and student organizations: Asian/Pacific Islander Media Responsibility Coalition; Union of Pan Asian Communities; Asian American Pacific Coalition; Pacific Islanders and Asians for the Rainbow; and the Asian/Pacific Islander Student Union. These groups realized they had common interests with other minority groups, especially the absence of stories on their community. The HRC report on the hearings stated: "Most of the testimony indicated profound concern about accurate portrayals of minority groups, as well as a pervasive sense of powerlessness in communicating these concerns to media decision-makers."

While the intent of the hearings was to present views on negative or inaccurate portrayals in the media, Asians, Blacks, and Latinos also addressed what they perceived to be unfair employment practices, which included a lack of hiring of minorities in visible or decision-making positions. An APAC representative complained that "local newscasters do not fairly resemble the faces of the community. I do not expect nor would I want employment to be based on one's ethnicity. However, there are many qualified journalists of Asian Pacific descent who are not seen in roles such as writer, newscaster, director, and actor." Catherine Henry of the San Diego Association of Black Journalists stated that she had presented a report to the commission on 21 January 1986 which dealt with the lack of Black, Hispanic, Asian, and Native American reporters employed in the local media; however, she had yet to see the commission take any action based on the findings. Ernesto Portillo Jr., president of the San Diego Chapter of the California Chicano News Media Association, also focused on the paucity of minority hires.[28] He urged HRC to survey the media in San Diego and assess the number of ethnic minorities and women employed in visible, decision-making positions and to publicize the statistics in order to convince the media to aggressively hire minorities. Many speakers commented that companies were not complying with national affirmative action guidelines and that the FCC was not enforcing these guidelines adequately.

It was obvious to Asian Americans that the media representatives they met with were highly unrepresentative of the population at large, and rectifying this problem was inherent in eradicating the media's racist depictions of them. In raising these concerns, the minority groups transformed the agenda of the HRC Media/Community Relations Task Force Subcommittee, which was to mediate disputes or complaints, and redirected its resources to advocacy-oriented activities. In November 1987, the subcommittee completed a media-employment survey of all the major newspaper, television stations, and radio stations to determine the ethnic composition of their staffs employed in visible and decision-making positions. They reported that minorities comprised only 4 percent of all managers and professionals employed at local newspapers and broadcast stations (Romero 1991) and met with the media to advise them on how to improve their employment practices. Changes would all be made on a voluntary basis, so some companies were more amenable than others. The HRC could not substantiate that actual intent to discriminate had occurred, but it was able to show that there was a discrepancy between the percentage of each group in the population and the number of individuals hired from these ethnic groups in certain positions. Using another approach, they presented awards to those in the print and broadcast media who hired minorities to encourage others to emulate these actions. HRC also initiated educational programs and panels to inform the public about media procedures and to educate the media about ethnic communities. They tried to establish a cooperative link, which had not existed previously, between the ethnic communities and the media.

Asian Americans seem to have been influential in bringing attention to the hiring practices of the media, but exactly how much influence they ultimately have had on this process is difficult to ascertain, for other factors come into play. Since these protests occurred, there have been several Asian reporters hired by the local television news stations and a few by the major newspaper company. Asians in San Diego, as well as in other cities in the United States, are still attempting to attain adequate representation in the media by asking for more Asian Americans to be hired and promoted; requesting the assignment of minority reporters to cover their ethnic communities; and trying to obtain accurate stories on Asians.[29] With the increasing deregulation of the communications industry as a whole, as well as the downsizing or closure of companies, and an increase in multimedia conglomerates that have reduced industry competition, power is concentrated in the hands of fewer decision makers. With a political climate that fosters less support for affirmative action programs, in essence rejecting the notion that racial discrimination and inequities exist, corporations are left to their own devices.

Putting out Fires: Still a Need for Collective Action

Although these protests and the subsequent hearing took place in the 1980s, the concerns about the cultural production of Asian Americans and Asians did not dissipate at the national or local level in the decade that followed. During the time I spent in the field, Asians in San Diego were upset about an illustration in a local publication about their community. The illustration accompanied an article about an organizational dispute within the Indochinese Mutual Assistance Association (IMAA), a nonprofit organization that assists Vietnamese, Cambodian, and Laotian refugees (Arnold 1993). The headline read, "Power Grab Stirs Strife in San Diego Asian Community," implicating all Asian Americans, not just the Southeast Asian or Vietnamese community. The illustration depicted two Asian male caricatures dressed in traditional Vietnamese peasant clothing posed on opposite ends of a seesaw balanced on top of a head figure wearing a traditional cone-shaped hat. Although it does not need explanation, it is worth noting that the ethnic leaders involved in the dispute discussed in the article wear suits and ties to work.

This depiction was particularly disturbing given that Southeast Asian Americans were experiencing racial animosity within their neighborhoods and that there had been a number of anti-Asian hate crimes reported a few years earlier (Lau 1990c). A key individual at UPAC was incensed about the depiction and planned to contact the publisher:

> That's the Asian community?! I'm just appalled. And I'm sure that it was not intentional, but it's a racist caricature of the Asian community. . . . It's this provincial kind of attitude, . . . the way in which the media presents it reflects where we are—the second-largest city in the state of California that places a caricature like that about Asians! . . . I mean, that's ridiculous. How backwards!

She remarks on the need for Asians to continuously monitor anti-Asian acts and advocates for Asian Americans to be astute and form coalitions:

> I hope they're [Asians] out there talking to legislators, looking at all the laws, the proposals for bills, or the bills that are coming up that are anti-immigrant types. I hope that they're paying attention to some of the statistics and violent incidents toward all Asians. It's not just Japan bashing, it's all over. I think that they're foolish if they think, "I'm protected because I don't know anyone or the incidence of violence has not been epidemic in my community." They may not be aware of it but it affects all Asian groups and they're foolish to look the other way. That's why the ethnocentrics in our communities are so devastating, because if you turn your back on another Asian group, it's like turning your back against your own group. We're beginning to realize that. The majority of folks [non-Asians] don't make distinctions that they make in terms of who you are. Middle America does not make distinction between one Southeast Asian or even between Filipino and Japanese. They don't make these kind of distinctions, and so making those kind of distinctions among ourselves and not supporting each other makes absolutely no sense. We are essentially fostering increased violence, fostering increased stereotypes; so you're as guilty as those that use violence by turning away from any Asian group.

Asian Americans are still concerned about the media coverage of Asian Americans, both their invisibility and the stereotypical portrayals of them. Since Asian Americans are seldom seen in the mainstream media, the few images available of them become even more significant. A Japanese American woman, a former president of the Pan Asian Lawyers Association, discusses the mainstream media's negligence, adding that the fragments that are shown depict Asians as criminals:

> I think that it's real easy to not even recognize that there is a very large population of Asians in San Diego. It's not addressed very much in the media or in the papers, especially not in the news. You wouldn't know that there were any Asians here in San Diego, other than they're involved in gang activity. That's about it. You never hear anything about Asians.

Media representations of Asian American gangs, which seem to be the most prolific image of Asians on the nightly news, present them as a threat to mainstream America—feeding into the anti-immigrant, anti-refugee, and anti-Asian backlash.

The same woman explains how she felt about the news stories in the local headlines about Chinese from the mainland being smuggled by coethnics to Mexico by ship and making their way by land to California to work as low-wage laborers in Chinatowns:

> What I think is interesting is with the Chinese coming over on the boat and I just see those parallels. You sort of want to keep a little distance between yourself and those people, because they're not quite one of us, but on the other hand, you see that they are, sort of. Well, hopefully people are opening their eyes, cause the dominant culture can't distinguish between the new immigrants and the people who have been here for a generation. So they just look at all of us the same way—we don't really belong here, we should go back to where we came from and that sort of thing, and I've had it said to my face.

The media coverage conveyed images of Asians as "coolies" and "illegal aliens" and presented sinister stereotypes of the "Chinese Mafia" and "crime-infested Chinatowns," feeding the anti-immigrant sentiment already present in the state and lending public support to anti-immigration legislation being considered at the time. As an acculturated, middle-class American of Asian ancestry, the former president of PALS acknowledged her hesitancy to identify with "fresh off the boat" (FOB) immigrant laborers. However, she had worked on immigrant rights projects, so she was able to understand that American-born and foreign-born Asians, irrespective of class differences, need to see their lives as interlinked.

Asian Americans may speak different languages, have different cultural practices, and be of different generations, yet anti-Asian incidents can affect them all. As one protester aptly put it: "The concerns of discrimination or civil rights are the same regardless of whether you're first generation or fifth generation. You look Asian." Racially motivated crimes against Asians have not waned, although there have been attempts to monitor and curb them (U.S. Commission on Civil Rights 1992).

Nor are they sporadic or confined to particular regions in the United States—they occur in places with few Asians and in areas with high concentrations of Asians. Different ethnic groups may be targeted in different areas, such as the anti-Indian attacks in New Jersey, the anti-Vietnamese attacks in Texas, or the anti-Korean attacks in Los Angeles, and this means developing different strategies for organizing. The 1990 Federal Hate Crimes Statistics Act means that local law enforcement is supposed to appropriately classify racially motivated hate crimes and report them to the Federal Bureau of Investigation for tabulation. In 1990, Asians founded the National Network Against Anti-Asian Violence to monitor, publicize, and mobilize opposition to hate crimes. In 1993, the National Asian Pacific American Legal Consortium, an independent organization, reported 335 violent hate crimes committed against Asians, and at least thirty individuals died as a result of the incidents in the United States (Chin 1994).[30] It is not uncommon to read in the Asian American media and on Internet networks about incidents of violence not reported in the mainstream media.

Asian American communities continue to expend their energies on countering racist cultural productions. In 1991, there was a New York City protest of the staging of *Miss Saigon*—a Broadway musical that depicted Asians as depraved, powerless prostitutes and pimps—and of the hiring of a non-Asian actor in the lead role. Korean Americans implicated the media for stereotyping and scapegoating them by blaming them for America's problems, thereby contributing to the material losses and emotional injuries they suffered during the 1992 Los Angeles Rebellion (Abelmann and Lie 1995). Asian American groups demonstrated against anti-Asian depictions outside theaters showing the movie *Rising Sun*, criticizing it for its blatant stereotypes of Japanese nationals as economic predators (Miller 1993). In early 1997 in Chicago, Asian individuals and organizations waged a successful protest against radio station B-96 after a morning show disc jockey created a character named Lem Chop who mocked Asians by speaking with a heavy accent and misusing Asian expressions. Asian Americans also protested the stereotypical characterizations of President Bill Clinton, First Lady Hillary Clinton, and Vice President Al Gore as a "Buddhist monk, Chinese coolie, and Chinese Red Guard" with slanted eyes and buckteeth on the 24 March 1997 cover of the *National Review*.

In 2002, Ohio-based Abercrombie and Fitch clothing company pulled from stores their line of T-shirts with "Orientalist" images and mocking slogans after a national protest by Asian American college students. In 2002, local organizers were part of a national Internet campaign and rally that protested the manufacturing and selling of a Halloween costume by a factory in northern San Diego County that distributed to chain stores nationwide. The "Kung Fool" costume, mimicking a kung fu or martial arts outfit, included a squinty-eyed and bucktoothed mask and a headband inscribed with the Chinese character for "loser."[31] In the summer of 2003, Fox Movie Channel suspended its plan to show the Chan Film Festival after Asian Americans complained that the Charlie Chan films, which debuted in the 1930s, featured offensive stereotypes with Whites in "yellowface." Then the Fox Television Channel premiered a new show, *Banzai*, that was filled with exaggerated caricatures of Asians, similar to those on the Larry Himmel show.[32] The list goes on—unfortunately, not much has changed.

Detecting Smoke: Naming Racism

Given these statistics and the prevalence of misrepresentations in the media, it would seem that protests would be more prevalent. In chastising the Asian American community for their inaction, Ling-chi Wang (1991) cites the increasing level of anti-Asian racism during the 1980s; this trend should have led to ethnic solidarity and mobilization, yet the community remains divided and ineffective. A number of experiences I had while doing my fieldwork, particularly during my interviews, offer an explanation for this inactivity. Although many interviewees recounted experiences of discrimination when asked, many at first denied having such experiences but later in the interview recalled incidents that could be classified discriminatory. Still others made efforts to dismiss or qualify these discriminatory acts. I expected these individuals, since they were involved in Asian American activism, to clearly articulate the meaning of racial discrimination, yet their responses revealed the multifaceted ways in which Asian Americans conceptualize racism and address it in their everyday lives.

In some cases, interviewees were dismissive of acts of racist bigotry and accepted them as part of their life in America. A Korean downplayed the racist slurs and gestures he received from individuals in moving vehicles: "Oh yeah, you get that occasional stuff in a car. But to me that doesn't mean anything." A Japanese doctor whose parents were interned during World War II and who is a longtime member of various ethnic organizations said: "Growing up I've been called names, but I think again one doesn't take that as a discrimination of them, but of local punks or kids or whatever it is. And that's not, I don't think, a significant discrimination." Although he considered exclusion of Asian Americans from medical schools a form of discrimination, he qualified his comments:

> When I was in medical school, some of the old-type professors would say, "Oh gee, you're so lucky to be able to get into medical school." Back in the old days, you really had some extra hurdles to get into medical school. And when I told them I applied to Albert Einstein medical school back East, they said, "You're crazy, they don't accept Asians at that school." Well, these are things that I did not grow up with or have any preconceived attitudes. And I think discrimination is some part of attitude. . . . Yourself and others.

In this somewhat simplistic analysis, he seems to indicate that those who look for discrimination will find it, whereas those who deemphasize its existence will be able to protect themselves from it. Yet he was also quite conscious of racial discrimination and willingly protested racist incidents. On several occasions I heard him tell the story of how he contacted a local news station manager after watching a news show in which he thought he heard an interviewee use the word "Japs" that he would later find out was actually "jobs."

An activist who is part Japanese and part Chinese, asked if he had experienced discrimination, replied: "Normally when people suffer discrimination that's very blatant, they remember it for a long time. I cannot recall such memories of blatant discrimination. My father is very conscious of discrimination. He thinks the world is very prejudiced. My feelings are, if you look for it, you're probably going to find it, even if it's not there." This resonates with the previous response, but like the Japanese American doctor, this activist goes on to explain a more complex perspective on discrimination as he rationalizes the treatment he received in the South:

> I worked for one summer in South Carolina. And if there's any prejudices, you'll find it out there. I never encountered any myself, but I did see the prejudices between black and white and that's clear. . . . They were very open to me. And the kids were very open to me. A lot of them thought I was Bruce Lee. It was funny. Their experiences with Asians are so limited that they were very curious about me, because all they've seen is what they've seen on TV, which is almost a negative portrayal. . . . You don't see them [Asians] in starring or costarring roles. You don't see them as being beautiful. You generally tend to see them as being peasants, laundry owners, martial arts [characters]. They don't show them in very diverse roles or occupations with the exception of Sulu in Star Trek. . . . And I think that's too bad, because television and movies is supposed to be a reflection of society somewhat and I don't think they're doing a very good job.

He, like other respondents, at first replied he could not remember incidents of discrimination but later in the interview recounted such experiences. A woman who remarked that the personal discrimination she experienced had been subtle then recalled: "Well, I did have an exchange of words with a neighbor of mine who was blocking my parking spot and I got impatient with her and she just said, 'I hate Orientals.'" Later in the conversation she discussed job interviews in which she felt she was being discounted because potential employers judged her based on their misconceptions of Asian American women, such as their inability to deal with management positions. She, like other interviewees, was reticent to discuss experiences in which they suspected discrimination but had no substantial evidence.

One interviewee raised in Alaska managed to be quite creative in dealing with being ethnically misidentified:

> I get mistaken a lot for Japanese. That's something you can't really blame them [for] because, you know, in a way, we do look alike, we have the same color hair, the same color eyes, the same body build or something like that, so that's why it's up us to make the distinction, "No, I'm not Japanese, I'm Taiwanese." People say why are we making this distinction, [and] that's a great opportunity to explain to them the differences of the different ethnic groups, the history.

Rather than connecting these mistakes to an educational system that neglects to include the experiences of communities of color in meaningful ways or to racial lumping by the media, he provides justification for them. Instead of challenging this discrimination directly, he has learned to alter his reaction from one of exasperation and anger to one of tolerance and patience.

These responses can be read as pragmatic survival strategies to contend with the multiple levels of discrimination Asian Americans experience. Sethi points out that "Asians often do not ascribe racist motivation to the discrimination they suffer, or they have felt that they could suffer the injustice of racial intolerance, in return for being later compensated by the fruits of economic success" (1994: 236). It is more than this, however. Some Asian immigrants know that they need to make sacrifices to start anew in this country, but they are often unprepared for the harsh racial discrimination they encounter, especially if they hold high ideals of American democracy. They may accept discrimination as part of an exchange for creating a better life for themselves and their children. Yet, for other immigrants and U.S.-born Asians, not naming or confronting racism is a strategy that allows them to survive emotionally. It seems almost to have become a psychological defense mechanism to thwart the pain associated with the barrage of cultural denigrations and verbal assaults. Naming racism means acknowledging that others might perceive one as "less than," not necessarily a facile notion for those proud of their culture, history, and people.

In some cases, having the vocabulary to identify racism enables individuals to make the connection between personal acts of discrimination and larger institutional structures of discrimination. A Filipino American provides an example of having a new discourse, along with a new ideology, to understand racism. He refers to an experience during his high school days when his family moved from National City, an ethnically mixed neighborhood, to Bonita, a primarily upper-middle-class White neighborhood in San Diego:

> I, for the first time, experienced racism. We had some people tell us, referring to me being Asian, being a "Gook," I should go back to where I came from; ... because I was different, because I was Asian, because I was a foreigner, [the person] pointed that out and told me to leave and that was the first time I ever felt sort of isolated. [I thought] Maybe we don't belong in this neighborhood. Maybe we should go back.... You know, sometimes it takes me a while to remember these racist incidences because I think back at that time when I was eighteen, I didn't think of it as a racist incident. I mean, I remember the feeling very well, but I didn't think of it as a racist incident. I didn't know what racism was at that time and I never really thought of that word and definition of racism 'til several years ago I took this Mexican American history class.

The community college course revealed to him a new political understanding of U.S. society and its treatment of minorities and gave him in his mid-thirties a discourse with which to identify his life experiences as a racialized Filipino American that eventually led to his politicization as a community activist.

Surveys that ask Asian Americans to provide yes or no answers to having experienced discrimination or to rate the level of discrimination by progressive scales cannot capture these nuanced understandings or perspectives on discrimination. To complicate matters, a number of respondents, when asked about anti-Asian racism, identified racism as more significant for other minority groups. For example, a Chinese American answered: "[For Asians] there isn't really prosecution like the slaves/Blacks and the community—they had it really tough. The Black community, you know, the history they had." I suspect that others who lack a language to clearly articulate racism or an understanding of the racism directed at Asian Americans also have difficulty making the connection between anti-Asian cultural productions and the injustices they experience. For organized resistance to occur there needs to be a naming of this racism and a connection made to its sources.

Although I do not disagree with Wang's comment at the beginning of this section about disorganization among Asian Americans, I think that the blame is misdirected. The campaign in this chapter shows the obstacles placed upon Asian Americans and the level of determination needed to successfully wage a battle against racism, even against local media entities. One activist commented on the radio incident that followed the television protest: "That's the kind of backlash that can happen that keeps people from becoming active." By highlighting the situation, they may make the conditions worse for themselves and, in fact, as has often happened, their protests lead to "free" publicity and more revenue for the culprits. In addition, Asians as a group, foreign-born and U.S.-born, are still in the process of teaching themselves about their history in this country, which has been absent from or distorted by educational and media institutions. They are also working to educate the U.S. public that Asian Americans are victims of racial discrimination and violence. For example, a poll conducted by the *Wall Street Journal* and *NBC News* found that most American voters polled did not think that Asian Americans suffered from discrimination, but they did think they were unfairly given "special advantages" (Polner 1993). Asian American groups often face racist incidents in localities where they have little or no political representation, even in places where Asian Americans comprise a significant population. The resources of the community are few, so it recognizes the need to be selective in its oppositional struggles.

Conclusion

It was the coalescing of the resources of various Asian American individuals and organizations that made this struggle against racism in the media possible. The chair of the UPAC board commented that "a positive outcome of all this has been the coming together of many Asian groups."[33] While organizations such as UPAC and PALS are still around, APAC and the ad hoc Media Responsibility Coalition disbanded. The Pan Asian Lawyers Association is still in existence and in its brochure lists as an accomplishment that it "spearheaded the Asian community's response to Asian racist remarks in the media." In 1994, PALS instituted an awards committee with a media division to reward the local media for "fair" press coverage. In July 2001, the Mayor's Asian Pacific Islanders Citizens Advisory Board and the Asian American Journalists Association of San Diego (AAJA-SD) sponsored "Understanding the Media: A Workshop for Asians and Pacific Islanders." AAJA-SD, which had been dormant for years, was officially reinstated as a chapter in 2000, hosted the sixteenth annual national AAJA convention in San Diego in 2003, and hosts the annual San Diego Asian Film Festival started in 1999. In addition, the San Diego Asian American Repertory Theatre celebrated its seventh season in 2002–2003, so the community, through these venues, has been able to create cultural representations that are more reflective of their experiences, even if it means doing so within their own realm.

Racial myths and stereotypes contribute to the exclusion of communities of color from mainstream society, but even more damaging is that these misconceptions weaken such communities' efforts to challenge a system of injustice and undermine their attempts to make demands of the state. The chair of UPAC at the time of this campaign explains why he felt they were involved: "Because that was important to us, putting down episodes like that where the media, however innocent, defames Asians. We took a strong role in that and went right to the source and dealt with it and did a very good job. . . . It affects all of us." Although some of these organizations were short-lived, the interconnections they provided at the grassroots level helped forge momentary bonds of unity, leading to the formation of networks that would become invaluable models for future mobilization efforts.

5

Economic Positioning
Resources, Opportunities, and Mobilization

n 1993, more than 300 guests, primarily Asian Americans, attended the yearly San Diego Asian Business Association (ABA) fund-raiser, "The New America: The Changing Faces of Asian Americans and Their Achievements," which was intended to highlight the growth of their population and to emphasize their economic success. Among the attendees were first- to fourth-generation Asians whose ancestry can be traced throughout Asia. Also attending were non-Asian local politicians; city and county representatives; Chamber of Commerce officials; corporate sponsors; and representatives from the Latino, Native American, and Black business organizations. The evening's events included the inauguration of four new officers, two of whom were born in this country and two born abroad; the new president still retained her Singaporean citizenship. A banker by profession, she was replacing an engineer who, like her, was born abroad and originally came to the United States for educational purposes. The evening's events included a slide presentation highlighting prominent Asian American community leaders. This organizational event reflects some of the most profound socioeconomic transformations occurring within the Asian American population.

In this chapter, I examine the development of a professional business organization, the Asian Business Association, to illustrate how contemporary demographics and economic circumstances, national and global, dramatically affect its

agenda and its ability to mobilize. As a nonprofit advocacy-based organization, it targets economic interests—whether it is to assist Asian
Americans find employment, make career advancements, increase their
business earnings, or create economic opportunities with Asia.[1] I examine how the ABA negotiates specific economic issues: racial discrimination, affirmative action programs, and trade with the Pacific Rim.
Part of its agenda was based on the idea that Asian Americans as a
domestic minority group still need to combat their economic exclusion
and, if incorporated, could be an asset to the U.S. economy. ABA's other
focus is based on the perception of Asian Americans as a resource in the
U.S. economy precisely because they are a transnational population
with economic links to Asia. In many ways, these internal complexities
forced the organizers to grapple with how to position themselves con-
currently as an *oppressed minority* and as a *privileged minority*. I also
address how this strategic positioning affected their ability to form coalitions with other racialized minorities in San Diego. These issues are a
reflection of the larger dilemma for those of Asian ancestry in the
United States who are negotiating their position in America and their
connection to Asia (Dirlik 1996; S. Wong 1995).

During the time of my research, I served as a volunteer for ABA. I
wrote an article on the organization and its attempts to preserve the historical Asian American community downtown for one of the early issues
of the ABA newsletter, and the president asked me to become editor of
their newsletter. Then at one of the dinner meetings I attended, a board
member nominated to me to be on the board. Although I was hesitant
at first to serve in these positions, I realized that to really understand
the inner workings of the organization, I would have to become an
active participant. These positions also gave me extraordinary access to
members, meetings, and information that would have been unattainable
otherwise.

The Politics of the "Model Minority" Myth

Asian Americans have been depicted as the "model minority," a myth
that Asian Americans are innately hardworking and family oriented,
and that they value education (Suzuki 1977). As an academic accustomed to demystifying this myth in my writings and teachings, I was
intrigued when conducting my research to observe the ways in which
this stereotype appealed to Asian Americans. To counteract the discrimination they experienced directly or indirectly in this country, they

conveniently embraced this image of themselves to show how their educational acumen and work ethic could help revitalize the local economy. Like cultural capital or material capital, it is a form of *image capital* that they have manipulated into currency to leverage some economic gain and political clout, conveniently overlooking its inaccuracies. It is possible for Asians to believe the public discourse about themselves and even begin to see this reflection in the mirror (Dhingra 2003; Loewen 1971). This manipulation was a precarious balancing act that came with negative consequences as well. Rather than taking these statements and actions at face value, in this chapter, I contextualize these beliefs against a backdrop of racial discrimination, global capitalism, and redistributive policies.

While some Asian Americans I interacted with used the term "model minority," others unfamiliar with the term were quite cognizant of its characteristics. When asked what commonalties Asian Americans have, a Taiwanese who grew up in Alaska answers, "I see family values as a common ground for Asians" and elaborates further: "Well, I think one thing the Asians do have in common as far as stereotyping is that we're all hardworking and education focused.... It doesn't matter if you're Japanese or Chinese. I guess that's a common stereotype of all Asian groups.... I think it's very true and I think it's a good thing." Another individual who is part Japanese and Chinese comments: "I'm proud that we do well academically. If you look at the list of valedictorians from the different schools, you see a high percentage of Asian males. I think they're associated with academic success. That's something to be proud of there." I was told by one individual that, given all the negative stereotypes that exist about various racial groups, Asian Americans should be "grateful" for being accused of being "intelligent, educated, industrious, family-oriented" people.

Some felt the myth had impacted their lives "positively." They mentioned how the perception of Asian Americans as *model workers* helped them land a job. A Chinese American engineer whose parents struggled with jobs in an ethnic enclave and who worked as a drafting assistant to pay for his education explains:

> I think there's always the aura of the work habits of the Asian culture being hardworking, studious, and successful, always wanting to achieve. I think that aura has helped me in trying to, I don't want to say maintain an image, but in helping me through my education and through my business practices.... I think overall, it's been positive for me because it again has reinforced my commitment to leading a productive life and that having the assurance, oh yeah, I can make it out of a "ghetto life."

Interviewees also spoke about this myth as providing common links for Asian Americans to come together and as an asset for organizing. The engineer just quoted intermixes biological and cultural traits as "inherent" to Asians: "I don't think we were forced into a situation where Asians have to unite to achieve something. I think it's more of a common ground. . . . I thought it was just a good group to socialize under or to have something in common that's Asian, having the almond eyes, the olive skin, straight black hair, of a culture that's family rigid and structured that stresses success and education." Another Chinese American adds that the myth has given Asian Americans a positive foundation for mobilizing, adding: "And all of the things about Asians being this and doing that and getting good grades. . . . There are somewhat positive images of Asians out there and that has created this empowerment."

Others express a contradictory stance toward the model minority myth. On the one hand, they repudiate it; on the other, they co-opt it for their own purposes. A Filipino American states:

> There's no positive Asian stuff, but maybe later on in the future, we're going to start appreciating Asian culture, the Asian history, the Asian language and our value system that is much different than American culture. And maybe that will wake up America, because right now we're seeing the breakup of the family, the traditional family unit. But hopefully in the Asian home, we'll continue bringing up the sense of family and I think that's where it makes us different, because we have that very family-oriented thinking.

When asked if he is referring to the model minority myth, he responds quite adamantly that it is a political illusion:

> Model minority to me is a concoction from the Euro-American-centric experience. You know, if you look at it from a global perspective, we are not minorities. The Chinese are the largest ethnic majority. . . . And I don't know what we mean by a model. . . . To me, it's a negative connotation. . . . [You're] a big contribution to American society as a consumer. You're paying your taxes to Uncle Sam. You're a good Asian family. You're a model. You're quiet. You're polite. You don't rant and rave. You don't argue. You don't take political stands.

While he is attracted to aspects of the myth, he is also skeptical of it. A woman officer of ABA comments: "I do know that a lot of people think Asians don't need help. There's a kind of perception that Asians do so well that they don't need any help." This myth perpetuates the idea that Asian Americans have assimilated and achieved parity with the mainstream population and therefore racism is not operating anymore and

Asian Americans are undeserving of special treatment as a disadvantaged minority group. It is an intricate balancing act to present themselves as simultaneously oppressed and better off.

Beginnings of the Asian Business Association

Scholars have discussed how ethnic solidarity can sustain capitalist entrepreneurship, yet for the most part, their analyses focus on single-ethnic enterprises in traditional occupations, such as grocery stores, and do not examine the role of pan-Asian networks in "nontraditional" professions (Bonacich and Modell 1980; I. Kim 1981; Light 1972; Light and Bonacich 1988; Min 1988). Resources such as rotating credit associations based on family name or regional, clan, or village affiliation are common among single-ethnic groups, especially for those in traditional businesses. However, for those entering nontraditional occupations or planning to expand into the "American general market," the need for class resources, such as education, savings, and loans from banks or government agencies, become more significant (Portes 1984; Portes and Manning 1986; Yoon 1991). Outside an ethnic enclave, contact and competition with other racial populations can increase a group's awareness of racial discrimination and heighten its level of ethnic consciousness (Kasinitz 1992; Portes 1984).

From its inception, ABA increased its membership because it was able to incorporate Asians who were not being served by traditional economic organizations. Traditional single-ethnic organizations tend to function as social clubs and concentrate on business concerns within an ethnic enclave, since they feel relatively powerless outside these confines (Light 1972), while Asian American organizations focus on a broader range of economic issues and are interested in reaching out to the mainstream society. As a U.S.-born Chinese American restaurateur explains: "It's still the same old group that's been around, with the exception of a few young people. . . . They're not real progressive; whereas newer groups are much more progressive and more willing to put in extra work. . . . One just wants the same status quo, and the other group wants to be more creative and find a solution. That's how I see ABA." Additionally, mainstream professional organizations often do not fulfill Asian needs; for example, a Chinese American, an officer in a local chapter of a structural engineering organization, notes that he was one of a few Asian Americans who joined the organization, even though this is a popular profession for them. As they enter the competition of the mainstream market, Asian Americans have relied on the resources and networks of others like them (Dhingra 2003; P. Ho 2002).

There were several attempts to gather the Asian American community around economic issues during the 1980s. Most notably, the Reagan administration, realizing the increasing affluence of the Asian American population, tried to organize a nationwide business organization with chapters in all major cities, especially in California. The formation of the Asian Pacific American Chamber of Commerce (APACC), with national headquarters in Washington, D.C., was funded by the Minority Business Development Agency, a division of the Department of Commerce.[2] In December 1984, local business people attempted to form a San Diego chapter and invited business owners and professionals to a workshop hosted by representatives from the local, state, and federal level to advise minority business owners on how to take advantage of government procurement.[3] While there was initial momentum for this pan-Asian business organization, the enthusiasm dissipated, partly because it was initiated and funded by the national government.

In contrast, the formation of the Asian Business Association in 1990 was initiated by the local Asian American community, and it was a statewide organization, rather than a nationwide one. The Union of Pan Asian Communities (UPAC), a social service agency (see Chapter Three), had invited Harold Yee, who owned a consulting company, to assist with strategies to obtain funding for an affordable housing project, and he informed UPAC of the ABA organization he had started in San Francisco. Meanwhile, Lynne Choy Uyeda, who owns a public relations company and started the ABA in Los Angeles in 1977, also encouraged UPAC participants to emulate her success locally.[4] Local individuals held a meeting in July 1990 at which they elected officers of Chinese, Japanese, and Filipino ancestry; enlisted members; and collected membership dues. ABA was incorporated in September 1990.[5] It continues to depend on the other contingents for direction, yet each ABA branch operates quite independently.[6]

A significant portion of the early participants were the same faces involved with the media protest, as well as with UPAC; as one organizer states, "ABA is an offshoot, a genesis of UPAC." As social workers involved with ABA, they were frustrated with the limitations of the social service system that kept their clients on welfare and in poverty, without focusing on more viable economic self-sufficiency solutions. An ABA supporter who once did social service work comments:

> I never really believed in social work, as much as I wanted to become a social worker. The real way to empower people is through economics. I know we've gone through this before, ... helping people start their own business, being self-sufficient and putting money back into the community, to help people get ahead. It's not just keeping them on welfare, but enabling them to be independent. So, I guess my values have changed since college.

Others had served on the board of UPAC and felt they could do more to help community members who were struggling economically and also that a network was needed for those attempting to move into middle-class professions.

In its early development, UPAC took on multiple agendas, but as the organization became more institutionalized and reliant on governmental funding and private foundations, it was more limited in the political projects it could pursue. The former chair of UPAC sums up why he helped to start a business-oriented organization like ABA:

> It's [UPAC] a diverse, sophisticated organization with a long history.... I guess it's like a tree that has grown substantially over the years, over time, and has survived all of the weather and disasters and elements. It adapts, its roots get stronger, and it knows when to produce another branch.... So there was a need, I realized, to form a separate body, another group, for an all-Asian business group to form; ... since we would not be dependent upon public funds, we would be free to speak up on issues that we felt that were important to the Asian community—Asian interests.

In his perspective, at that time, Asian Americans were not ready to organize a strictly political organization: "On political issues itself, we would not survive, but on the issue of money and how to band together to survive as a business community, that I knew would bind them all together."

The first president of the organization, who is a fourth-generation immigrant whose father was Chinese-Hawaiian and whose mother was Japanese-Filipino, wanted to get the American-born population involved first, then target the immigrant population, which he believed would get involved only after they saw tangible benefits from organizing. Experienced in other coalition projects, he explains his strategy:

> For them [American-born Asians], I knew it's a matter of believing that they can be effective, that they can participate, they can have a voice.... And so I focus my attention on the second through fourth generation because they are equipped educationally, they have their own business or about to have their own business, they understand the culture.... And it was a matter of nurturing them, getting them to believe that an organization which works

together can become a very powerful voice in the city. I knew that the first generation ... would never do it themselves because it's out of their experience; but I knew that they would come around once they see it happening.

As he predicted, those active in the organization incorporated both groups. The second president was born in China, raised in Hong Kong, and came to the United States for educational purposes. The third president was born in Malaysia and raised in Singapore, went to college in the United States in the 1970s, and—although she married a Chinese American and has the option of becoming an U.S. citizen—retains her Singaporean citizenship. The fourth president was a fourth-generation Japanese American who had been involved in the 1970s Asian American movement and began his career as a social service worker. By 1994 approximately half of ABA's twenty-seven officers and board members had been born abroad. Some immigrated during childhood, others came for college, and some were immigrants or refugees who came as adults. A noticeable commonality was that many active participants were in their twenties to forties and were in their prime working years. The American-born and the foreign-born are able to use their educational and professional skills, along with their financial resources, to start and manage an organization.

In the early 1990s, they held their monthly dinners at two tables in a small banquet room of a Chinese restaurant, but by the mid-1990s they were occupying ballrooms in motels and hotels or occupying large restaurant spaces. A handful of core participants and members mushroomed to numbers in the hundreds with varying levels of participation. Other gatherings included seminars, committee meetings, board meetings, a Toastmasters division, and community work. Depending on the event, the participants might include lawyers, accountants, caterers, graphic designers, translators, dentists, architects, journalists, restaurateurs, bankers, financial consultants, political representatives, students, realtors, insurance agents, journalists, law enforcement officers, nonprofit representatives, communication specialists, engineers, medical professionals, social service professionals, and sales representatives from a variety of companies. I participated in and heard lively conversations about personal histories, family matters, leisure activities, and breaking news stories. Between this "getting to know one another" socializing, I observed the exchange of business cards and arrangements to meet for lunch and overheard discussions of employment opportunities and business barriers.

Socioeconomic Mobility and the Glass Ceiling

Jennings Hom, whose family opened a grocery and merchandise store in San Diego in the late 1800s, explained that before World War II, "all jobs were denied to Orientals except as houseboys, gardeners, working in laundries and restaurants. Being a professional was unthinkable" (cited in Clifford 1990b). During the civil rights and power movement eras, antidiscrimination legislation was passed, affirmative action policies were instituted, and minorities demanded equitable treatment. Asian Americans were gradually given new educational opportunities, allowed to enter new professions, and permitted to expand their businesses beyond the ethnic enclaves (U.S. Commission on Civil Rights 1988).

The disproportionate percentage of entrepreneurs who are Asian Americans has been portrayed as having fulfilled the American dream. San Diego reflects the national increase in the number of Asian-owned businesses. With a total of 6,053 Asian-owned businesses in San Diego County, the breakdown in 1990 was Filipino 1,819; Chinese 1,255; Japanese, 1,168; Vietnamese, 837; Korean, 525; Hawaiian, 94; and other Asian, 385, representing a total of close to $400 million a year in gross sales, almost double the total of ten years earlier.[7] While Asian Americans have the highest percentage of minority business ownerships nationwide, some of these are highly profitable, while others struggle to survive. Many turn to entrepreneurship not by choice, but because they encountered linguistic, degree equivalency, and racial discrimination problems in professional occupations.

The socioeconomic conditions for Asian Americans have improved overall since the 1940s, with later generations attending college and with the influx of more college-educated immigrants; however, their career trajectories must be measured in relative terms (Hurh and Kim 1989). In comparison to their White counterparts, Asian Americans, as a whole, have not obtained occupations or incomes commensurate with their level of education or experience (Der 1993; O'Hare and Felt 1991). While Asian American professionals are found in entry-level and mid-level technically oriented positions, they are less likely to acquire senior-level decision-making or top management positions in either the private corporate or the public sector, hitting what is referred to as the glass ceiling (U.S. Commission on Civil Rights 1992; Vartabedian 1992).

An engineer from Hong Kong recognized that in the workplace, Asian immigrants face linguistic barriers that prevent their advancement, yet he adds that they are uncomfortable or uninterested in par-

ticipating in the work culture, such as sports talk or after-hours socializing with coworkers, often crucial to receiving a promotion. However,
U.S-born Asian Americans who spoke fluent English and were socialized in U.S. culture spoke of similar barriers in the workplace. A longtime employee of Teledyne in San Diego states: "I've never had any,
what they call, overt discrimination, but there is a glass ceiling in the
industry. I'm an aerospace engineer and there . . . seems to be never an
opportunity to move into management. Asians always are good techni-
cians and what have you." A third-generation Japanese American born
in 1940 whose grandparents and parents owned family farms in San
Diego explains the problems he encountered in trying to get promoted:

> I had reached mid-level management, as program director level–type, deputy
> director. I think that was all, because there was no other Asians that were in
> CEO or director capacities in public [social service] agencies in particular.
> They were all good accountants and they were all good deputies and they
> were all good support people to the director, but not the *director*. . . . I had to
> do it [get another job] in order to get out of a bureaucracy where I didn't feel
> I was going to move up, where I wasn't viewed as being a director, but just a
> support type.

A Filipino American born in 1959 in the Philippines and raised in
San Diego who remembers the discrimination his father faced as a store-
keeper in the U.S. Navy sums up his observations about discrimination:
"The point I'm trying to tell . . . is sometimes, especially with Asians,
you know, they will shut the door, they'll make an assumption. They'll
make an assumption, for example, during a promotion to . . . [a] super-
visory position [in the police department]—Asians are docile, they're not
leadership material so maybe they can't lead." As one of the highest-
ranking officers in a police department with approximately seventy-five
Asian American officers, he served as the liaison between the police
department and the Asian American community, including ABA. He was
the vice president of the Law Enforcement Alliance of the Pacific, a support and network group, in 1993; a lieutenant who was the highest-
ranking Asian American officer was president (Lau 1993b). This Filipino
American told me the department decided to mobilize Asian American
officers after the suicide of a Korean American sergeant that many
believe was associated with his impending demotion and other pressures
of the job.

Asian American women, foreign-born and U.S.-born, described
experiences with race and gender discrimination in their workplaces. A
female accountant who is an immigrant and speaks impeccable English

explains her experience applying for work at a corporate firm in New York City: "I'm qualified, but they didn't take me. The irony of it was they took my assistant who worked for me in the Philippines because he was male and I was a married woman of childbearing age who didn't practice birth control. During those times, they could ask you your religion, what you did [for birth control], how many kids you have, how old are you." It became even more difficult for her to find work when she moved to San Diego, since there were few accounting firms and a firmly entrenched "old White boys' network," so she worked for non-profit agencies with a lower base salary.

A U.S.-born woman of Japanese Filipino ancestry explains: "Although we're all from so many different walks of life and experiences, there are some commonalties that we share; .... our relations with the majority culture, that's one thing we have in common, how we relate to majority culture, trying to succeed or progress, move up the ladder careerwise and maybe we all kind of face that glass ceiling, I know we talk about that a lot—hitting that glass ceiling." She adds that "we [Asian American women] look younger than we are. In some situations, it might be a compliment. In an office setting, they tend to look at you like a child and discount what you say. And it's not just our look, but our height. So I think Asian women have a lot to compensate. We need to dress more professionally, and do a lot of things to counter those perceptions."

As newcomers, minorities, and females, Asian American women also faced obstacles trying to start businesses in San Diego. Some found ways to circumvent the obstacles placed in front of them. For example, a Chinese immigrant CPA could not find work in the competitive San Diego market, so she opened up her own firm and purposely hired an Anglo salesperson to help her market to a diverse clientele that might hesitate to hire a firm owned by an Asian American woman.

Male business owners explained that they started their own companies when they could not find work in the public or private sector or when they were frustrated with being passed up for promotions. A Vietnamese American who came as a refugee in 1975 and had been a high school science teacher in Vietnam recounted how he decided to open up his own electronics-manufacturing firm after being overlooked for promotions repeatedly in previous jobs, while White employees with less education and less experience got promoted. A U.S.-born Korean American, who moved to the area in 1971 from New York City where he had an established career, decided to open up a graphic design business even though, he said, "starting a business here in a Republican town is not easy. And coming from L.A. and stepping in a very small competitive turf, I didn't get the kind of response that I liked to."

A Chinese American who decided to go into the grocery business like his parents comments:

> I think, as Asians, the opportunity only exists if you're in the private sector and in business for yourself. I don't think as Asians we're going to rise in a structured environment.... Once you get into that position you will never rise to the top. There would be direct competition with the Whites.... I believed that when I went into the [U.S. military] service I find out that somehow the Whites are always going to get above you quickly, much faster than you. I learned that there.... In any organized company or organization, they would always be put in a position to rise above you, no matter what qualifications or how you do your job.... That's the way it is.

His wife and business partner quit her corporate position in a petroleum company, and they found more opportunities in self-employment. Even though they initially went into a "traditional" business for Asian immigrants, he comments that they used their educational training to reinvest their profits to venture into other businesses. Since then they have become very successful with their real estate business, travel agency, and Hong Kong–style restaurant. Clearly, Asian Americans recognize that attaining a supposedly "higher" class status does not necessarily protect one from de facto discrimination, personal and institutional (Omi 1993).

In 1996, there were 1,573 complaints of racial discrimination filed against San Diego County employers with the state Department of Fair Employment and Housing, a 19 percent increase from 1995, translating to about 54 complaints per 100,000 residents, the highest of any county in Southern California (Braun and McKinnie 1997). A Chinese American county employee who processed these legal cases informed me that although Asian Americans filed a small percentage of these cases, this does not represent their experience with racial discrimination, since he was aware of other situations in which they were hesitant to take legal action. A Japanese American comments: "We were too damn quiet. I get passed up on a promotion and somebody else gets passed up on a promotion; ... it's different than passing up a Black or a Hispanic because they have support groups out there and they're going to go to them and that agency will be called on the carpet. And we didn't have that then. Now, we've got that through ABA." A third-generation Chinese American restaurateur born in 1952 also expresses the need to develop new strategies to combat their exclusion: "As much as I hate yelling and screaming, 'We don't get our fair share,' it's something I deal with more. . . . Because if you don't scream and yell, you're not going to get a piece of the pie. . . . There may be a few that will make it up above the ceiling, but the majority of Asians get above that by screaming and yelling."

Given their limited resources, ABA activists used a proactive approach that encouraged the public and private sector to hire and promote more Asian Americans. The glass ceiling is one issue that can unite the native-born and foreign-born populations, yet organizers disagree over how stridently they should approach these matters. In their country of origin, Asian immigrant professionals were most likely racial majorities and were unencumbered by racial domination, so protesting gender and racial barriers in their profession is outside their repertoire. However, having once been a part of a racial majority population can also have the opposite effect; they are less willing to simply accept the racial discrimination they experience and have more confidence to contest economic inequities and challenge their subordinate status in the United States. The forms of discrimination that U.S.-born and foreign-born Asian Americans experience affects their strategies; for example, those born abroad may encounter biases based on their language skills or degree equivalency. Immigrants note that U.S.-born Asians have advantages over them, as in this comment: "They [Asians born in this country] have a lot more opportunity because they speak the language. They share the culture. Other than how they look, everything's American. These people move up." However, there are immigrants who speak fluent English and have material and human capital that their U.S.-born counterparts do not possess. ABA allows them to share experiences with those in similar circumstances and to discuss various strategies to contend with their exclusion.

Debating the Benefits of Affirmative Action

To counter economic marginalization, one major strategy adopted by ABA was to be included in affirmative action programs in public contracting; however, as I found out, this can be a controversial tactic. In the late 1960s, President Johnson created programs to help stimulate the growth of businesses owned by minorities (racial minorities and women) and this program was expanded by the Nixon administration, which created the Office of Minority Business Enterprise in the Department of Commerce (Jones 1988). The public sector, namely government entities at the state and city level, was encouraged to grant contracts to minority-owned firms and could award them extra points when they made bids for a project, which were tabulated along with points for factors such as estimated cost, level of experience, and quality of proposal. Since minorities or women own few large contracting or consulting businesses, prime contractors are encouraged to hire minority- and women-owned businesses as subcontractors, another way to acquire additional points. To enforce these policies, federal funding would be withheld from local and state governments that did not comply (Graham 1990). Although San Diego County had an affirmative action program, the San Diego city program received more notoriety.[8] Responding to pressure from local minority groups, at that time primarily Latinos and Blacks, the San Diego City Council established the Equal Opportunity Contracting Program (EOCP) in March 1985 to achieve parity in the representation of minorities and women in city contracting.[9]

One of the central issues that brought the organizers of the Asian Business Association together was to ensure Asian Americans received their "fair share in terms of economic opportunities," especially in the lucrative area of government contracts. The first president explains the speech he made at the preliminary meeting of ABA organizers:

> I told everybody, as I do now, that the Asian community is missing out on a lot of opportunities and that's because either we're not participating, or that we're afraid to participate or that we're inexperienced or whatever; but the opportunities are there. And we've got to participate economically, we have to be part of the mainstream, be part of the politics. . . . All the resources that the city gives to businesses and development, it's all Caucasian, no Asians in sight. And these were deals that were unbelievable. . . . I thought it was wrong and now that as I realized that there was a big Asian community, we've got to get our ass off our chairs and start getting involved.

They were aware that the model minority myth assumed Asian American business owners were not in need of any public sector assistance, and hence they had been excluded from affirmative action outreach programs. As a Korean American who owns an advertising company explained, ABA would "let the government and agencies know that yes, we support affirmative action," and that they wanted to be included in such programs. For some Asian Americans, minority contracting became more important, because with the recession in the early 1990s, private industry work had dried up; these contracts could save a struggling business such as those in catering, printing, office supplies, construction, engineering, architecture, and janitorial services. As one officer of the organization states: "Our obligation as business leaders is to bring the Asian American community into the mainstream. . . . Asian businesses aren't all just mom-and-pop small restaurants. They compete with American companies for projects."[10]

Institutions often alleged they could not fulfill their goals due to the lack of Asian-owned businesses. Asian Americans dismissed these claims, however, stating that more often Asian American business owners did not know of these opportunities, had difficulty with the certification process, or were inexperienced in the bidding procedures, so they tended to underuse these services. In 1991, the city manager stated that in 1990, 28 percent of the city's certified M/WBE (Minority Business Enterprise and Women Business Enterprise) consultant/professional services firms were Asian/Filipino, and they received 1.5 percent of all contracts.[11] So the problem was not the number of available businesses, but ensuring that certified Asian American businesses were selected for projects. By sharing their resources and experiences, they could help one another with the daunting paperwork required to be certified as an MBE, a designation that must be updated yearly. Having this network allowed members to be informed about procurement opportunities, learn how to write up their proposals, and become familiar with how to bid for projects. Asian Americans argued that the public and private sectors did not seek the involvement of business owners, so ABA also made efforts to compile a list of Asian-owned businesses to provide to mainstream institutions.

Since the laws implementing and monitoring these race-conscious programs were vaguely outlined, these programs have been challenged legally and have led to vociferous public controversies about whether they are remedial or preferential. In the precedent ruling, *City of Richmond v. J. A. Croson Co.*, in 1989, the U.S. Supreme Court decided that minority set-aside programs were unconstitutional if communities failed to prove a history of discrimination in awarding public contracts.[12] The court ruled that a statistical outcome was invalid without documented evidence proving the *intent to discriminate*, so the burden of proof is on the "victim." Although this case was decided in Virginia, it has had repercussions on affirmative action contracting programs nationwide.[13] The San Diego city attorney, who did not support the plan before it was implemented in 1985, made his recommendation based on the Richmond decision: "The City would best be served by reevaluating its MBE/WBE program with an eye to eliminating race and gender conscious goals and instead substituting criteria that are race and gender neutral."[14] In the early 1990s, a group of Anglo engineers sued the city for discrimination, objecting to the EOCP program on the grounds that it unfairly disadvantaged them.[15] Upon hearing the case, the U.S. District judge dismissed the city's eight-year-old program in September 1993, declaring the goal-setting policies unconstitutional, since they were tantamount to an illegal quota system (Cantlupe 1994b). Like other cities, San Diego conducted a disparity study to assess the program (Cantlupe 1994a; LaNoue 1991) and the city instituted an interim "voluntary" program that relies on the "good faith efforts" of prime contractors to provide subcontracting work to minority- and women-owned firms (Cantlupe 1994b, 1994c).[16] The most drastic blow to race-conscious public contract programs was the 1995 *Adarand Construction v. Pena* ruling, in which the U.S. Supreme Court ruled five to four in favor of a "reverse discrimination" claim by a White-owned engineering company against a Latino-owned company in Colorado. This was followed in 1996 by the passage in California of Proposition 209, which eliminated race-based programs at the state level. Both legal moves basically allowed local governments to dismiss their affirmative action programs.

Not only did ABA organizers have to contend with external undermining of these set-aside programs, they had to contend with contentious debates within their ranks. During my research I found varying opinions about affirmative action policies for educational or employment purposes. More often than not, individuals supported the need for affirmative action–type programs, yet were highly critical of the facilitation and monitoring of such programs in both the public sector and private sector. A Chinese American whose engineering company works on projects for transit, water, and sewer districts for the city, county, and state government states:

Well, I think the first time I was made aware of it was I'd say about three, four years ago where we did lose a project. Again, there is no official statements made, "Yeah, you lost it because you're not [a minority- or women-owned firm]." We thought we were the best-qualified candidate for a certain job and the firm that ultimately got it was a White-owned firm who had women-owned business status. In other words, he sold the business to his wife. That's when I first noticed it. I said, wait a minute, that's not fair. We were the most qualified. We gave the best interview presentation. We had the most background and so forth and so on. . . . Right after that we started choosing our subconsultants or our team members based on their minority- or women-owned business classification. And we, quite frankly, had to substitute a lot of the team members that we used to deal with before. So all of a sudden all these subconsultant firms go, "What have we done? Why aren't we being used by you guys anymore? Is it because we messed up?" "No, you guys did good work and you helped us a lot but you're the wrong color of skin and we have to fulfill the points." And it's about that blunt.... [When we work with subcontractors] the first questions we do ask is, can you do the work, do you have insurance, and do you have certain cases of minority or women-owned business? Again, the intention is good but that's not the way it was meant to be, I don't think.

He added that he is supportive of the "goal" to achieve equity but complained about the lack of monitoring of the programs: "I think it's good to have an affirmative action program if it is administered correctly and if it is intended to do what it is supposed to do and that is help disadvantaged minority- or women-owned business that need the help."

Another individual active in ABA comments: "I am for affirmative action programs. At the same time, I think there's a lot of waste and inequities in the system. I don't think there's very much monitoring of how our tax dollars or private dollars are being spent. I just hope that the resources go to where they need to go." Ironically, a Taiwanese vice president of an Asian-owned bank that hired mainly bilingual Chinese immigrants and whose clients were mostly Asians was concerned that affirmative action policies would force him to diversify his loans to include non-Asian minorities, in addition to diversifying his staff. Another individual complained that the majority of employees in his company were women and minorities; however, it was not minority owned, so it could not be certified a minority business. These comments reflect the widespread criticism regarding the program, ranging from the monitoring of prime contractors to the advertising of projects.[17] The criticisms are focused less on the validity of a color-conscious policy, but more on the implementation and enforcement of such programs.

It is difficult for foreign-born populations who arrive without an understanding of U.S. race relations and Asian American history to conceive of Asian Americans as an oppressed minority population, and less likely for them to support affirmative action programs. Newcomers have concerns about being classified as a domestic American minority group and are often uncomfortable using language associated with racial injustice and racial oppression or the struggle for civil rights in the United States. Those with resources buy into the model minority myth as a positive image, pointing out that Asians were successful because they had a good work ethic, valued education, and respected their family and therefore do not need affirmative action programs.

This echoes the sentiments of the Anglo engineers who filed the law-suit against the city: "A rich person from India, a rich person from Japan, can come over here and automatically get preferential points over someone who's been struggling—and there's no way you can say that's fair" (quoted in Traitel and Cantlupe 1992). Those with long-established roots in this country or those who may have been born abroad but were raised in this country may easily be able to conceptu-alize their claims for economic parity based on their rights as Ameri-cans—a concept not so easily adopted by Asian immigrants. Yet I also found that, like the foreign-born population, younger generations of U.S.-born Asians who lack an understanding of the racial discrimina-tion and the historical struggles against discrimination are reticent about supporting race-based programs.

The existence of a new generation of Asian immigrant groups raises complex questions about whether or not long-established but recently included groups, such as South Asians, and newly included immigrant populations with a shorter history in this country, such as Hmong, Cam-bodians, Laotian, Vietnamese, Thais, or Indonesians, qualify for affir-mative action programs. When I was helping to put together a flyer for ABA, I wanted to create a decorative border that listed the various eth-nic groups. The president hesitated when I mentioned Asian Indians and told me to consult some board members; when he raised this concern at the next board meeting, an unsettling discussion followed. Many thought of Asian Indians, the largest of the South Asian American pop-ulation, as "Asians" (the group includes individuals from Pakistan, Bangladesh, Sri Lanka, Nepal, and so on). Other members protested their inclusion based on what they perceived to be cultural and histor-ical differences between Asian Indians and other "Asians." For exam-ple, two Chinese individuals, one raised in Malaysia and one raised in Singapore, where there are substantial Asian Indian communities, felt Asian Indians belonged in this category; a Chinese raised in Hong Kong who had little contact with Asians Indians felt they were their own dis-tinct group. In private, a Chinese American told me: "I think you would agree with me there's more of a similarity between a Hmong or a Viet-namese and a Japanese and Korean and the Chinese than there are with the Asian Indians." A Japanese–Chinese American woman gave a response that reflects the ambivalence of many: "You know, I think they're [South Asians] lumped together for political reasons, cause you have power in numbers, but I consider them their own category.... I know for practical reasons it's probably a good idea, but I just see them as their own race also, because they are just so different from Asia per se. And I know they're facing a lot of hate crimes and discrimination."

A Chinese American felt that South Asians do not qualify for affirmative action programs, whereas other groups qualify because "their ancestry has been discriminated against in America and their ancestry are part of the pioneer that built this country; . . . the Chinese built the railroad, the Japanese got internment." There is ample room for debate, since Asian Indians arrived in the United States in the early 1900s, and they experienced forms of social and legal discrimination similar to the Japanese and Chinese experience (Chan 1991; Takaki 1989a).[18] The 1923 Bhagat Singh Thind case ruled that although Asian Indians could categorically be labeled "Caucasian," they were not commonly perceived as White, so they should be barred from citizenship, immigration, and intermarriage with Whites—like other Asians in the United States at that time (Mazumdar 1989). In the 1980s, the U.S. census included South Asians in the Asian category; in the 1990s, San Diego County counted South Asians as Asian Americans or minorities for employment statistics, yet ironically, Asian Indians could not be certified as minority business enterprises. Regardless of state-defined categories, those classified as South Asians will have to negotiate to "belong" in this category, a task that will become more pressing for ABA as more South Asians move to San Diego.

While some ABA participants question the incorporation of relatively new immigrant groups in programs, others point out that the legacy of discrimination directed at Asians in this country affects a new generation of Asian immigrants and Asian Americans in the contemporary period. A Japanese-White ABA board member explains these connections:

> My feeling is if the group, whatever it happens to be, has been discriminated then I think you need to have a certain amount of affirmative action to counteract what that negative stereotyping or whatever that negative, you know. For so many years, Asians were discriminated against, particularly in California, there were laws against them owning land. You know, being Japanese American, even though my family wasn't in the U.S. in that period, that impacts on all of us who are Japanese American because all of that negative stereotyping, all that stuff that happened, the internment during the war, everything goes back. It impacts on us even today. . . . They treated us just the way they did the Indians, the Blacks, every other minority of color. When the white majority had the power to do it, they did it. They had fear, they had resentment, you know, whatever it was, they locked us up and put us away in a little box so they wouldn't have to deal with us. And so I feel real strongly that when we have that kind of history, you know, where people would treat

us that way, … the kind of attitudes linger much longer after that generation. It just continues and continues. And so in order to address that, I think
you really do have to have a certain amount of affirmative action, because
there's still to this day, and I have felt it myself, this feeling that we're not
good enough.

This board member felt that new immigrants, even those from newer
Asian groups with some financial resources, should be included in the
Asian American category and in affirmative action programs. A Chinese
immigrant also noted the need to correct past problems: "I agree with
affirmative action. … But I want to do away with it because a fair society shouldn't have affirmative action."

Homeland experiences affect their perceptions of affirmative action
programs, for example, an ethnic Chinese woman from Singapore and
an ethnic Chinese from Malaysia have contrasting views. The banker,
a former president of ABA, explains:

> In Singapore, as I said, there is no such thing as affirmative action. Everyone
> does have that equal opportunity. Our cabinet of ministers, for instance, is
> well represented by Chinese, Indians, Malays and so on. They don't even have
> to come up with a quota that says, oh, just because the population, 70 per-
> cent of them are Chinese and therefore, we have to have seven out of ten to
> be Chinese. There's no such thing. They're basically qualified, based on their
> academic and professional qualifications if they want to be ministers, noth-
> ing to do with race. Our presidents have also been of various ethnicities.
> We've had an Indian president. We've had an Eurasian president, a Chinese
> president. Our prime minister has always been Chinese, but that sort of goes
> without saying. So for me, when I came up to the States and meeting or learn-
> ing of these affirmative action acts, affirmative action here and there, and all
> of that, sometimes it's kind of ridiculous to me, but I do understand.

She adds:

> It's important that we're being thought of in affirmative action. There's a lot
> of, for instance, making loans, using that as an example for affirmative action,
> very often people are fighting for their rights for lending for Blacks, Black
> communities, lending to Hispanic communities and such. Hardly anybody
> stands up for lending to the Asian community because the perception is that
> Asians are rich. … But we forget a lot of times that there are the new immi-
> grants that are not. And they fall into the same financial category as the His-
> panics and/or Blacks in the lower income sections, but nobody stands up to
> fight for them.

In contrast, an ethnic Chinese male who was born and raised in Malaysia states that U.S. affirmative action programs are "harmful rather
than helpful," comparing them to policies in his homeland:

Well, I guess the policy of the government, because it's controlled by Malays, that the policies tends be slanted toward encouraging or trying to help the Malays gain economic efficiency. Traditionally they have been rural people, farmers and such, fishermen. As a result, they have not been able to catch up. The Chinese were mainly traders so they went into business easily and as a result they managed to climb the social and economic ladder faster. The Malays, most of them had a hard time being in business, they didn't know how to conduct business so all of the policies are geared toward bringing the Malays up to a certain level, in order to compete. As a Chinese of course I didn't like that. I resented that. . . . I think in the long run, . . . and it's been about twenty years since the policy was openly enforced, I don't think it's done very much to bring the Malay populations ahead, to get them to be where they want. There is a percentage of them that has achieved professional-type jobs and are very affluent, but by far the majority of the Malay population is no better off.

He felt it was unfair that educational slots and scholarships were reserved for Malays, because "the Malays would get preference even though their grades would be lower" at the expense of the ethnic Chinese—one of the reasons he chose to go to New Zealand for his college education. Many of his criticisms about the Malaysian system parallel those directed at U.S. programs. Numerically, Malays were the majority in the population and in the government, while the Chinese were the minority, so this case differs from the U.S. case; however, the projection that communities of color will become the predominant group demographically in the near future—already the case in California, according to the 2000 U.S. census—raises even more complicated questions about affirmative action programs. Clearly with the increasing ethnic, generational, and socioeconomic diversity of the Asian American population, it becomes more difficult to reach consensus on the interventionist approaches they should use to attain economic parity and how they should position themselves in the debates.

The Marketing of Asian American Consumers

As Asian Americans entered new economic arenas, they realized they shared similar problems and have promoted the sharing of both class and racial resources. They are using *racial economic solidarity* through ABA to reach out to each other for professional support, as well as to target other Asian Americans as consumers. Because minorities have been and continue to be excluded residentially, educationally, economically, socially, and politically from the mainstream, they have chosen their "comfort zone" within their racialized groups. In this way, they were breaking out of the ethnic enclave mode, but they were not necessarily mainstreaming. In this pan-Asian model, they were encouraging economic interchanges with other Asian ethnics. ABA organizers were encouraged to assist one another financially, by conducting business with Asian American professionals and patronizing Asian-owned businesses, which are dispersed throughout San Diego County.

Often they do not know what other Asian-owned businesses or professionals exist, since entering nontraditional fields is still relatively new for them. As one restaurant owner remarks: "A lot of us were so busy doing our own little things we didn't know who the other players were. On the one hand, we could do business with this company that's White or we could do it with this company who's Asian. And a lot of us didn't know that the talent was there in the Asian community. And surprisingly enough there is. So I think that's one thing that the networking did." Some involved with ABA provided consultation on the creation of the first San Diego Asian Business (Telephone) Directory in 1993, providing multilingual listings of local businesses.

Meeting members from other ethnic groups can create avenues for ethnic business owners to reach out to more Asian consumers. A Chinese lawyer, half of whose clients were Asian Americans, explains why he was active in ABA: "Because it's mainly a business networking group. And it was a good way to meet different Asians in the community. First of all, it's easier to sell to your own ethnic group. If you want to move outside of that, without an introduction from the other ethnic group, it's very hard to break in." Three Asians banks in San Diego were owned by either Chinese or Taiwanese, yet in order to survive, they cannot cater only to their own ethnic subgroup; they needed to branch out and do business with other Asians. A manager of one of the banks who actively participated in the ABA explained the necessity of targeting a wider Asian American market: "San Diego is different because it's quite spread out and the Asian population is quite spread out and also businesses are quite spread out, so you have to keep an open mind, be very creative."

In addition, mainstream companies noticed the increasing Asian American population, especially with the influx of prosperous immigrants, and realized that local Asian American consumers were perhaps an untapped market with substantial buying power. A Korean American individual who works for a mainstream financial planning and investment firm explains that his involvement in ABA is "just important in our overall picture of what we're trying to do to earn money to be the premiere company within the Asian market, so we need to be in that environment. We need to have the recognition from the different communities and we need to know who's who." Noticeable were the non-Asian representatives from mainstream companies attending ABA meetings, recruiting possible ethnic employees whom they perceived to have the necessary language and cultural skills to initiate contacts and "infiltrate" the Asian market. Asians manipulated the model minority image to promote themselves as *model minority consumers* with purchasing power, so corporations would target this market.

Mainstream companies and agencies began to capitalize on this market by giving their employees, especially those in insurance and financial planning, titles such as Asian Marketing Manager. The advantage for employees was it allowed ethnic populations to do business with someone of their own racial background. The disadvantage was that it segregated Asian American employees into "ethnic" positions and markets, and left a perception that they could not target mainstream markets. If the ethnic markets did not pan out, they were fired rather than repositioned within the company, which explains why numerous individuals with these ethnic market titles were constantly changing jobs or companies during my research period. With the pressure to reach their "quota," sometimes these representatives misled or deceived their clientele. In addition to finding new employees to target what they thought was a capital-rich group, mainstream companies saw ABA as a way to diversify their workforce. Private corporations are not accountable to state or federally mandated affirmative action programs, so they can narrowly promote their version of corporate diversity or multiculturalism when it is profitable. And those that have superficially incorporated diversity can conveniently disregard it when they deem it "unnecessary," especially when it is not mandated.

Other Asian Americans were more hesitant about ABA connections, even if it did bring corporate donations, as one critic notes: "Every time they [companies] want Asian [consumers], they have a perception that ABA has all the Asian market, which is not true at this time." Many corporations are eager to target minority populations when they recognize their profitability, as is evident in their advertising campaigns that increasingly include ethnic faces and ethnic languages. However, this limited form of *corporate multiculturalism* can exploit ethnic communities, for example, by trying to sell naïve Asian immigrants unnecessary insurance policies. ABA organizers also practice a precarious balancing act, demanding that companies hire Asian Americans because they are a growing, affluent consumer base, especially if they are unable to justify these claims, rather than demanding they include more Asian Americans in their company based on sound principles of racial equity.

Capitalizing on Asian American Transnational Connections

The need for San Diego to diversify and revitalize its economy, along with significant economic growth in Asia, provided Asian Americans with new opportunities for mobilization. Since World War II, the largest nonmanufacturing employer in the area has been the U.S. government, including both active duty military personnel and civilian employees working for the military.[19] At the end of the Cold War, the high-tech defense industry, a mainstay of the local manufacturing economy, was severely destabilized by cutbacks in defense spending. Officials noted the loss of 20,000 jobs alone in 1992 and at least 9,000 more in 1993. With the economic recession of the early 1990s, business failures and bank closures increased and real estate prices dropped for both private and commercial property. Some local officials suggested that the capital gains tax stifled entrepreneurial growth, a primary factor in the region's economic prosperity. The higher regulatory costs for businesses and the high tax environment have impacted negatively on maintaining companies and attracting new ventures. Others have attributed the decline to the antigrowth climate in the area, which enacted housing restrictions in local communities that resulted in increasingly higher housing costs.

As a consequence of the economic downturn in San Diego, city officials tried to capture the resources of the ethnic community, especially the Latino and Asian populations, and turned to them for help in boosting the region's economic recovery by providing connections to new markets abroad and by attracting international investors to establish businesses in San Diego (Novarro 1993). By the late 1980s, the Pacific Rim region surpassed the Atlantic as the main trading partner with the United States, and Asia was perceived as a vast economic market, given the large population that could serve as a labor pool and a consumer base (Nakanishi 1991; Ong and Liu 1994). New Asian immigrants bring investments that can improve the sagging residential real estate market and provide an entrepreneurial boost to the economy, especially with the creation of new jobs (Schoenberger 1993). In turn, political and economic instability in Asian countries has led capital investors to seek more secure investments overseas (Zhou 1992). In the early stages of ABA, organizers were concerned with domestic issues, but by the third year there was a major shift in emphasis to international issues. With the influence of foreign-born Asians, increasing trade with Asian countries identified as the "tigers" or "dragons" became a primary function of the organization, especially since city officials encouraged it.

Asian Americans became aware of their new economic status and tried to benefit from the perception by the public and private sector that they had connections to the Pacific Rim. A Chinese American woman entrepreneur active in ABA took personal pride in the economic growth in Asia: "It's not because we are sitting here and make that happen over there.... We are really taking advantage of what's over there that makes us look better, so we are gaining the respect and the recognition of being an Asian." A Chinese American lawyer and restaurateur agrees: "When they look at us, even though we're Asian American, I think they look as Asians as a broad group that includes Asians from the Far East and this gives us that perception, a total perception of probably more power than we really have today." As one ABA member wanting to capitalize on the economic potential of the Pacific Rim states: "I mean, like it or not, people label Asian with money, with business opportunity, especially today. So, why not take advantage of it?" Local officials began using rhetoric that described the Asian American community as the "bridge for the Pacific Rim into San Diego" at public events.

Previously, single-ethnic groups often hosted economic and political delegations from their home country, yet they complained that politicians, including the mayor, ignored invitations to meet with these dignitaries privately and declined to attend functions hosted in honor of the delegates. ABA leaders began hosting Asian business delegates and holding forums for these economic exchanges which attracted city leaders.[20] A number of Asian immigrant entrepreneurs had ready-made contacts; some sustained their small businesses by relying on products made in their former homelands where lower wages and lower production costs allowed them to compete in the domestic market. ABA members wanted to be a resource capable of creating not only a business climate amenable to Asian investors, but also a social and cultural environment attractive to them, which would also bring indirect profits from the tourism trade. An officer of ABA explained her experience in the 1980s in Vancouver, Canada, which managed to attract a substantial number of entrepreneurs from Hong Kong: "If you want to attract those people to dump money in your community, you've got to package yourself, saying, Look, we think you're important, there's a lot of people that are similar to you over here, [and] they're accepted. We'd really like for you to work with them." Unlike California cities where there are large ethnic residential and commercial centers, San Diego was a riskier venture, without an ethnic concentration.

The San Diego Chamber of Commerce's desire to focus more on trade with Mexico and the Pacific Rim placed Latinos and Asian Americans in a more favorable position. Historically, the Chamber had not been receptive to any of the minority communities, including the Asian American population. On 4 March 1882, the San Diego Chamber of Commerce held a demonstration at the downtown Horton Plaza, encouraging businesses and stores to close to show their support of the Chinese Exclusion Act, which barred further immigration from China (Chu 1982). One Asian American individual who attended the Chamber meetings for a brief period during the late 1970s noticed the lack of minorities:

> The board of directors was all White and very established, very establishment.... There were no Asians, no Latinos, and there were no Blacks.... It was just very, very Caucasian. I always knew that I stuck out like a sore thumb.... And I always knew that they ignored me, which bothered the hell out of me. But I had no choice. I had to go along with the way the rules are set. Aside from that, you have to make a living, so I just went along with it, but my heart, my enthusiasm, was never really there. I just went through the motions and because they never really accepted my ideas, I knew that I would never be in a serious dialogue with the decision makers. I never really participated in a meaningful way.

A Taiwanese comments that right before the formation of ABA, some Taiwanese had joined the Chamber, "but subsequently a lot withdrew their membership due to the fact the Chamber was not very receptive to their business interests. That may have been the old boys' network at the Chamber, the fact they are predominantly Caucasian. There was no representation of Asians or Asian organization in the Chamber."

In 1992, with the president of seventeen years leaving, the new leadership at the Chamber decisively placed an "emphasis on international trade" and the need "to develop more foreign markets for San Diego businesses" (Kraul 1992; Shaw 1992). In 1993, the Chamber's annual dinner, whose theme was "In the Spirit of Cooperation," was cosponsored by ABA, the Black Chamber of Commerce, and the Hispanic Chamber of Commerce, with proceeds split evenly among the four organizations.[21] With 800–900 attendees, this unprecedented event had the highest attendance of any Chamber event.[22] A number of Chamber board members objected to these joint endeavors, since allowing "minorities" to share economic power would undermine the role of traditional power brokers and the racial power dynamics of the city. One of the main joint ventures with the Chamber of Commerce was support of the 1993 North American Free Trade Agreement (NAFTA) signed by the United States, Mexico, and Canada, which was to remove trade barriers; this created disagreements among ABA members. Some thought the agreement would improve the quality of life in Mexico by providing jobs, making the economy stable, and helping the country clean up its environment. Those who disagreed argued that NAFTA would not protect workers' rights, only allow corporations to move their factories to countries where wages were lower and where there were fewer workplace and environmental regulations.

Whether the "transnational" image of them is real or symbolic, Asian Americans continue to take advantage of it. Although some ABA participants, foreign-born and U.S.-born, have connections to investment or trading opportunities in Asia, others clearly do not. There are also cultural differences between Asians in America and those in Asia that make these connections challenging and personally uncomfortable. For example, a Chinese American immigrant woman who was helping to host delegates from mainland China stated that all the delegates were men who were uncomfortable with her as a younger woman, and they complained about the inauthentic Chinese dishes served at the luncheon and criticized her for not speaking the dialect with the correct accent. Scholars have argued that it is precisely their racial exclusion and marginalization from U.S. employment structures that forces Asian Americans to find alternative economic avenues abroad (S. Wong 1995). Hence, some members of ABA were interested in pursuing this agenda, while others did not consider it to be a primary or realistic goal for the community or for the organization, advocating instead that domestic problems should be the focus of their attention.

As a racially discriminated group, it seems appealing for Asian Americans to be considered an asset and a possible savior of the local economy based on their connection to the Pacific Rim. Asian immigrants opportunistically positioned themselves as having the potential to rebuild or revitalize the U.S. economy, constructing themselves as *model immigrants* worthy of becoming *model U.S. citizens*. The irony is that to prove their value, they highlight their connections to Asia, showing that they have "foreign" connections by maintaining their ethnic cultures and languages, which has the potential to remarginalize them. Other participants of ABA expressed concern that associating Asian Americans too closely with Asia can also reinforce the perception of them as "foreigners," which can be a contributing factor to hate crimes, and so they were cautious about being too closely identified with Asian trade issues. Asian Americans were mindful of the Japan bashing prevalent in the 1980s, when the perception was that Asians were sending too many exports to America, imposing stiff tariffs on U.S. imports to Japan, and invading the U.S. economy.[23] Their celebratory stance as resource-rich Asian immigrants is taking place at a time of economic uneasiness about the loss of U.S. manufacturing jobs to Asia as a result of "flexible production" as well as loss of professional positions in the high-tech and bio-tech industries known as "offshoring" or "outsourcing" (Somers 2003). Additionally, focusing on Asian markets can be a very risky venture, since it is impossible to predict the social, political, or economic stability of the region.[24] While Asia is still considered an economic threat, by the 1990s this view was tempered by the image of Asia as a potential economic ally, and these contradictory dualities persist for the community.

Negotiating an Organization: Gender, Ethnicity, Class, and Perspectives

I observed tensions between ABA members, board members, and officers based on multiple factors—background or personality differences or ideological perspectives. Although men still outnumber women in ABA, noticeable is the number of active women who serve as officers and board members. In the third year, of the four officers, only the vice-president was male; however, the board members were primarily male. At a planning meeting, an officer used the word "chairman," but quickly corrected himself by using the term "chairperson," commenting that this was more correct since the current chair was a male but the chair-elect was a woman. At another meeting to organize an upcoming dinner meeting, a male member stated that there were too many men speaking at these events and revised the agenda to give women a turn to speak, to encourage them to take a visible role at the functions. His wife, a Filipina, was a high-ranking officer in the sheriff's department so he understood the importance of gender and leadership dynamics.

Nonetheless, women involved in ABA have had to contend with gender discrimination in the organization. A woman officer explained what happened when she received a list from a male officer of potential ABA panelists for a career-day workshop for Asian American teenagers: "So after we got through the list, I found out that there really were no women. It's extremely important that we get a woman to get up there on the panel, a woman who is Asian; . . . we have to show them [the teenagers], not just in terms of having an Asian role model, but that Asian woman as a role model." One of the most active women in ABA comments:

> It's very apparent that we don't have enough women on the board itself. The few that we have are definitely vocal, but we need more because women, well, women to me, do come with always a different point of view. Women, also, unfortunately, tend to do more work. Men tend to take the more strategic planning role, generally, I think, in most organizations, which I think is unfortunate. We have, I feel a lot of times that the women's opinion in the organization, sometimes I value even more than the men. And I have to admit that on occasion, I have, you know, turned toward other women in the organization for their opinions and then represented them as such on the board meetings. . . . Because I am holding an office of position . . . I feel that whatever I say will be heard. It may or may not be followed or respected or what have you, but it will be heard.

She mentioned that ABA was an improvement over the meetings or events she attended with single-ethnic groups, which were primarily composed of new immigrant groups and where the wives of the male leaders were usually the only other women in attendance.

A common theme expressed by ABA leaders is the desire to become incorporated or integrated, individually and as a group, into the economic mainstream; however, it also leads them to disassociate themselves from particular segments of the Asian American community. A Chinese American man finds that "it's so exciting in ABA these days because we have a very active group that wants to blend into the mainstream. . . . That's kind of exciting because now, rather than just saying, well, the Asians are coming, are rising and want to have power, it's more like, hey, we can fit in as well." Ironically, in their desire to become incorporated in the mainstream, some try to disassociate themselves from those "less assimilated" or "less well-off." A Chinese immigrant who works as a lawyer and serves many Southeast Asian clients articulates these distinctions:

> I think, as an individual they probably see me differently, maybe because I dress differently. I'm more educated than some of them [Asian refugees]. . . . I think most of the people can distinguish between an Asian who has assimilated into the American culture and one who hasn't and they tend to classify the group in a different light than ones that have. . . . The one group who has assimilated, people who are professional, people who are successful in business, they have a lot of respect for. People who are new immigrants, people who are not as well off economically, socially, they probably tend to look down at them.

When I was collecting advertising for the ABA newsletter, a Korean American who worked for an investment company and had previously put in full-page ads told me he wanted to change the photograph of his Chinese American coworker in the ad because "she looks like some damn refugee, you know, a boat person!" His comments stem from ethnic and class factors, and he felt it was appropriate to make this statement to me, regardless of my being Vietnamese.

I heard similarly framed remarks from other individuals; for example, a person who came to the United States as a college student explains explicitly why he wanted to economically disidentify himself from Southeast Asian refugees:

> I don't think of refugees as being Asian Americans, so in a sense, I'm prejudiced against other Asians, but it's because I like to be more associated with successful Asian Americans that are doing things and going somewhere. People who are integrated well. People who are successful in terms of business or who do well academically. Who speak very fair English. . . . Sometimes I don't think of those [boat] people in those same terms, right or wrong. I might be misinformed. But I probably hold the same general perception that most people, American people, most White people do. . . . It almost causes you to be resentful because the Vietnamese are boat people, and people developed a stereotype of boat people. . . . I realized that people might look at me as being Vietnamese. I better be very clear on not having an accent, being very different. I guess I learned to be more dynamic and very succinct with my English so that I wouldn't get mixed up with a boat person, which I had a negative perception of.

Although there are class reasons for this disidentification, his comments indicate that his resentment stems from the racism directed against Southeast Asian refugees. Even though he wanted to distance himself from the refugee population, he adamantly defended the need for ABA to support UPAC's programs, many directed at Southeast Asians, when others at a board meeting felt that working with the social service organization on a collaborative project would hurt the image of "successful" Asian Americans that ABA was trying to project to mainstream corporations.

The organization has been criticized for being too elitist, "too acculturated," and "too Americanized," since it is involved with mainstream issues. Critics may question if a business organization primarily interested in socioeconomic mobility for a select fraction of the Asian American population is able to address the concerns of working-class Asian Americans who must contend with chronic unemployment or underemployment. It would be impossible for a single organization to be attuned to the wide array of economic needs of all Asian Americans.

Working-class Asian Americans who are more critical of the capitalist system and its exploitation of workers have formed their own organizations (K. Wong 1994). The local chapter of the Asian Pacific American Labor Alliance, the first national Asian labor organization within the ranks of the AFL-CIO, was started in 1992.[25] Asian Americans are becoming more socioeconomically heterogeneous, and the likely scenario is that they will form varied organizations with differing class interests, that some will share resources, and that others will be ideologically opposed to one another (Louie 2001).

There was disagreement in ABA over basic organizational strategies. For example, while some wanted ABA to continue its political advocacy agenda, others preferred focusing on improving their economic networks. A Japanese and Filipino American woman who helped establish ABA comments:

> [With the first president of ABA], it was a very politically orientated organization at the time, lobbying for a lot of things. . . . [Now] I see it more networking with other Chambers, small-business Chambers. [The first president] was out there meeting with every council member, every supervisor, with the mayor. . . . For some people, I know it was a little too political.

Another individual of Japanese and Chinese ancestry who also helped start ABA comments on his reservations about its direction:

> Our leadership was focusing on areas that involved political awareness, understanding how the political system works, and making the political system demand that we have some attention; and I think our prior leadership did a great job at that. The reason we have key Asians in these positions now, are because of the efforts done by the people before. It's not so much of what's been happening now. . . . I don't see the awareness of what's happening in city council becoming a priority for us anymore. I don't see ABA going to city council and saying, "We demand this." That's something we used to do—good or bad or indifferent. We've gone to a very socially focused organization, I've noticed, where networking plays a very key role.

The original organizers started ABA precisely because they wanted to take on more controversial issues; however, as they became more established with the Chamber of Commerce and had corporate sponsors, they toned down their political advocacy work, yet this can fluctuate depending on the organizational leadership.

A vociferous debate occurred during an ABA planning meeting in July 1993, in which the question of using "Asian" or "Asian American" was raised concerning the mission statement, exemplifying the disagreements about how Asian immigrants and Asian Americans should position themselves. One immigrant officer thought the term "Asian" reflected the whole community, since it included recent arrivals who have been in the United States five years or less, such as Southeast Asians, who may not identify with being American and would more likely accept a term which emphasizes their Asian roots. Another immigrant argued vehemently that they should use the term "Asian American," stating that he had raised his children to think of themselves not only as Asians, but also as "Americans." His great-grandfather and grandfather had worked as laborers in the United States, so for him, it was important to emphasize their historical and cultural connection to this country. While no consensus was reached at that juncture, in late 1993, the board members agreed without much debate that "Asian Pacific American" would be used in the mission statement, although the name of their organization remains the Asian Business Association.

This issue was raised again at another meeting. A Korean American born in Hawai'i told me of how he was outvoted: "What's missing from ABA is Americans—Asian Americans. And that was my first statement to the summit people in attendance, . . . 'You want to be called Asian Business Association?' They said, 'Yes, we want to be called Asian Business Association, not Asian American.'" As a graphic artist, he created the new logo for the local ABA since he thought the previous one with the U.S. flag motif in the bamboo was too crudely "Orientalist." He created a logo with a yin-yang design, a more subtle "Asian" reference with a modern twist, which ABA still uses. Asians in this country, especially evident with the Asian American movement in the 1960s and 1970s, struggled to be treated legally, socially, and politically as "Americans" and are sensitive to their portrayal or treatment as "foreigners"; yet they grapple with how to be sensitive to the perspective of newcomers.

As in many collaborative endeavors, the problems encountered revolve around personal goals being given priority over the interests of the organization, the same issue that almost splintered the Los Angeles ABA.[26] Similarly in San Diego, tension arose over a failed financial dealing and the fact that certain members did not share contracting opportunities with organizational members. According to one member: "There have been people involved with personal agendas other than for the good of the community. I think when you get individuals like that, that put their personal and business goals ahead of the goals of the organization, I think there are going to be problems." When I asked another interviewee if ethnicity created tension among members, the reply was: "No, I think it may be not necessarily the ethnic group itself that is the problem, it may be the different personalities of people, you know, . . . I mean it may just be an excuse for some people to not trust other people." As the organization developed, and with such a small network, conflicts among individuals have been unavoidable.

Race Relations and a Tenuous Economic Basis of Solidarity

ABA formed coalitions with other racial groups, and this has enhanced their status with the mainstream sector; nonetheless, there was not consensus among participants about whether or not coalitions were valuable goals. From the beginning, ABA was intent on establishing connections with other racial communities, as made clear in its mission statement: "Its [ABA] programs and effort will be directed toward both business and community-at-large issues that affect the economic interest of the Asian Community, as well as the Latino, African American and Native American communities in San Diego."[27] In November 1990, at one of the first ABA meetings, Mateo Camarillo, founder of the Chicano Federation, and attorney Dan Guevera of the Mexican American Business and Professional Foundation, were the keynote speakers. In 1992, ABA held an Asian and African American business mixer and an Asian and American Indian business mixer, according to an ABA flyer, with the intent of "breaking down cultural barriers; improving race relations; promoting inter-business opportunities; develop forums for future discussions; and get to know each others respective communities." Like other similar functions I attended, it was the "converted" who attended, showing the difficulty of creating a widespread coalition.

Coalitions have been most successful working together on limited, short-term projects to ensure representation by protesting the exclusion of "minorities" in employment, procurement, and contracting practices in the public and private sector.[28] For example, in 1991, ABA helped form an ad hoc organization, Communities United for Economic Justice (CUEJ), with African Americans, Latinos, Native Americans, and White women to protest the exclusion of "minorities" in contract opportunities with the Port Commission.[29] In 1991, CUEJ effectively prevented the Port Commission from automatically extending their contract with Host International/Marriott, a private company, which had the contract for the food and beverage concessions and gift shops. Although the contract was eventually given to Host for $30 million, the company agreed to include a Minority Business Enterprise and Women Business Enterprise (MBE/WBE) plan. This endeavor was so successful that CUEJ organizers decided to maintain the group to pursue other joint economic agendas.[30] They worked with the San Diego Convention Center, which awarded a contract to the Service America Corporation for food service, helping them monitor their MBE/WBE goals. CUEJ assisted San Diego Gas and Electric (SDG&E) in developing the Emerging Business Enterprise (EBE) program to increase the participation of nonminority women, minority, and disabled veteran business in employment, procurement, and contracting policies.[31] SDG&E initially sought representatives from the Latino community, and it was the Latino representative who suggested a joint committee with other racial groups, including Asian Americans.[32] As one Filipino American explains: "CUEJ, for example, would have not been perceived as being credible if it was an organization that was just made up of Hispanic organizations." Within CUEJ, participating Asian Americans have not been unified, and there have been conflicts among African American leaders and also between African American and Latino leaders over whether they were truly sharing opportunities, which eventually led to a breakdown in this coalition effort.

These activists recognize the power of collective action, yet their suspicions and stereotypes about one another make it difficult to work as a cohesive bloc. In the 1990s, Latinos composed the largest minority population in San Diego and Asian Americans surpassed the African American population, although African Americans still have the most political positions and appointments of the three groups in the city. In his speech at an ABA dinner on 21 February 1992, Hal Brown, a longtime activist who was president of CUEJ, discussed a reciprocal relationship in which African Americans can provide Asian Americans with political strategies, while Asian Americans can provide African Americans with entrepreneurship strategies—in essence an exchange of economic and political power.[33] He urged Asian Americans to get to know other racial communities and stated that "we in the African American [community] are not doing this. I know people in the African American community who are saying, we've struggled and fought, and so we should get 90 percent of the pie." Brown was expressing the sentiment of some members of the African American community who do not want to share economic resources with "foreigners" whom they perceive to be "advantaged." He echoed the same message at the CUEJ meetings: "We're not here to fight for separate pieces of the pie. We're here to try to get the best deal we can for the overall collection of [our] communities."[34] A Filipina American ABA board member reiterates this feeling of distrust:

> I think a lot of Africans and Hispanics, to a certain extent, are wary of the Asians because of the stereotype that the Asians are sharp and that they're really great businessmen.... Unfortunately, there are people, specifically in the African American community, that state, "Well, the more that goes into

their pocket, is less in our pocket; therefore, we should not be encouraging them." I think that's a big mistake. I think again unity in numbers can only help all three organizations, all the different cultures. But I think there's going to be resistance, more from the African Americans than from the Hispanics.

The Los Angeles rebellion of 1992 (about an hour and a half away) impacted ABA members' understanding of coalition efforts in San Diego, especially of how racial misperceptions can have a negative impact on race relations.

Some ABA participants, more swayed by negative stereotypes of other racial groups and positive ones of their own group, are convinced that Asian Americans have enough resources without having to negotiate with other groups. The following statements from two individuals involved with ABA indicate these sentiments:

> [In terms of] government programs, especially the Latinos and African Americans, they have much more per se than the Asians. But that's something that I wouldn't advocate, "Well, hey, give me an equal amount," because I think in a sense [that] will make us grow much weaker. But I think in programs, for example, scholarships and something constructive, I think I'm for that. But as far as giving money to the poor and all that, I don't think that should happen. I think we have to learn to stand on our own feet. We have to learn to work. We have to learn how to care for our children.

> I think that we should not only build a coalition between the other ethnic [groups]. . . . Don't just get yourself involved with the minority. I think that's very unhealthy. I think, at this time, you don't need that anymore. Before, because of the numbers, you need to join to leverage with the Whites, but you really don't need to do that anymore. . . . In fact, I don't like that label "minority" because I don't like the word "minority" anymore. Be Asian American— I think we have more powerful force than just minority because you know how minority is like "You get your quota, you get your disadvantage," but I think that I have so much pride in [being] Asian. We are no longer disadvantaged. . . . I think we are really getting into a time that Asians have lots of value outside of just being [labeled as] a disability; . . . because you really don't need to just link up with so and so, because you can link up with the majority.

Such persons were not interested in playing coalitional politics, believing that Asian Americans could go it alone. This attitude caused friction when an Asian American woman privately told me she refused to go along with a "quid pro quo" in which Asian Americans and Latinos would support each other's appointments, one of them for her, on prominent economic boards in San Diego. For the most part, these individuals felt that coalition building was futile and disadvantageous; however, they were hesitant to express these views openly to the general ABA membership.

While dissenting opinions existed, what I noticed during my research was how the U.S.-born and foreign-born managed to form an ad hoc reciprocal relationship to help them negotiate with other racial groups. Established individuals and groups can assist newcomers. For example, a Taiwanese immigrant who purchased a hotel downtown was experiencing problems with the employees and their union, composed of mainly African American and Latino workers, and asked if ABA could assist him in negotiating the crisis. As a Filipina involved with the negotiations process explained at an ABA board meeting, apparently there was a "no labor successor clause in the new owner's contract, hence the labor Union approached it from an aggressive/confrontational angle" and passed out flyers with anti-Asian slurs, mistaking the new owners for Koreans. American-born Asians, in this case a Filipina American who grew up in a multiracial neighborhood in south San Diego, are more likely to be familiar with other racial groups, so they can provide information about local issues and can intercede on behalf of the Asian American community. In one case, a Chinese immigrant from Hong Kong asked a Japanese American whose family settled in San Diego four generations ago to replace him as the liaison with CUEJ. The Japanese American, who had dealt with these longtime activists from other ethnic and racial communities since the early 1970s, comments on this replacement: "Well, I can talk to them [other racial groups] on their level. You know, I kind of understand where they're coming from." Interestingly enough, when they needed a representative to work with the Hispanic business organization, ABA board members selected an individual of Chinese ancestry born and raised in Peru whose first language was Spanish, who attended college in the United States and then opened a graphics production company. The leaders from these other racial groups feel more comfortable negotiating with someone who understands the history of their communities and who speaks their language, literally and figuratively. These economic cross-racial coalitions are often circumstantial and born out of necessity; nevertheless, racialized misconceptions that groups have about one another pose almost insurmountable obstacles for collaborative endeavors.

Conclusion

Asian American socioeconomic resources changed dramatically by the early 1990s in the San Diego area, which made Asian Americans "visible" and gave them new possibilities for mobilization. In 2003, ABA continues to thrive, with an office in downtown San Diego and an ethnic

Chinese Vietnamese American executive director, a Filipina president, and an extensive list of national, state, and local corporate sponsors. The goals of the organization remain the same: "unites and links Asian business owners, professionals and those who do business with the Asian business community," "advocates the interests of the Asian business community," "links the Pacific Rim and the San Diego business community," and "develops community leaders."

The realities of transnational migration and the global economy force Asians in this country to consider how they are to define their political identities and their connection to both America and Asia. If ABA wants the support of newcomers for glass-ceiling issues or affirmative action programs, the group needs to address newcomers' valid concerns about being classified as a domestic American minority group. With the current attacks on affirmative action programs and the legislative push for a "color-blind" society gaining ground across the country, regardless of the racial inequities that persist, ABA must take a firmer stance on these issues if the group expects to preserve threatened programs or be part of the dialogue on finding new directions for racial equity. In turn, the organization also needs to understand the social and political ramifications of promoting economic relations with the Pacific Rim for Asian immigrants, as well as for established Asian Americans, in addition to the potential exploitation of those in Asia. Mainstream society has mixed feelings about the increasing number of Asian American business enclaves and residential settlements. Members of mainstream society recognize that these new immigrants can play a vital role in building the local economy, and some may welcome the establishment of these vibrant communities; yet many are afraid of being overwhelmed by these "foreigners" and their demands for power sharing. The ebbs and flows of the domestic and international economy and the political climate can determine the economic options available to Asian Americans. They must interrogate the dangers of employing the model minority image, even as an act of resistance, to improve their economic circumstances, especially if they want to form coalitions with other racialized communities.

ABA as a nonprofit voluntary organization began to wield some economic influence and inadvertently filled the political vacuum in the San Diego Asian community. A Filipina comments on the need to translate their economic strength into political leverage: "I think we've demonstrated very well we can succeed very significantly, independent of each other, in terms of economics, but those economics mean little unless we're politically empowered, working together, and moving forward."

6

"Where Do We Stand?"
Politics, Representation, and Leadership

n the early 1980s, San Diego Asians were not considered an important group in the traditional paradigm of electoral politics, yet by the early 1990s, they were being perceived as what one interviewee describes as an "untapped political reserve." One advantage that they had in terms of collective action was that the rapid demographic growth brought new resources, such as numbers of potential voters and contributors, which made their agenda more "visible" to politicians. Leaders tried to pool their limited resources and to reorganize accordingly, using an accommodative political approach; they began demanding political access and better service for their communities. In effect, they were beginning to directly and indirectly turn their economic currency, real and perceived, into a leveraging tool for political power. A Chinese immigrant comments that "individuals have been involved in politics, but not the community as a whole. So because of that, . . . I think other communities perceive us as being disinterested . . . because we've always just been rather silent in the political arena." So even if some Asian Americans voted or gave money, they did so as individuals, which does not have the same impact as doing so on the basis of representing a constituency.

Race has always been a part of political life in the United States, even when it was dominated solely by White men— they had to decide which racial groups they would include or exclude from political power. It has long been assumed that, over time, class would replace ethnicity as a primary determinant of political participation in American life (Dahl 1961). Some scholars contest this model, arguing that ethnic political alliances can persist, even with class differentiation among successive generations (Levy and Kramer 1972; Nelson 1979; Parenti 1967; Wolfinger 1965). While some scholars have analyzed the political incorporation of single-ethnic Asian subgroups, others have examined political coalition building among Asian Americans.[1] Their groundbreaking studies indicate that Asian Americans have the potential to be a viable political force on multiple levels, depending on their resources and networks; more important, they note that Asians are invested in becoming part of U.S. civic society.

During my research, I found that individuals engaged in social, economic, and cultural concerns in the community were also the ones involved in the political terrain in various ways, such as running for office; working for politicians at the local, state, and national level; lobbying politicians; donating money; holding or attending fund-raisers; organizing political forums; holding voter registration drives or working on phone-a-thons to call voters on behalf of candidates at election time; inviting politicians to their community functions; and even putting bumper stickers on their cars. I was busy during my ethnographic research attending weekly organizational meetings, fund-raisers, political forums, briefing sessions, community-planning meetings, and formal and informal political gatherings. These were not always explicitly "political" functions but could be social events where politicking occurred. Although a viable Asian American political organization has not emerged, there exists a lively history of political activism by these political workers.

Asian Americans lack not only a political agenda, but also experienced leaders who could provide them with direction (Nakanishi 1991), so leaders involved with various other pan-Asian organizations filled this political leadership vacuum. While there are certain actions leaders can take that require few Asian American participants, such as pushing for Asian American appointments or lobbying on crucial issues, others, such as fund-raising, necessitate the involvement of Asian Americans with finances, and still others, such as voting, need the participation of the general Asian American population. Participants at all these levels include the American-born activists, an increasing number of the so-called 1.5 generation, and even first-generation immigrants. Cultivating this culture of participation and sustaining a political momentum has been a major challenge. An individual who organized Asian American political forums states: "They [Caucasians] have the liberty of saying, 'Well, I don't want to get involved in this community, this and that.' Well, there's so many Caucasians. If 50 percent say they don't want to get involved, so what? They already got 50 percent in there, they'll control 100 percent. It doesn't matter. But if we say, 'We don't want to get involved' . . . there's nobody there."

Asian Americans were learning and testing the rules for political participation, representation, and access. Clearly, the existing social, economic, and political structures of power affect the opportunities for political mobilization (Kasfir 1979). In this chapter, the question Where do we stand? can be understood in the political realm to mean a consideration of: (1) how we evaluate Asian American political ideologies; (2) how we measure Asian American political progress or the lack of it; and (3) how we assess Asian American political leadership. I examine what Asian Americans in San Diego thought about electoral politics and how they became involved in the process, in addition to considering the internal challenges they faced and the difficulties of forging multiracial alliances.

Working against a Legacy of Exclusion

Asian Americans are attempting to enter an already established political terrain that has excluded minorities historically, and when it included them, did so selectively (Lien 2001). The Naturalization Law of 1790 denied first-generation Asian immigrants the right to citizenship, and hence the rights to vote, hold elected office, or become incorporated into the political system. Although the native-born second and subsequent generations were given the right to vote, it was difficult for them to make a political impact when their parents' generation, who were the majority, was disenfranchised. It was not until World War II and afterward that the discriminatory ban was lifted, giving first-generation Asian immigrants citizenship rights, that is, the opportunity to participate in the electoral process; however, by that time, Asian Americans lacked participation habits and struggled to enter an American political system that was already established (Uhlaner, Cain, and Kiewiet 1989). The 1965 Immigration Act substantially increased the percentage of Asian Americans who could become political participants; nonetheless, these immigrants are only beginning to make their entrée into the U.S. political system.

There are multiple explanations of why Asian Americans are not incorporated into the U.S. political system, ranging from their homeland experience to racism in America (Erie and Brackman 1993). Although a preoccupation with homeland politics has been commonly blamed for their lack of political participation in the United States, this was not the general opinion of my interviewees. Some of the first generation I interviewed paid attention to political issues in their country of origin, yet none were actively involved in politics abroad and actually complained that compatriots in the United States need to pay more attention to how political events in this country affect them.

Many activists note that Asian immigrants are suspicious and distrustful of politics and politicians in their home country and bring this cultural attitude with them. For example, an individual who is politically active discussed how his mother, who was as a "twice migrant" forced to emigrate after experiencing persecution, once by the Communists in China and then in Cuba, was hesitant to become involved with politics. A multiethnic Asian American who was involved with Patsy Mink's campaign in Hawai'i when she first ran for office states that the same problem exists in San Diego: "I think because when you're dealing with the first generation, it's very easy to understand politics is dangerous, people can get shot. They come from countries where politics is dangerous. They mind their own business. Stay away and feed the family, especially from Vietnam or Southeast Asia. I knew they would not get involved in politics." A Vietnamese American who has worked at getting co-patriots involved agrees: "Politics is a dirty word and politicians [a] dirtier word to them. . . . The newer immigrants tend to stick to themselves, don't want to be involved. If nothing else, they are more concerned on how they can get food on their table than who's going to get elected." So in addition to homeland issues, a major reason for lack of participation is the "new immigrant" syndrome, in which immigrants are concerned with adaptation and daily subsistence issues like maintaining a job, finding a safe neighbor to reside in, and raising their children, so they have little time for or interest in political issues.

Not only homeland issues, but also U.S. government policies against political agitators and other negative interactions with the U.S. government have dissuaded some from engaging in political participation. These lessons were not lost on an immigrant who came of age in the United States in the tumultuous late 1960s and early 1970s:

> The Asian population was so small in the U.S., I think that any protest would construed us anti-American and it would be very, very much in the limelight

and therefore, the implications are that you are un-American. And therefore you would be open for a lot of political pressure, you know, like maybe harassment and like that, FBI and things like that. And I've known many cases in that sense. . . . So most of the Asians at that time were, whatever their political feelings were, they were really hidden agendas.

Although he was aware of leftist Asian American politics, this man was afraid at that time to become active, fearing persecution and also wanting to be a "good son" to help out his immigrant parents. As he got older and more financially stable, he became involved in politics. The legacy of being denied citizenship rights and their treatment as racialized subjects by the state instilled in Asian Americans a sense of caution and negatively impacted their desire to become involved with politics; this individual's example shows, it takes time to overcome these feelings. It is precisely their experiences in the United States that have deterred their participation.

Often their unfamiliarity with the political process or lack of contact with those who are involved leads to their inactivity. An individual who immigrated here in college explains:

> I just don't know how. Because there is no channel. . . . Because I don't know anybody. Nobody contact me. . . . It's not that I don't want to, it's just that it's not part of the routine, you know. I'm not involved. Like, Tom [American-born Chinese], for example, they grow up in an environment and his family is involved with politics or something, so it's natural for them. But to a lot of people, it's not, unless you get involved with a group, you don't know what a fund-raiser is.

When I asked a Chinese immigrant why he became involved, he responded that some Asian Americans friends mentored him, and it became particularly salient when he felt the negative impact of the political process:

> [They] educated me on the basics of how local government really works. You know, again, coming out of college, I really didn't care. I paid my taxes. I wasn't happy about that but I didn't want to be bothered with it. And then it affected my [engineering] project more and more and now, I think, with ABA [Asian Business Association], it's taught me that there is a potential to do something about it or at least, to have your voice heard.

Participation is contingent on the extent to which others like them have already entered the political process. The U.S.-born generation and immigrants who are mainly socialized in the United States do not have a legacy of electoral participation to guide them. It is erroneous to assume that Asian Americans, even the newer groups, are disinterested or disinvested in the political process. Their involvement in anticolonial struggles and other resistance movements, along with the wars in their homelands, indicate they are politically engaged, which dismisses any cultural arguments that Asians are "naturally" passive or apolitical. For many, it is merely a question of how to become involved with the political system.

Potential Swing Voters?

The Voting Rights Act of 1965 removed the legal barriers to political participation for Asian Americans and was intended to protect their right to participate in the political process and pave the way for a new electoral era for minorities (Erie and Brackman 1993; Hamilton 1982). Political workers recognize that Asian Americans are growing in numbers; however, this numerical increase does not necessarily correlate with greater political clout or power unless the majority of them vote. A Chinese American who has organized several political fund-raisers argues that they have yet to become a viable political force: "If we can say, 'This is how many votes we can deliver,' if we can say that, any politician will listen. And we can't say that. If anything, the numbers count against us. I mean, it's a fact that the Asians don't vote ... so I think the key thing is to get us to vote, to get the bloc of votes that we can deliver to a politician." In 1990, Asians were 10 percent of California's population but represented only 7 percent of the state's eligible voters, 4 percent of registered voters, and 3 percent of actual voters (Erie and Brackman 1993: 39).[2]

Asian leaders in San Diego realized they needed to establish a stable political base and organize voter-registration and turn-out-the-vote drives. In late 1991, a nonpartisan group calling itself the Asian-American Non-Partisan Voters League was created; it joined forces with Latinos and was renamed the Asian-Latino-Filipino-American (ALFA) Voters League.[3] As one Filipino male organizer recalls, it was not whom they chose to include in the coalition that was controversial, but whom they chose to exclude:

> Now that in itself pissed off the African American community because they found out about it. And I had encouraged them to include African Americans in this. And I was told, "Oh, well, we don't want to include the Blacks, they have their own political structures already." So, you know, here were some Asian, Latino, [and] Filipino, and there were a few women that were involved. And I made a motion to have cogender chairs and then it went hay-

wire, "Oh, we don't need to do this; we don't need to include women." These were the same kinds of, you know, people who were experiencing discrimination and they were willing to subject women of the group to their sexism.

The disagreements over the exclusion of African Americans from the coalition and the considerations regarding a gender balance in the leadership undermined the organization. In ALFA's short existence, many of the Asian American participants, primarily Southeast Asians and Filipinos, tried to register voters.

Even though their voting participation is fragmentary and limited, Asian Americans are being wooed for their potential as a crucial swing vote (Nakanishi 1991), at least locally, where it is possible to win a relatively close election with just a small number of the electorate voting in one's favor. A Filipino who was a former aide for Democratic Assembly Member Steve Peace from San Diego explains why he was hired as a liaison with the Filipino and Asian community: "They [politicians] saw the Asian community as a force, you know, a voting bloc. They saw them as a voting bloc, and you know, as a potential swing vote, so they wanted to make sure that they covered all of their bases." San Diego City Council Member Tom Behr won a seven-way race in a special election in District 5 by 304 votes and credits Asian Americans, who comprised 20 percent of his district, with giving him a "winning edge" (Huard 1991a, b). A Chinese immigrant adds: "If there is a candidate in town that . . . does not court minority votes, they'll never win. . . . Nobody can afford not to court minority votes anymore. It's getting to a point where the minority votes are the determining votes on closely split races."

In the 1992 mayoral race, Susan Golding beat her opponent, Ron Roberts, by a slim margin in the general election. A Filipino explains: "She had built a rapport with the Asian community over the years as a councilperson and as a supervisor. I think that it paid off for her. When you look at how close that race was, I think the Asian community definitely made a difference."[4] Quite a few Asian Americans noted that Golding, who also served as a city council member and as a county supervisor in San Diego, formed a relationship with the Asian and Filipino communities early on.[5] Without statistical evidence available to verify how individuals voted, there is no way to validate these claims by either the politicians or by members of the Asian American community. What mattered in these cases was the perception that Asian Americans can be a crucial electorate, yet swing votes require disciplined voting, and Asian Americans are still being tested for their ability to deliver the votes. In order to be more effective, they have continued to work to have voting materials translated; to push for bilingual assistance at the ballot box; to organize voter registration drives, to ensure that politicians pay attention to them as voters; and to support research on their voting patterns.

Divisions over Partisanship

Unlike other minority groups, Asian Americans are not aligned closely with either party, which has weakened their political clout (Cain, Kiewiet, and Uhlaner 1991; Tachibana 1986). In 1990, while only one-third of White voters supported the Democratic Party, over 90 percent of African American and two-thirds of all Latino voters were Democratic supporters (Cain 1991). Overall, the Asian population was more or less split between Democrats and Republicans (Cain and Kiewiet 1986; Mendel 1994; Nakanishi 1986). Among the thirty Asian Americans I interviewed who were willing to state their party affiliation, a few were Independents, but the rest were almost evenly divided between Democrats and Republicans. Scholars suggest that Asian Americans' alignment with either party is connected to factors such as socioeconomic status, perceptions of discrimination, recruitment by these parties, and homeland politics (Lien 2001; Saito 1998). Many post-1965 Asians arrived during a period of Republican presidential dominance and this, along with their more conservative understanding of political issues from their experiences in their home countries, affects their political affiliation. Immigrants from China, Korea, and Southeast Asia—countries affected by Communist regimes—will select the Republican Party because of the party's stronger anti-Communist stance (Cain, Kiewiet, and Uhlaner 1984). Asian Americans are not necessarily enamored with either party; however, they recognize they need to engage in the partisan system if they are to counter their underrepresentation and marginalization.

In the 1990s, Filipinos, the only Asian ethnic group to form partisan organizations, had a Republican organization and a long-standing Democratic one. Few Asians attended the Democratic or Republican Central Committee meetings at the local and state level, so their knowledge of and access to the Democratic and Republican Parties was still unsystematic. Few Asian Americans had run for office, which is another method for gaining a position on the Central Committee and would allow them to advocate for state and national appointments. This second-generation Filipino who was appointed as a delegate for the state Democratic Party, with the assistance of his father who was also involved with Democratic politics, explains:

We need both parties. And I say that, I say that emphatically. Not that we're going to tear down our communities, but we have to be perceived as a community that is involved in both groups because there are elected officials from both sides of the fence. And to play politics, you have to play the game. You've got to know the game rules, you've got to know the rules, and the rules are it's basically a bipartisan party rule.... And if we don't have ... the structure of both, we're never gonna see any kind of power whatsoever. We're never going to be recognized by the political people.

In March 1993, along with others, this Filipino formed the Asian and Pacific Islander Democratic Club.[6] Their intent was to register more Asians, have a voice in the Democratic Central Committee, including the national Asian Pacific American Democratic Platform, and eventually help Asians run for office.[7] The catalyst for the organization was the San Diego Democratic Central Committee's endorsement of an Anglo candidate for city council, without giving an Asian American running in the same race an opportunity to gain their endorsement (Braun 1993a).[8] Their point was not that the Asian American candidate should have been endorsed instead, but that the process was inequitable, since no one in the Asian American community was notified when the committee vote was taking place. The first president of the Asian and Pacific Islander Democratic Club was an attorney of Filipino and Chamorro ancestry who worked in Washington, D.C., as a lobbyist for the governor of Guam and also as chief of staff for a Guamanian senator. He comments: "Unless you get in there at the mechanics level, policy level, you are going to find out that the decisions are already made. I mean, you really have to be part of that mechanics process, that grassroots process." They felt their priority should be becoming part of the partisan political structure, and they actually offered to help Asian Republicans form their own group.

Others contest the idea of splitting the Asian American community along party lines and prefer organizing nonpartisan political organizations. As a Chinese Democrat explains: "I mean, it's a tight line to walk but I think it's the right course. Instead of trying to be, hey, I'm a Republican or I'm a Democrat, ... I think the Asian today, as a group, ... should focus on issues. See, Asian candidates are different. I go for an Asian candidate whether he's Republican or Democrat." He disagrees with forming partisan Asian organizations, remarking:

They say, "Let's form a Democratic Asian club or a Republican Asian club." That's one thing I'm not ready for and I won't be active in it. That's a narrow focus right now. Until you get the bodies, maybe it will happen. They

> have it in San Francisco, they have it in L.A. But I think, right now, you work
> with what we are and once you start trying to splinter, I think it's—it's going
> to weaken the Asian empowerment, so to speak.

Like others, he believes that with their small population, forming Asian American partisan organizations or partisan political action committees (PACs) would diminish the effectiveness of the community and divide its limited resources.

Although the Asian American community was split between Democrats and Republicans, there were examples of nonpartisan racial politics. Organizations like ABA have tried to maintain a balance; for example, in 1991 at the first ABA Annual Installation Dinner, Republican Matt Fong, member of the State Board of Equalization, was the keynote speaker; in 1992, Democrat Michael Woo, a Los Angeles City Council member, was the keynote speaker. An individual who is half Japanese and Filipino comments on Asian ethnic ties in a political context: "I think when you're dealing about non-Asian candidates, that party lines are a lot stronger; but when there's an Asian candidate, I think party lines are crossed." An ad hoc group calling itself the San Diego Asian Committee of 100, which included many ABA members and was comprised of Chinese, Japanese, Filipinos, Koreans, and Vietnamese, raised $10,000 for Michael Woo's bid for Los Angeles mayor in 1993, a race he lost to Richard Riordan. Although Woo was a liberal Democrat, there were conservative Republicans at the fund-raiser. At particular moments, Asian Americans can cross party lines, making common racial or ethnic affiliation stronger than party affiliation.

Local politics are different, since parties do not play as prominent a role. A Vietnamese American leader sought after by mainstream San Diego politicians for endorsements states: "I'm Republican. But local vote . . . it doesn't matter. I'll vote either one. Local, I consider who is friendly and good for community; but president and senator and congressman, I consider a party." Like other Asian Americans, such as the Chinese and Koreans, this leader supports Republican candidates because of the party's staunchly anti-Communist stance and the perception that the party is pro-business, yet party loyalty is not primary for him at the local level. However, San Diego is a Republican town (Hornor 1994).[9] Here, former California Governor Pete Wilson received his political training as mayor in the early 1970s, followed by Republican Mayors Roger Hedgecock, Maureen O'Connor, and Susan Golding into the 1990s; traditional political structures still dominate. San Diego is well known as a Republican stronghold, although at the

time of my research, there was a realignment that made Bill Clinton the
first Democratic presidential candidate to carry San Diego County since
Franklin D. Roosevelt (Horstman 1992).[10] Being a Democrat in San
Diego has been a challenge, as a Japanese Filipino American woman
remarks in 1993:

> Oh, gosh, I remember about eight years ago I was so frustrated with this com-
> munity being so conservative, because at that time, it was predominantly
> people who were retired who moved here. It was a very old community, very
> military, so very conservative. So it was frustrating, being a liberal. . . . Well,
> with this new [Clinton] administration, it's almost like all these closet Democ-
> rats have come out. And I was down at City Hall during the celebration when
> Clinton got elected, it's like, where have all these people been over the years?
> And they were so diverse.

The debate within the local Asian American community regarding
whether it should concentrate on partisan politics or focus on being unified as a racialized group reflects national political organizing as well.

Donations and Fund-raisers

A Filipino notes how the electoral system works in the homeland: "In
the Philippines and in the culture, . . . politicians give you money to vote,
but here in America, politicians ask you for money and [ask you to] vote
for them. . . . I mean we come from countries where we don't trust politicians." A Vietnamese American leader expressed the same dilemma in
Vietnam, where the government paid for campaigns and politicians paid
the voters, so "people don't put in money to support [a] candidate." Only
U.S. citizens and permanent residents are eligible to make political contributions, which does limit the participation of some newer immigrants,
although some unaware of this policy have made contributions. The
younger generation of U.S.-born Asian leaders, in most cases, does not
have the financial resources to donate substantial amounts. While single-ethnic groups held fund-raisers for their own ethnic candidates, the
community as a whole began to organize pan-Asian fund-raisers for candidates.[11] Filipinos and Taiwanese were the only two Asian subgroups
that organized separate fund-raisers in 1992 for mayoral candidate Susan
Golding, yet some among their ranks also participated in pan-Asian
fund-raising efforts.

With no long-standing political organization in existence, Asians
have formed ad hoc committees to organize each political fund-raiser,
and the committees' leadership overlaps with existing Asian American

organizations. As nonprofit organizations, UPAC and ABA cannot directly endorse candidates, although members of these organizations have been principal participants by planning fund-raisers and donating money as individuals.[12] Politicians have focused on ABA for support because they associate its members with money and want to tap into their pocketbooks. Informal discussions of political matters were a constant at ABA gatherings, and ABA scheduled politicians as speakers for its monthly events as a way to meet the politicians.[13] In March 1992, individuals involved primarily with ABA organized the Asian Business Leaders Ad Hoc Political Caucus to sponsor a fund-raiser for "political candidates running for offices who have supported Asian business agenda and those with large number of Asians in their district."[14] They managed to raise several thousand dollars for mayoral, city council, and congressional candidates.[15]

A local Chinese American restaurateur whose father owns a popular restaurant opened in 1939 in Sacramento dubbed the "third house," because it was frequented by state politicians, was immersed in politics growing up and has been one of the primary organizers of these fund-raisers. He went to law school with Robert Matsui, a Japanese American, who was a city council member from Sacramento and who has been in the U.S. House of Representatives since 1978. As a fund-raiser for Matsui, his job was "to raise money from the Chinese to support a Japanese candidate," which he explains was next to impossible:

> It was very difficult to tell a first-generation Chinese to support a second- or third-generation Japanese, or for that matter, a Japanese—"Why should we support them, when we still feel that anxiety, that bitterness because of the war?" And that's when I started giving my own, you know, deal about Asian empowerment. From that day on, I've been speaking the same language. . . . I'm a firm believer that we've got to go for the strength. And unfortunately, Asians, if they're all scattered, do not have a lot of strength, and so you've got to go as a group.

He adds that "now, when Bob [Matsui] comes into town and goes to a fund-raiser, it's automatic—I mean the Chinese and Japanese and the Korean, they all go." When this activist moved to San Diego, there were no Asian politicians, so he organized Asian American fund-raisers at his restaurant for mainstream political contenders. He comments:

> We've had Asian functions here [at his Chinese restaurant] and it was dominated by Filipinos, believe it or not. And that's why I'm saying, it's a stepping-stone. What you see today is not what happened when I came here in '74. Now you see, you know, more of a trend, Chinese, Japanese, Vietnamese. . . . Now

you can even network; before when you wanted to do a fund-raiser, it was just who do you call real quick to show that there's Asians here.

Earlier, his adjoining restaurants, Fat City and China Camp, were primary locations for local Asian activists to plan their strategies and hold fund-raisers.[16] This seed money and grassroots support for local and state Asian American candidates is crucial, since they cannot always rely on the political machinery to support them financially. While they have made inroads in organizing more fund-raisers for Asian American candidates and non-Asian allies, the events are still sporadic and the sums raised are minimal in comparison to the resources available.

Political Forums as Public Articulations

While Asian Americans lobbied politicians on an individual basis, they also began to sponsor public forums to make politicians accountable to the interests of the Asian American community. They wanted to provide a comfortable space for Asian Americans who would not necessarily attend a mainstream forum to articulate their needs and make politicians respond to their questions. In late 1984, Vernon Yoshioka, a Japanese American Republican, and Glenn Barroga, a Filipino who was state chair of the Asian Pacific Caucus of the California Democratic Party, formed the Pacific Asian Voter Education (PAVE) organization.[17] They used the UPAC office as their address, since some of the organizers were affiliated with this social service organization. An organizer explained that the group encountered problems mobilizing support: "That's a lot of work, trying to get people together and we ended up at one forum, with UPAC board members, JACL [Japanese American Citizens League] board members, and COPAO [Council of Pilipino-American Organizations] board members, and that was about it. And we had about as many candidate speakers as audience [members]. That was embarrassing." He adds that "it was a little early, the awareness wasn't there."

Since the early 1990s, there have been more consistent attempts to sponsor political forums. Asian Americans held nonpartisan forums for both the primary and general elections.[18] At the San Diego Asian Communities Candidates' Forum held at the University of San Diego in 1992, the candidates included candidates in the primaries for mayor, county board of supervisors, state assembly, and San Diego Unified School District who were running in districts that had at least 10 percent Asian American population and two Asian American candidates running for National City Council and U.S. Congress. The planning meetings were held at the UPAC offices, with ABA taking the lead in cosponsoring the event with other organizations. Similar to previous forums, few Asian Americans attended and most of the seats in the large theater remained empty, which only reinforced the image of Asian Americans as apolitical. Attendees remarked to me that the site, a private college campus removed from any Asian American population, was perhaps too isolated and uninviting.

In October 1992, the same group hosted the "First All Ethnic Asian American Communities Forum in the History of San Diego's General Elections" at Mira Mesa Mall; participating were candidates for mayor, county board of supervisors, and U.S. Congress. The Mira Mesa community has a large Asian American population with many Filipinos and Southeast Asians, and attendance was improved over the earlier forum, although it is not clear whether the audience intended to come to the forum or inadvertently came upon it while shopping at the open mall. In my assessment, this forum was awkward, since there were passersby who were European Americans whose presence may have tempered the answers given by politicians who did not want to offend them and perhaps subdued the mood of Asian Americans present in expressing themselves. The direction of the forums depends on who is coordinating the events and their perception of what the needs of the communities may be. Additionally, there were thirty-six ethnic organizations cosponsoring the event and the complexity of coordinating such events became more difficult. The group has managed to build some momentum for these events; however, questions have been raised regarding the effectiveness of these forums for raising the political consciousness of the community or for ensuring that politicians pay attention to Asian American needs.

Articulating Needs and Demands

The Asian American community has been heavily criticized for naïvely donating money or supporting politicians, but not asking for anything or receiving little in return (Nakanishi 1991; Wang 1991). However, I found that this was not necessarily the case. Activists were quite aware that communicating their needs to politicians was an important task. As a Taiwanese immigrant who was previously a legislative aide for a Black Oregon state senator states: "I don't think any one of them [local politicians] truly understand the Asian community. Again, that is, well, I don't know how much effort they put into trying to understand the Asian community, but on the other side of the coin, it's also our responsibility as Asians to let it be known what our needs are, to voice our opinion." A Filipina, a board member for a social service organization who has attended many fund-raisers, explains how her forthrightness and finances are finally paying off, in this case for job-training programs:

> I think I am redoing my priority again, you know, I have never asked anything from them. Well, now I'm visible, I've been asking, you know, you were at the dinner at UPAC? Two weeks before that, we were before the city council asking for funding for the $150,000 for economic development. They gave us $75,000. It was really a surprise when we got [another] $75,000 right there [at the dinner]. So I keep saying finally, finally, our money [is effective] because now we are becoming visible.

A Filipino and Guamanian activist was quite explicit about making mainstream policy makers accountable for their hiring and placements:

> Well, one of the things that I'm getting involved in Pan Asian Lawyers association as the vice president, I guess I'll be president-elect next year. I know that some people are sort of worried that I'll make this organization just a little bit more political—but not in terms of Democrat or Republican—but political in terms of posturing for our just desserts as Asian Pacific Islanders here. How many people do we have working for county council? How many people are working for city council? How many people do we have working for public defenders? How many people work for the big firms here. . . . You have a growing gang problem here with Filipinos, Laotians, Vietnamese, Asian Pacific Islanders. Where is the active recruitment, okay, in those departments—get out there and make your organization that either prosecutes us or defends us representative of that community so we have someone to relate to.

This man was active in organizing political forums, as well as on the board of ABA and an officer of the then newly formed Asian Democratic organization.

In the flyer concerning the Asian Pacific Islander Candidates' Forum, the group's stated agenda was to find answers to such questions as: "How responsive and sensitive are the Candidates to the *concerns*, *needs*, and *demands* of the Asian-American Community? How aware are the Candidates of Asian-American *goals*? Where do the Candidates stand on the many pressing issues (i.e., underrepresentation of Asian-Americans in key county and city departments, Asian-gangs, and hate-crimes) faced by the Asian-American Community?" More specifically, repeatedly asked at these forums is whether the candidates support the hiring of more Asian lawyers, more Asian police officers, more Asian contractors, more hiring of Asian staff by politicians, and more appointments of Asians at both the city and county level. At a 1992 mayoral Filipino American political forum I attended, these pointed questions were reiterated:

> Asian Americans are the 2nd largest ethnic group in San Diego as well as in California. As of 1989, Asian Businesses contributed into the local economy over $384 million dollars. In light of this however, there are almost no Asian Americans on significant decision making bodies in either government or in business. 1. Please provide a concise opinion as to why you think this is so. 2. Tell us 3 specific actions you would take to ensure greater Asian representation. 3. Tell us how many Asian-Americans are actively participating in your campaign committees. As mayor, how do [you] propose to more effectively involve the Filipino and overall Asian community in the political system?

Other questions often asked of the candidates involved support for social services, particularly funding for gang prevention and AIDS education, along with issues related to support for Pacific Rim trade and small businesses.[19] Incumbents and others who had held political office tended to list their "diversity" record, while other candidates seemed receptive to working with Asian American needs; however, some side-stepped the issue, saying they are interested in the most "qualified" individual or would do what was best for the "general economy or community." My perception was that many were uninformed about the issues of this racial community and had a difficult time even understanding the basic questions or demands. For example, one mayoral candidate, frustrated by such questions, repeatedly answered that he had learned to communicate with his deaf son and would use the same approach to deal with the Asian American community. Was he suggesting that Asian Americans were like "children" or that they have problems "communicating" or that they are a "handicapped" group?—all possibilities that can be regarded as insulting in this context. His response showed the low level of racial sensitivity of some of the candidates and justified the community's feelings of the need for vigilant educational campaigns about the community.

Demands articulated in these public forums were reiterated in letters sent to the candidates. For example, in their letter to a mayoral candidate who wanted their support, ABA leaders specified that more Asian Americans need to be hired in the city minority contracting program and appointed to boards and commissions, and supported "the utilization of local Asian Americans as a resource to major city committees that deal with Pacific Rim Trade."[20] In the same letter, they voiced their cultural and social needs, requesting support for the development of the Filipino Cultural Center, funding for the Japanese Friendship Garden, and approval of Community Block Building Grants for social service organizations such as the UPAC, Indochinese Mutual Assistance Association, and (Southeast Asian) Linda Vista Community Development Corporation. While at the national level, it may be difficult to articulate specific claims and demands, Asian Americans, like those in San Diego, have not been shy about asserting, even in rudimentary terms, their local demands publicly and privately to political contenders, using their limited resources as leverage.

Creating Inclusion: Appointing One of Our Own

Securing political appointments is one way in which Asian Americans, who have had difficulty winning elections, have been incorporated into mainstream institutions and political processes. Depending on the position, appointees can promote affirmative action programs, support city contracts to minority businesses, create private sector job opportunities for minorities, guide public investment in urban infrastructure and housing that serve and protect minority populations, direct cultural and economic downtown redevelopment, and funnel money to nonprofit organizations. In the past, UPAC was the primary organization to contact for recommendations and endorsements on appointments, yet this changed as ABA gained prominence as the organization to contact for nominations.[21]

In fact, the main problem was finding enough interested Asian Americans to volunteer to serve. In one case, an African American city council member who wanted to get more minorities on boards and commissions offered to nominate an Asian American architect to a prestigious position on a city board; the fourth-generation Asian American was not interested in political issues and declined the offer. He explains the reaction he received from the Anglo owners of his architectural firm; when he told them about the offer, "they looked at me and they said, 'You know, that's what's wrong with this city, they're putting all these immigrants on these boards and commissions.'" He adds:

> I was really shocked by what they said. . . . I didn't say anything but I was particularly hurt by what they said. . . . I remember leaving there and that whole night I thought about that. And it just struck me right then . . . what it means to me personally. It just kind of fell altogether, you know, we have a problem here. We have a real problem here. And how are we going to change this. Here we've got the politicians who want to try to make changes and do it

right and they may ask the wrong person, but they're trying to get minorities on the commissions and boards.

As a result of the reaction he received at work, he decided to accept the appointment overseeing downtown redevelopment and a month later also decided to quit the firm, even though he had just received a promotion.

This architect was involved with UPAC at that time, and this seemingly small event motivated him to move beyond social service endeavors and become involved in mobilizing the community politically. Although he has never sought an elected political office, he was the driving force behind many political actions in the community, either on the front line or behind the scenes. He explains the rationale for his involvement:

> Well, the sacrifices are necessary. I'm not trying to paint myself with this big ego. I do see myself having a unique ability, maybe by fortune, because of how things have occurred in my personal and professional life, to see what's happened in the Anglo community and the Asian group. It is my feeling that I can't advance myself up to a certain level unless the whole level of Asians are willing to rise up. I've been there in a sea of White faces and it's not comfortable. I don't like being ignored. And that's what happens when you're the only minority. If the community rises as a level, as a whole, there would be more Asian faces and voices in the boards and commissions and in politics, we'd have equal grounds, equal footing at the table, then the more we have to do with the dialogue, to be listened to.

As a consequence of the time and energy he spent on political activities, he sacrificed his thriving architectural business and made some unwise financial decisions that affected other Asian Americans. Many mentioned to me that he has been their "mentor" in the political process and, in their eyes, has been one of the most instrumental leaders in mobilizing the community. Ironically, although he has paved the way for the advancement of individuals in the community, many have distanced themselves personally from him.

The community has encouraged politicians and city officials to hire Asian Americans who can serve as liaisons, realizing that this would give them political access. The San Diego chief of police hired a Filipino American sergeant to be his liaison with the Asian American community, and before that a Chinese American was hired.[22] The sergeant feels his position has "opened a lot of doors" in regard to recruiting and promotions by the department, as well as improving community policing issues. But, he adds: "Until we put Asians in these key policy-making positions, a lot of what we want, a lot of what we need, is not going to get accomplished." The mayor, along with various city council members, county supervisors, and members of the California legislature, appointed Asian Americans to be contact persons with the community.[23] A Chinese American restaurateur and lawyer who has been appointed to several prestigious committees states: "People do call me from time to time and say, 'Do you recommend some Asian for this post or this commission?' ... which is good and I'm proud of my role because, you know, where did we have this dialogue ten years ago? We didn't, from the Asian [community] to the mayor's office." Since politicians or organizations can often afford to create only one position, they prefer to hire someone who is endorsed by Asian American organizations, rather than by just one ethnic organization, because the individual is expected to work with all the Asian subgroups.[24]

The appointment of a Chinese American businesswoman who helped with the creation of ABA to the San Diego Port Commission board, one of the most coveted appointments in town, was, as one Chinese American states, "a great victory for the community."[25] She was the first Asian and first minority appointed to the board, reflecting the influence that first-generation Asian Americans have in local politics. Her grandfather had worked in the United States as a laborer, but she was born in Canton, China, raised in Hong Kong, and came to the United States in 1965 after marrying a Chinese man born in China who immigrated as a child with his family. Her longtime involvement in mainstream organizations, her entrepreneurial enterprises locally and in Asia, and her participation on the San Diego County International Trade Commission made it possible to get the coveted nomination, which was approved by city council members. It did not hurt that her firm managed portfolios worth more than $80 million in real estate and other property. While ABA initiated the appointment process, others such as the Japanese American executive director of UPAC, a Vietnamese American leader active in city politics, and a Filipina chief of staff to a councilman lobbied on her behalf as well, although in private she credits herself for swaying city council members.

An individual involved with mainstream organizations, this businesswoman has always been quite aware of the role race plays in perceptions about her, especially since she was often the first and only minority or Asian American representative in most of these organizations:

> To tell you the truth, they intimidate me from the beginning and that's why in some of the big [mainstream] boards, I'd become very quiet. You know how vocal I am [around Asians] . . . but in some of the very heavy powerful boards, I become very quiet. Because I feel, yes, I'm the only Asian and I better be careful what I say. Are they listening or do they just want me to be window dressing? So I have to be extra sensitive and careful when I talk, express my opinion.

She recognizes that how she behaves and what she says not only is a reflection upon her, but also is associated with her race. It is difficult for her to separate her personal identity from her racialized one, because even when she speaks for herself, it is assumed she is a representative of her racial group.

These appointees can gain valuable political experience, the community is able to gain access to once untouchable institutions, and mainstream society is able to fulfill its diversity agenda. But the real issue is how this symbolic representation will translate into long-term political clout and inclusion. As someone who has served in these positions states: "The recent, you know, the staff people and appointments in the city council and whatever are not proactive. They're more like yes-men. They're there because of their color, they're more like social workers. They're not political workers." He concedes that he played a token role for a local assemblyman: "I was their local Asian representative. I was a field representative, liaison for him, and providing our services to garner more votes in the Filipino community primarily. So I saw myself, in a sense, a pawn; but also, by getting the position, I was able to use that later on to do other things." While Asians previously were able to push for appointments to ethnic bodies like the Mayor's Asian Advisory Board or as representatives from the minority community, they are beginning to contest their image as merely a special interest group by pursuing appointments to mainstream boards and committees that make decisions on the whole community, not just Asians. For many, this is the litmus test that will indicate their acceptance as U.S. citizens.

Drawing the Lines: Reapportionment and Redistricting

According to the 1990 U.S. census, Asians had increased by 127 percent since 1980 in California (Lopez 2002) and, for the first time in San Diego and other parts of the state, were involved in reapportionment and redistricting battles in which districts were redrawn to match population shifts.[26] Asians comprised 12 percent of San Diego city's and 8 percent of San Diego County's population; Blacks, 9 percent and 6 percent; and Hispanics, 21 percent and 20 percent (U.S. Bureau of Census 1990b). Unlike Latinos and Blacks, Asians do not reside in concentrated areas, making it difficult for them to impact city council and county board of supervisors elections, which rely on district voters.[27] After the 1990 census, Asian activists followed the direction taken by other minorities, engaging in gerrymandering, and tried to cluster themselves racially, rather than by individual ethnic group. For example, while there is a concentration of Filipinos in the South Bay, there is also a major Filipino population in North County, so the strategy has been to cluster Filipinos in their respective areas with other Asian subgroups.

Redistricting became important for Asians locally in 1988 when the San Diego City Council voted to change its election process from an at-large to a district election process (Christensen and Gerston 1984; Smolens 1991).[28] The move to district elections meant that candidates would be elected by voters in each district and provided minorities with the incentive to redraw boundaries according to the density of their population.[29] The original reapportionment and redistricting map proposed by the city council following the 1990 census fragmented the Asian community throughout the eight districts. To counteract this gerrymandering, Asian leaders focused their energy on District 5, which covers the northern part of the city. There had been an increase in the Asian population in the last ten years in this vicinity, so they wanted to make this the district not only with the largest Asian population, but also one with the largest minority group.[30] By lobbying and testifying at the redistricting hearings, Asian American leaders managed to keep particular areas together, especially Linda Vista, giving District 5 a 20 percent Asian population. However, this was hardly enough for many, as the publisher and editor of the local *Asian Journal* critically remarked:

> With hardly any opposition from Asian Americans because of apathy on the latter, the city council drew and approved new council districts that divided and diluted and therefore diminished the potency of the Asian American's voting or political power. The heavily concentrated Asian Americans in Mira Mesa were separated from the Asian dominated district of Rancho Penasquitos. Other heavily Asian populated districts in San Diego like Linda Vista, North Park, Paradise Hills, Southbay San Diego, and Nestor were distributed to different council districts singly. (Silverio 1991)

In the drawing of boundaries for city council districts, there was some overlap, but overall, Latinos, Blacks, and Asians had separate districts where they were each the majority racial group (Flynn 1991, 1992; Granberry 1990).[31]

Unlike the district boundaries for city council where racial groups could stake out an area, the district boundaries for the San Diego County Board of Supervisors were not so clearly delineated.[32] In the county redistricting process, a ten-person advisory committee made up of individuals from the Latino, Black, and Asian communities was appointed to advise the five county supervisors on the needs of their ethnic and racial communities. The president of the Asian Business Association, a Filipino involved with COPAO and the Filipino Republican Club, and a Vietnamese leader represented the Asian American contingent. An Asian coalition consisting of ABA along with the Asian American Political Coalition and the Associated Asian American Leaders—two political ad hoc groups whose members were primarily Filipinos—submitted its proposal for county redistricting. In addition, proposals were submitted by other minority groups, such as the Chicano Federation, the San Diego Black Political Action Committee, the (largely Latino) Camino Real Group and the (African American and Latino) Harborview Community Council.[33]

Dissatisfied with the new reapportionment plan, the Chicano Federation filed a lawsuit in September 1991 against the board of supervisors, charging them with deliberately diluting minority voting strength and preserving incumbencies.[34] Although Asian Americans were asked to join the suit, they decided that they lacked sufficient data on voting trends to prove their case. One of three Asian lawyers from the Pan Asian Lawyers Association in San Diego who advised Asians leaders on redistricting noted another problem: "They [Asians] are spread out in this city; you don't have a concentration of Asians in any particular location, they're sort of all over. They are more in a corridor than a concentrated mass." The Chicano Federation wanted the supervisors to adopt a redistricting plan that contained a "super-majority minority district" with a 75 percent minority population, primarily Latino (Pierce 1991g).[35] Yet they did not have the support of other minorities, who felt that the plan favored Latinos only (Pierce 1991a, c, d). Federation representatives wanted to maximize minority voting strength, noting that "Blacks, Asians, and Hispanics have common interest and should be grouped in a single district when practical." A coalition consisting of the ABA, Asian American Political Coalition, the Camino Real Group, and Harborview Community Council presented another proposal, stating that "each racial community has unique needs and interests" (Pierce

1991e).[36] Instead of creating one minority district, the coalition wanted to create two districts with a 45 percent minority population in each—in one district, Latinos were the dominant minority group, in the other, Asians were the primary minority (Flynn 1991; Pierce 1991b, f; Wolf 1991). At various points, the groups changed their allegiances; some dropped out of the controversy, and others joined, which showed the lack of unity among the ethnic and racial groups. Given the internal animosity, the groups decided to allow each coalition to submit a map and agreed not to attack another's plan publicly. In late 1991, the same judge who ruled in the case against the city decided to let stand the redistricting map approved by the county supervisors, which had smaller percentages of Latinos and Asians in each district than any of the maps proposed by the minority groups (Bernstein 1992). The difficulty of the battle, in which minority groups had to show "proof" of deliberate discrimination, was captured in the San Diego deputy county counsel's comment that the Chicano Federation "will have the burden of demonstrating that minorities are politically cohesive and that the white voters vote as a block to defeat minorities in the district that they propose" (quoted in Pierce 1991g).[37]

On the one hand, communities of color in San Diego realize that if they intend to influence the political process, they need to collaborate; yet on the other hand, having few resources to share can undermine their coalitions. They are especially skeptical about electing a single minority politician who would represent all minority groups; throughout my fieldwork I heard grumbling from Asian Americans that Black politicians in office neglected Asians in their districts. Blacks in California have always been the smallest of the minority groups, but they have been the "most unified, aggressive, and successful in their various campaigns" (Anderson 1991: 56). In San Diego, while African Americans were the smallest of the groups, in the 1980s and early 1990s, a Black representative served on both the city council and the board of supervisors, while Latino representation has been inconsistent. With the Asian and Latino populations increasing, and the White and Black populations decreasing proportionally, there will be contentious struggles over reapportionment and redistricting in the foreseeable future, especially in California with its multiracial neighborhoods and ethnic communities that commonly border one another. In California, a fair number of elected minority officeholders have gained their seats in districts with a majority, or near majority, minority population, so the outcome of reapportionment and redistricting is crucial (Guerra 1991).

The contentiousness and complexity of these struggles explain why few individuals, including Asian Americans, are willing to tackle the redistricting issue. One of the primary representatives of the Asian community was Gil Ontai, who was identified with ABA and was the only Asian quoted in the numerous articles on redistricting in the local press. Another was Jim Cua, whose father was a second-generation Filipino American and whose mother was a Japanese war bride. Cua, who was instrumental in shaping my understanding of redistricting politics, found the San Diego Democratic Club was predominantly White and sought other political outlets. He had been involved extensively with gay and lesbian Democratic politics, serving as the president of the Harvey Milk Democratic Club, working with it and other gay and lesbian organizations to confront their racist practices and to include minority agendas:

> Almost every institution in the gay-lesbian community did not have diversity—the Metropolitan Community Church, . . . the gay and lesbian center, . . . pride parade board, so things have changed immensely in the gay-lesbian community because we've organized as ethnic peoples. . . . In '88, I did the first racism forum in the gay community and that was something that hadn't been dealt with in our community, and after that particular forum, I decided to found an organization that would support gay and lesbian Asian Pacifics [Gay and Lesbian Asian Social Support].

Cua, who testified on behalf of the Asian community in city redistricting hearings, explains the dilemma confronting him:

> I didn't get active in Asian community politics until we had the hearings for redistricting. . . . That was a very, very difficult time for me because I was basically forced to choose between the gay-lesbian community and the Asian community. The gay and lesbian community wanted to create a gay district and basically combine areas that were in two districts and make it into one [Hillcrest, North Park, Kensington, Golden Hill, Normal Heights]. . . . They wanted to adopt a map that would have split the Asian community in the north into four districts [Mira Mesa, Linda Vista, Scripps Ranch, Rancho Pensaquitos]. I mean, they were willing to sacrifice the Asian community and what the Asian community wanted. . . . They totally ignored the ethnic communities in working with the plans with these politicians. The ethnic communities were not consulted by our [gay-lesbian] community. . . . And I said we need to hammer something out or find some kind of compromise or open up a discussion, and they wouldn't have anything to do with it. They said they were going to be pushing their own agendas. And this was after the human dignity ordinance had passed where we had been soliciting support from all of these [ethnic] communities to support gay rights in the city, and here they were . . . turning their backs on these communities. And I was

furious. . . . I testified against them and I was branded a traitor to the gay and lesbian community.

Although he was able to laugh about this situation during our interview, it was evident that he was extremely upset at being forced to make this choice and hurt by the criticism he experienced as a result of his decision.

Later Cua would become president of the Filipino American Democrat Club and the Asian Pacific American Democratic Club; however, he was not without criticism for the Asian American community. His experience in gay politics taught him the importance of strategic organizing and of preserving a group's district struggles, which ultimately allowed the gay and lesbian community to elect one of their own to office:

> The benefits of coalition building are that elected officials will take us more seriously. When we're organized and we're raising money and we're getting out to vote. . . . I mean, I think that's one of the reasons why the gay and lesbian community has been able to make so many advances is that they give tons of money to politicians. . . . And they're used to doing it and Asians are just not used to doing that, and there are so few that really give or that try to make a difference in that respect. The gay and lesbian community in particular for this one [city council] race, this one district, they raised one-third of the money. So, I've also seen that in the gay and lesbian community—the party lines are crossed if there's a pro-gay candidate or if there's a gay candidate.

He also comments on the redistricting process: "We just don't have enough people who are astute enough to realize, you know, this is how it hurts our community when we're not politically involved." At the time of my interview, Cua was HIV positive but had been healthy for many years. He worked as the executive director of COPAO and for a Filipino American newspaper and considered running for office. His untimely death in 1994 from AIDS-related complications left a void in many communities, evident from the diversity of people who showed up at his funeral.

"Outside Looking In?" Electing One of Our Own

Tom Hom says of his father, who opened a produce business in San Diego in 1918, that "he always felt that, as an immigrant, he was on the outside looking in." The younger Hom, who served five years on the San Diego City Council starting in 1963 and one term as an assemblyman, goes on to say his father "would have been proud that we were on the inside looking out" (Clifford 1990b). Hom was born in 1927 in San Diego's downtown Chinese district, became the first Asian American real estate agent in the area in the 1950s at a time when restrictive covenants maintained segregated neighborhoods, and also became the city's first elected Asian American official (Showley 1980). While San Diego Asians point to him as a role model, they are unable to explain why Asian Americans are still "on the outside looking in," since there has not been another Asian American politician elected to a major office in San Diego since the 1960s.

In California elections in the 1990s, Asian Americans ran for office and won some crucial seats, yet San Diego has not matched this success. A third-generation Japanese American in San Diego who unsuccessfully ran for an assembly seat in 1981 comments that, although he received support from different Asian ethnic communities, many could not vote at the time, and as recent immigrants, many did not have money to donate. But in his perception, "the time is right now" for an Asian to get elected in San Diego, because they are more politically astute and more established economically.

A Filipino American, a liaison between the community and the police department, explains his rationale for having minority politicians in office by referring to a local White politician: "He listens, but he's not Asian. . . . You can almost guarantee that a[n Asian] person is very conscious, very concerned about the Asian community when you put them in that position of power, when we say, 'Hey, we need this done,' we don't have to explain to him why we need it done, why this community wants this, or why this law or this thing is going to offend this community. . . . If you have to explain why to somebody, he can't argue why as forcefully or with that much emotion because he doesn't really understand." The publisher and editor of the local *Asian Journal* echoed these sentiments in his column: "Experience tells us that people take care of their own kind. Whites take care of whites, Hispanics take care of Hispanics, Blacks take care of Blacks, and therefore Asian Americans should take care of Asian Americans" (Silverio 1991).

This should not be interpreted as blind support for any Asian candidate, since many emphasized the need to have "qualified" candidates. A longtime Chinese American political organizer states:

> I was at the point where I would support anyone [Asian] who would run, who had the guts to run, qualified or not. Now, I'm not. So, now I think, because things have changed, we have to raise the level up for the Asian community as a whole, through hard work and by doing things right, by building it up on the basis of credibility and reputation and the image that we do things right and we continue to do things right. So now I've backed off from just

supporting any Asian that's running because now I realize that things have changed. . . . I think it's important that we get qualified Asian candidates identified and somehow help the process where we're nurturing them to get to the point where they will run.

Others expressed similar sentiments and were sensitive to the criticism directed at "unqualified" minorities being given positions as a result of affirmative action programs. A Taiwanese American also comments on the need to make judicious choices: "You're running for the office as an 'Asian,' and then you go there and you don't do a good job, you're immediately going to ruin the image for the future for any Asian candidates." With so few Asians in prominent positions, he was aware of the process of racialization in which outsiders interpret the actions of a politician from one Asian ethnic background as representative of *all* Asian Americans.

Minority candidates cannot address the concerns of only their own ethnic group, they must broaden their platform and appeal to a diversity of mainstream and minority supporters (Pinderhughes 1987). There is still a sense that Americans in general do not feel comfortable with Asian American politicians, as one of my interviewees remarked: "I think there just needs to be . . . a comfort level for middle America to see that there's an American [politician] up there that doesn't look European." If minority candidates are perceived to be engaged in the "politics of victimization" as their political platform, for example, for redistributive programs such as social services or affirmative action, they will alienate the White middle class, who often compose the voting base and who are less willing to share its resources with disadvantaged nonwhite populations. Asian American candidates face harsh public scrutiny from mainstream society, and there is still public skepticism about whether Asian American politicians can be loyal, patriotic citizens who can represent "all" Americans.

Electing One of our Own: Race, Ethnicity, Gender, and Class

The case of Villa Mills is a compelling example of how gender, ethnicity, race, and class intersect in politics. In 1993, when Tom Behr, the incumbent city councilman for District 5, chose not to run for reelection, he endorsed his chief of staff, Villa Mills, a Filipina and the highest-ranked Asian official in the city, who decided to run for his seat. Two years earlier, the publisher and editor of the *Asian Journal*, a local

newspaper, wrote: "If we Asian Americans unite together by supporting one single Asian American candidate in the 5th district, we might
yet elect, with the help of many enlightened White, Hispanic and Black
voters, the first Asian American council person in San Diego after many
years. One who might look after our interests, and hopefully, the rest
of his or her constituency. Should an Asian American decide to run, it
would be inconceivable not to support our own" (Silverio 1991).

Mills lost the election in the primary, and her case exemplifies many
of the difficulties and contradictions that Asian American candidates
encounter. Mills was born in the Philippines and came to San Diego as
a child when her father, a U.S. Navy recruit, was transferred to San
Diego. Raised in the low-income section of south San Diego, she
dropped out of high school when she had a child and then endured an
abusive relationship with the father of her child. After her divorce, she
supported herself working for a telephone company and, as she describes
it, "climbing poles and fixing telephone lines." She eventually went back
to school and received a master's degree in social work. When she
decided to run for office, she was married to a White doctor, had three
more sons, had just become a grandmother, and was living in the affluent section of Scripps Ranch. For years, she had been involved with
mainstream organizations, particularly those that dealt with affordable
housing and business issues, and with Asian American organizations as
well—she was a board member of the Filipino-American Chamber of
Commerce and of the Asian Business Association.

When I asked Asian Americans before the primary if they would support Mills's candidacy, they revealed divergent views. A Filipino American stated: "She's capable, she's intelligent, but she's inexperienced. She
doesn't have enough experience in the community, Asian community. I
think she needs to put more time into the community, for us to get to
know her." A Chinese American said: "I think Villa has the potential for
the future, but I don't think she's ready for it... And not just the political experience but just the experience of being out in the community."
A Japanese American commented that "she's not experienced enough and
she doesn't have the support. She hasn't done enough for the Asian community to show that she can do the job." These respondents did not support her because they felt she was unqualified in terms of dealing with
mainstream politics and of working for the "Asian" community.

In contrast, there were Asian Americans who supported Mills on the
premise that she had enough political experience and she could represent the interests of the Asian American community. A Filipino involved

in the Filipino Democratic Club stated: "I think that Villa is well qualified. . . . I think she'll represent us well." A Chinese said that "Asians have to support her; she is qualified. . . . How many Asians in the last fifteen years have run for city council? She's the first one. And I say, you've got to get behind the candidate." A Korean American who lives in the district added: "She seems like a very conscientious, sincere person who is going to be able to do something good for the community. . . . I think to me, it's more important that she's Asian and that she's running." An individual of Japanese American ancestry was "supporting her mostly from the perspective of being a Filipino candidate, the potential of being the first Filipino Asian on the council."

This was a significant political race, the first to test the redistricting map in which Asian Americans had struggled to keep intact the Asian population in the northern part of San Diego. In district elections, an Asian American candidate needs the support of all Asians in the area for funding, even though only those Asians living within the district can vote. At an ABA dinner I attended, City Council Member Tom Behr, the Anglo politician who had hired Mills as his chief of staff, gave a speech explaining how redistricting occurs once every ten years; in the last one, he said:

> I made sure that Linda Vista was included in District 5 to allow an Asian American to win for the empowerment of the Asian community. . . . I was hoping that some Asian would have the guts to run. Next redistricting, I'm sure that the districts will be redrawn differently and Asian American power will be diluted. Last time there was an Asian in city council was twenty-five years ago with Tom Hom. It doesn't matter if you're Korean, Chinese, Japanese, Filipino. . . . I don't care about your commitment to the other [Anglo] candidates. Your support for them will save an Anglo face and lose an Asian one. Asians should have somebody representing them.

After the speech, I heard varied comments. A Chinese American pointed out that "you've got Tom Behr that's going out of his way to support Villa Mills. We're Asians here and we should do the same thing." Another response was, "I don't think she is the best candidate. I disagree with the idea that she's the only Asian, so we have to support her."

Asian Americans rarely run in Asian majority districts, so they usually cannot afford to be perceived by their non-Asian constituents as only an "ethnic" or "racial" candidate, nor can they ignore Asian coethnics (Uhlaner, Cain, and Kiewiet 1989), as the foregoing statements show. While the newspapers stated that Villa Mills was "endorsed by Asian-Americans" (Braun 1993b), she knew that she could not win with only the Asian vote: "I'm not putting all my focus on the Asian vote for this campaign. . . . I'm definitely putting a lot of focus and energy on the majority vote. I'm not running as a minority candidate." While Mills recognized the constraints imposed on "minority" politicians, she still had a difficult time constructing a political agenda that balanced these components. She explains that the reaction she received from Whites at political forums and in door-to-door campaigning was that she was too focused on "ethnic" issues, yet often Filipinos and Asians thought she did not focus enough on "ethnic" issues. She realized that she could not send her young Filipino American volunteers to campaign door-to-door in groups, since the presence of four Filipinos, particularly if they were males, in affluent White suburban neighborhoods would be read by wary residents as a "gang" invasion (even when the youths were formally attired). In terms of votes, about 20 percent of the approximately 35,000 people in the district were Asians—many Southeast Asians who had arrived recently. Many Asians lived outside the district as did half the Filipino population, so they were unable to vote for her.

Yet not just race but gender affected how others perceived Mills's electoral possibilities. Asian American women had been appointed to some of the more powerful position in the city; however, none had been elected to the city council or county positions. One of Mills's campaign flyers that stated she would focus on improving education was sent back to her with comments scrawled over it: "We'll educate ours, you educate yours," and "There's an overpopulation problem here, go back to the Philippines where they need you"—a reference to her country of origin and her reproductive abilities. To the mainstream community, Mills's being a woman of color made a difference, and she states that "people in North County have been very nice, but it's because I'm a female, not a Filipino male." When I asked one Vietnamese leader who lived in her district what he thought of Mills running, he stated that he did not think she was a good politician yet, but also questioned her ability as a woman to handle the job: "She can do something else. . . . I tell you, if she [was] my wife, I [would] tell her, no, don't ever touch that. That [being a council member] will not make you happy—lots of headaches and you have to deal with so many things." During her door-to-door campaign in the precinct after she explained her age and number of years of experience, she overheard an elderly White woman say to her husband, "She is the sweetest cutest little Japanese thing and she's running for city council. Isn't that cute?"—hardly the ideal image for a woman politician, even if she were Japanese. Mills further explains the age and gender dilemma: "Someone said, 'Gee, you look like you're twenty-three years old.' . . . It doesn't matter what I say. . . . 'I've been around this community for a long time. . . .' They're not hearing even when I tell them, 'No, I'm forty-one years old, I'm a grandmother, I have children, I have a son who is twenty-four years old.' None of that."

Cognizant of these stereotypes, Mills was aware that she needed to present herself as a serious politician to the larger community and also had to negotiate how ethnic markers might be misinterpreted or purposely used against her by the mainstream society. Her reaction to being informed that she was to be the grand marshal of the Filipino American Festival parade was mixed:

> Nobody asked me if I wanted to do that and then they wanted me to put on this [frilly] Filipino dress. Great. That's the last thing I need is to get my picture taken with my opposition putting my picture up, "Do you want this beauty queen to be your council member?" . . . So I did not purposely wear a native dress during the parade, I wore a suit. And I did concede to wearing one [a native dress] for a picture in the [Filipino] newspaper, but I wasn't going to be a beauty queen.

At forty-one, she was close in age to many of the first-generation immigrants, but because she was raised in the United States she states that she "doesn't act like them" or "have the same style," which has created a "love-resentment-envy" relationship between her and other Filipinos of her generation. She comments that "they don't really know what the hell to do with me," explaining what impact this also had on her as a Filipina running for political office:

> In essence it forces Filipino people to come to terms with who they are politically and personally. It really rubs against our grain to be out there, fully visible and having to be knowledgeable and accountable for concrete facts and political issues when really one of our [accepted] areas of expertise is looking pretty and knowing about things that are absolutely apolitical. And there's this feeling of discomfort because it forces people, in terms of the outside world, to really look at us to see who we are. That's really uncomfortable for people and they resent that. And they don't realize it, but they resent that on my part that I am forcing them into that situation by the mere fact that I'm out there saying, "I'm a Filipino and this is what Filipinos ought to be, I'm what Filipinos are, I represent this and we are to be taken seriously, we are a force to be reckoned with. You cannot deny or avoid or not acknowledge who we are because we are here in numbers." And it's a real uncomfortable thing for both sides. And I see it over and over and over again.

Further, she connects these problems to the enduring legacy of colonization in the Philippines:

I'm recognizing certain traits in the Filipino community that are vestiges of the colonial mentality. That feeling of insecurity and feeling less than that the Spaniards instilled in us. . . . One of the ways in which the Spaniards made sure that we never united against them was to divide and conquer. They cultivated a sense of differentness, superiority, and conflict in all of the various different groups. . . . So, they really instilled that, you're so-and-so group; you're so-and-so class, and you're different, and one's better than the other. And part of that was attached with we are the Spanish, we're better than you. And so that the learning around the identity of who we are is based upon a comparison of being better than or less than other people. It's not based upon in terms of identity, we are all one, equal, and so forth and so on. So in the process of what I am doing in terms of the election, the arrangements and problem solving and just the sorting out of who we are politically is still very rooted in that very basic perception of who we are, in terms of the culture. Its cultural underpinnings are rooted in the Spanish divide-and-conquer strategy, whether it's acknowledged, intentional, or whatever. . . . Very, very interesting to watch, because as Filipinos see me out there, unafraid and being outspoken, they feel very proud about it and very good about it, hey, we have an identity; at the same time, it creates an internal conflict because it doesn't jibe with their meanings. It just does not jibe with their definitions with who they are and who they are as a group. . . . We've had Americans being the superior presence in our country for so many years. We had the Spanish before them. Throughout those years the underlying message was we were always the ones that were less than, that others were always superior. That hasn't changed. It was really an ingrained piece of the identity.

Additionally, while some Filipinos are the descendants of laborers, others came through the U.S. military, and more recent immigrants arrived as professionals. This mix adds to the class differences, along with the fact that they come from various regions or provinces in the Philippines, making it difficult to unify them politically.

While Mills managed to raise over $10,000, her major opponents raised more than twice as much. A number of the U.S.-born generation, many college-age students, supported her and volunteered for her campaign, but they were not established enough to contribute financially to her campaign. Two of the primary individuals who organized her fund-raiser, which advertised her as "San Diego's Only Asian American Candidate," were Chinese, and listed as part of the cohost committee were Chinese, Japanese, and Filipinos. Support among Asian American leaders was divided between Mills and one of her opponents, Fred Colby, a European American who was a community college trustee. Colby's mother, a local philanthropist, had developed good relations with many individuals in the Asian community, and as a result, many Asian Americans who could have supported Mills decided to support her opponent or decided not to support either candidate publicly. When Mills came in third in the primary election, which put her out of the race, Asian Americans, including those who had originally supported her, held a fund-raising event for her opponent, "Asian Americans for Fred Colby."[38] Barbara Warden won the election. She was a newspaper publisher from the affluent Rancho Bernardo area where 30 percent of registered voters, primarily non-Asian, and 40 percent of likely voters in the district live.[39]

Those unfamiliar with the political process often ignore smaller elections, as a newcomer from Hong Kong who is an engineer notes:

> If you don't support Villa Mills to sit on the city council, how do you expect that there will be an Asian running for the governor of California if they don't go through little races, get elected, build up their reputation, then go on a little bigger one? [As a structural engineer,] if I don't get a small bridge job, how am I going to do a big bridge? The Asian community to me, just within the Chinese community, [they think] if you're big and going for big things, you've got a big name, we support you. But if you're little, [they say] I'm not sure if I can support you. . . . [With Villa] they think it's not enough, it's just a small [city] council seat, and no big deal, we only support those big races. But they don't understand that without those small races, nobody will come out to be a contender of the big race.

An old-timer Chinese American who has been involved in Asian American political issues since the 1970s and helped organize a fund-raiser for Villa Mills agrees and expresses his frustration:

> Asians have to get together, because there are not enough of us; . . . we're lucky to find a qualified candidate—an Asian candidate—to run to begin with. So when we have someone qualified, whether it's Japanese, Chinese, Filipino, or whatnot . . . then I think the Asians should rally around that person; . . . there's not enough of us, we have to help each other, if he [the politician] does a good job and shows a strong showing, I mean, let me tell you, it makes all of us look good. And it will build up our own image as qualified Asians down the road, instead of having to always be on the defensive. And it's going to help your kids, and your grandkids, and so forth in this country. Are you going to live in this country or are you going to go back to your old country? I said, "You've got to help." And that was my argument. And I'll tell you, that's why it's frustrating because I say the same argument. Sometimes I say, "Why can't they think like me and I don't have to do this argument? Why can't they just say, 'God, it's an Asian guy, help him!'" I'll tell you, there's obstacles all down the road. Sometimes I get so frustrated, I say, "Why am I doing this?"

With the intense internal and external obstacles facing them, it is quite transparent why there are few Asian American political contenders.

"No One Represents Us": Dilemmas of Leadership

Along with a new generation of U.S.-born leaders becoming spokespersons for the community, there are immigrants who are also becoming involved, and this creates conditions for conflict as they struggle to define who can speak for them. An activist critical of the conduct of a first-generation Asian elder and the reception given him at a city council meeting states: "He basically, like, rambled and he didn't even take a position. I mean, he was just there to basically hear himself talk but he made no points. Plus he speaks with a heavy accent and you can see the mental shutoff in these people—the council members—the moment they hear, like, an Asian speaking with a heavy accent, there's something that automatically turns off." Another organizer acknowledges the problem as well: "I hate to admit, they [the Asian American community] need some type of leadership training. What I mean is, we need to learn the finer points of how to organize meetings, how to run meetings so things get accomplished, how to address the city council, how to address the mayor, how to address the chief of police, ... what's the protocol. ... How do you get things accomplished politically?"

These viewpoints reflect comments I heard from 1.5-, second-, third-, and fourth-generation Asian Americans who were critical of how the community was being represented by the first generation, whose political leadership styles do not translate well in the mainstream. They also voiced awareness of the racism that casts them as "foreigners," an image they consider the first generation to inadvertently perpetuate. The younger generation acknowledges that they are novices in this process; however, they saw themselves as advantaged by their socialization in the United States and their English proficiency. Younger generations who were experienced with the pan-Asian format in San Diego developed organizations to address these concerns. In 1991, the organizers of the Filipino Alliance for Community Leadership, in their initial letter inviting participants, wrote that they saw the "need for more effective representation of the Filipino community" and saw problems with the current "level of sophistication, political and social experience, and personal insight necessary to adequately participate in the political arena." In 1992 after the Los Angeles rebellion, the Korean American Professional Association stated the goal of the group was "to get politically aligned and affiliated with all the power sources, so to speak, so that when we need something . . . we know who we can go to who will listen and who can make things happen." In turn, there are concerns raised that U.S.-born Asians, although they may be empathetic to the immigrant experience and can assist immigrants in certain instances, are unable to adequately address their needs.

New immigrants, particularly professionals, have been labeled conservatives, yet they represent a wide spectrum of political viewpoints and life experiences, and their motives for getting politically involved are diverse. For example, an engineer, an immigrant from Hong Kong, who had no intention of running for political office and sacrificed his business and family time, was becoming politicized. He realized that for someone with little leadership experience, he would be criticized—and he was. However, he was learning about the political process: "I guess I'm transforming from an engineer into the business-like person [and] getting more involved with politics, understand how to play the game and how not to say something and how to say it. And it's making me sharper, to be able to look at more things [from] a different perspective than just from an engineer's point of view." He identified himself as a staunch Democrat, has conservative views on economic issues, and makes tentative remarks about labor unions. During our conversation, he explained the importance of advocating for equal rights for gays and lesbians, of defending affirmative action programs, and of trying to improve race relations. Individuals like him have used their material resources and institutional connections to bring attention to the racial inequities that affect Asian Americans. They can force the public and private sector to listen and, at times, to take action. We cannot disregard them merely because of their class status (Takahashi 1997). I acknowledge the criticism that these immigrants can stifle the potential of progressive Asian American activism; however, it is important not to assume they are "essentialized ethnic elitists" and to recognize the variety of their experiences and politics, as well as to acknowledge that they are a growing population that will shape Asian American activism in the future.

Being a self-appointed or appointed leader of the Asian American community, or one who is perceived as a leader, is not an enviable position. Such individuals have to constantly balance their credibility with the mainstream society against internal factions and inevitable criticism by other Asian ethnics. A leader who is half Japanese and half Filipino born in Japan was generous in stating that "nobody represents the community. One person cannot represent everything within such a diverse community, all the different ethnic groups. . . . So, I don't think one person can represent every aspect of Asians in San Diego, but to a certain extent, they deserve to be heard if they put in their dues"—meaning they have put time and effort into Asian-based networks and organizations. Leaders I interviewed were hesitant about being considered representative of the Asian American community and its issues. They were pragmatic and realized that they speak from a certain position, and that there are a multitude of voices in the community that they cannot represent.

Conclusion

The period in which I conducted my fieldwork was one during which Asian Americans were finally making significant inroads into the political arena, after an extensive history of legal exclusion and struggle. There are varying criteria to measure the "success" of political integration, ranging from the ability to extract resources from politicians to the election of an officeholder from one's group. While other generations of leaders have, to some extent, been involved with the political system, the current generation of leaders was the first group to gather momentum in affecting political policies and to attract more than token attention from mainstream leaders. As Asian Americans made modest gains, they were encouraged to continue organizing, as conveyed by one longtime participant in San Diego politics: "When I came into the act, Asian was considered nothing as a force. Nothing. Zero. Nothing. . . . I mean, they look at us as just another voter but never really grouped us, grouped the Asians as a power group. . . . [Politicians] looked at us as a group now, only because we've agreed to become a group in our political approaches." While their mobilization efforts have increased at various levels, their victories have been small; yet there has been a marked change from a decade earlier, when they were not even considered political contenders (Daniels 1997).

As Asian Americans are forging new paths to political participation, they encounter both old barriers and newly devised ones. The 1996 campaign funding-raising scandal, when Asians, immigrants and U.S.-born, were accused of illegal donations and of espionage or conspiracy, is indicative of the barriers they continue to face. During this time, Americans of Asian ancestry, particularly contributors to both parties, endured probes about their citizenship status, income sources, and loyalty merely as a consequence of having an Asian surname; they also faced racially biased and offensive remarks by the media and politicians

(Chang 2001; Zia 2000). Asian American politicians, and especially their donor lists, were scrutinized closely as well. The interchanging of Asian nationals ("foreigners") with Asian Americans resembled the historical period of the "Yellow Peril." The issue I am raising is not about the need for campaign finance reform, which requires little debate, but the way Asian Americans were treated and represented in this process. Were Asian Americans being held to a higher standard and being unfairly scrutinized or facing selective harassment? This incident has had a chilling effect on local Asian American communities that were just beginning to become involved in the political process, making it more difficult for leaders to encourage political engagement.

The power of the initiative and referendum process, referred to as direct democracy, still dominated by California's white middle-class interests, can undermine the legislative gains made by minorities and symbolizes new political challenges faced by Asian Americans (Cain 1991). Ironically, by the latter part of the 1990s in California, when statewide propositions were supported by voters against affirmative action programs, bilingual education, and social services for immigrants, Asian Americans had larger constituencies to bring in votes, were registering to vote in greater numbers, were creating political leaders, were making substantial contributions, and were volunteering their time. Race and racialization still matter deeply in the American polity. Sustaining political momentum and contending with generational, ethnic, immigrant, class, sexual, gender, and ideological differences, as well as facing countless external obstacles, can be daunting. Mobilizing a splintered group that lacks a tradition of involvement in electoral politics is no simple task. In this realm, Asian Americans accept the need to work on accommodating strategies, but they are still willing to rely on confrontational strategies if necessary.

7

Mapping Asian America

In Search of "Our" History and
"Our" Community

At the turn of the twentieth century, were one looking for Asian Americans in San Diego, one would have gone to the heart of the city's downtown area, next to the red-light district with its lively saloons, brothels, and gambling houses. There existed a thriving, bustling community—with Filipino migrant laborers relaxing in the pool halls, Chinese fishermen bringing in their catch of the day, and Japanese grocers selling produce in their markets. Yet by the early 1990s, only a few remnants of this past remained, and the Asian communities were scattered in pockets on the edges of the city or in the suburbs. If one looked closely at a few of the buildings downtown, one might notice a red tile roof arched at the edges, a sign with Chinese lettering, or ironwork with an Asian motif on a patio. And one might see a few elderly Chinese taking walks to escape their tiny apartments or shopping in the neighborhood stores, but overall, one rarely saw Asians downtown. What happened in the intervening years? And what prompted Asian Americans in the 1990s to mobilize in an attempt to recapture this almost forgotten past?

In the late 1980s, city leaders, as part of the downtown renovation, were celebrating Asian American contributions to the city's history, as a memo from the city's planning department explains: "The establishment of this Thematic Historic District provides an opportunity to maintain and enhance the unique urban character of Centre City, San Diego, by featuring a historical resource that was important to the development of downtown San Diego, the Chinese/Asian community."[1] Mainstream elites expected local Asians to play a peripheral role in the revitalization plans; non-Asians, they thought, would orchestrate the preapproved plans. Unwilling to be relegated to the sidelines, Asian Americans challenged one of the most powerful mainstream institutions in the city in order to be incorporated in the process. Asian American activists wanted to reestablish their physical presence in San Diego's downtown and to restore the district to recreate it as a cultural and economic center for Asian Americans, as well as attract investments from Asian nationals. They were not against commercializing the district; rather, they wanted decision-making power in the district and they wanted to benefit from its commercialization. What ensued was a struggle of accommodative resistance, as Asian Americans worked toward becoming integrated into the political structure while also retaining their autonomy.

This case demonstrates the dilemmas of mobilization for a racialized group with a large immigrant base, especially one that has been consistently tokenized in city politics. There are preservation projects of Japantowns, Chinatowns, and Manilatowns across the country, but the San Diego project is unique because it includes the redevelopment of an area shared by the Chinese, Japanese, and Filipino communities. This was a highly charged political issue that brought together a mix of core participants: old-timers who were original residents of the district; their children who were raised in the district and still live in San Diego; migrants who moved to San Diego; and more recent immigrants of Asian ancestry. The first two groups were relatively small but had an attachment to the site, so the addition of supporters from the larger Asian American community helped to substantiate their objectives, although their connections were more ambiguously defined. Some newcomers of Chinese, Japanese, and Filipino ancestry feel that although they are not directly linked to the district, the preservation project is part of their shared history in the community. For other ethnic groups without historical roots in this district, the connection is more complicated.

Specifically, I highlight three aspects of the creation of an "Asiatown" in San Diego: the development of the Chinese/Asian Historic District; the controversy over a building in the district; and the formation of a pan-Asian organization in the district. I arrived on the scene during the latter part of the controversy and, along with informal and formal interviews, rely on multiple resources for this chapter, including documents from the city development agency and Asian American individuals, newspaper accounts, formal meetings, and informal discussions at which I was present. During the early stages of my research, I wrote an article about the district for the Asian Business Association newsletter, which gave me entrée to later meetings.[2] It was often awkward for me to attend formal meetings, since these were small official gatherings and I was the only one without an official title; however, my attendance provided me with a critical analytical perspective. I argue that this spatial revitalization project illustrates the complex challenges confronting Asian Americans as they attempt to reconstruct their collective history and to make claims on their communities in sites across the country.

History of a Segregated Settlement

The San Diego Asian community, originally established in the mid-1800s, is a significant part of the city landscape, but much of its history is undocumented or lost (see also Chapter Two). The Chinese were the first to settle this area of the city, in 1860, and the Japanese and Filipinos later also settled in this segregated section (Brandes, Carrico, and Nagel n.d.). There are three periods of structural growth in the area that coincide with periods of immigration and with immigration restrictions: 1860–1890, 1891–1910, and 1911–1930 (see Figures 2, 3, and 4). Beginning in the 1860s, there were at least 24 Asian buildings in the downtown area, bound by E and K Streets and Second and Sixth Avenues, which would continue to define the western and eastern boundaries. In the second period, 1891–1910, the number of businesses and/or buildings had grown to 50 and many of the new settlers were Japanese merchants who expanded to Broadway and K Street. During the third period, 1911–1930, there were approximately 100 Asian businesses or buildings, with most concentrated between Market (Martin Luther King Jr. Way) and J Streets. Fifth Avenue was the main thoroughfare for what was then called New Town, San Diego, and many Asian American businesses and buildings were located in an area that covered approximately eight square blocks.[3] Reports on the area state that "there is a congenial combination of many Asian ethnic groups. Chinese, Filipino, Japanese and Hawaiian businesses flourished during this time side by side with remarkable concentration."[4] While laws prevented first-generation Asians from owning any real estate or land, as tenants, some incorporated modest Asian architectural designs on the buildings, leaving behind a visible reminder of their presence.

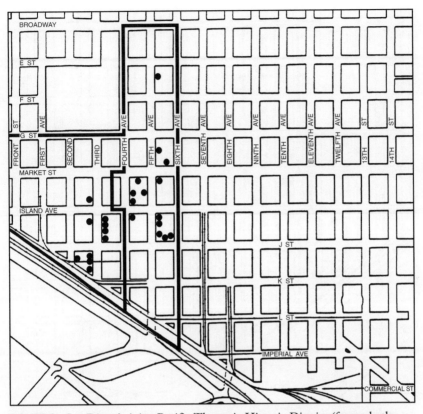

FIGURE 2. San Diego's Asian Pacific Thematic Historic District (formerly the
Chinese/Asian Thematic Historical District), 1877–1890. Heavy lines demarcate
the contemporary Marina District (wedge-shaped area at left center) and the
Gaslamp Quarter District (between Fourth and Sixth avenues) in the downtown
area. Dots identify Asian American businesses.
Source: San Diego City Planning Department, 1987.

During the Depression, the downtown area began to decline, and after
World War II, the area was abandoned for new affordable housing in the
suburbs. It was estimated that, "at its peak, right before World War I,
4,000 Chinese, 10% of the city's population, lived in the district and until
the early 1960s, more than 1,500 people of Chinese descent lived there"
(Novarro 1986). After World War II, younger-generation Japanese Americans, released from the internment camps, were prevented from or were
not interested in opening the kinds of businesses their parents had owned,
so the Japanese presence never reestablished itself downtown. For example, Joe Yamada, a second-generation Japanese American who once lived
in the district, became an architect and would later work to revitalize the

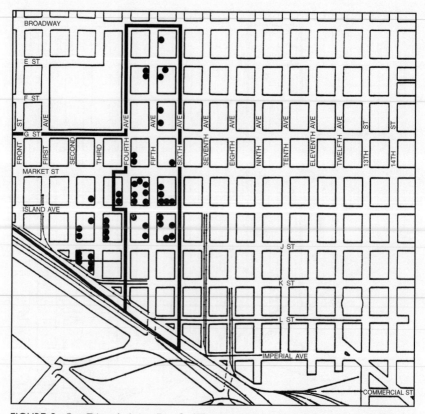

FIGURE 3. San Diego's Asian Pacific Thematic Historic District (formerly the Chinese/Asian Thematic Historical District), 1891–1910. Heavy lines demarcate the contemporary Marina District (wedge-shaped area at left center) and the Gaslamp Quarter District (between Fourth and Sixth avenues) in the downtown area. Dots identify Asian American businesses.
Source: San Diego City Planning Department, 1987.

district. His father had owned Frisco Café on Fifth Avenue, but during World War II, FBI agents took him away for two years and Yamada's mother was forced to sell the business before she was interned at Poston, Arizona. When race-restrictive housing covenants were declared unconstitutional, many Asians living in the city's core moved to the suburbs. Anna Wong Lau, daughter of the owner of the Nanking Café, San Diego's oldest Chinese restaurant until its closure in 1993, remarked: "Gaslamp [downtown] was scary. The rescue mission was there. It was skid row. People didn't go down there. We hopped in the car at night and went home to live in Hillcrest. A lot of Chinese moved to better locations once they could afford it" (quoted in Lau 1994). It was the elderly, poor Chinese who had nowhere to go, along with some organizations serving them that remained behind in the dilapidated city.

Downtown Renovation, Centre City Development Corporation, and the Preservation of an Asian American District

During the first part of the twentieth century, San Diego's downtown, also referred to as Centre City, was an active and prosperous place, but like other metropolitan areas, with the Depression and suburbanization

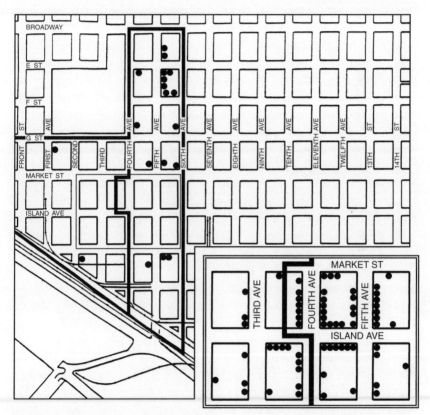

FIGURE 4. San Diego's Asian Pacific Thematic Historic District (formerly the Chinese/Asian Thematic Historical District), 1911–1930. Heavy lines demarcate the contemporary Marina District (wedge-shaped area at left center) and the Gaslamp Quarter District (between Fourth and Sixth avenues) in the downtown area. Dots identify Asian American businesses. *Inset (lower right):* Enlargement of the shaded area, showing densely clustered Asian American businesses. *Source:* San Diego City Planning Department, 1987.

after World War II, it gradually became a blighted area. The district was known for its rescue missions, rundown warehouses, empty buildings, and a few antique stores. Many of the clientele of the main businesses, such as the X-rated movie houses, adult entertainment shops, and seedy bars, were navy personnel with shore passes from docked ships. In the 1970s during Mayor Pete Wilson's reign, when he dubbed San Diego "America's Finest City," efforts were initiated by the city council and its redevelopment agency to renovate the downtown.

By the 1980s, the area began to show visible signs of change as old buildings were demolished and new ones were erected, especially with the establishment of a landmark open mall, Horton Plaza, which housed shops, restaurants, theaters, and a supermarket. The gentrification of the downtown area also included the development of office buildings, luxury apartments, townhouses, condos, hotels, and later the new Convention Center. The opening of more restaurants, coffee houses, bars, nightclubs, art galleries, and boutiques on Fourth and Fifth Avenues followed. Within less than ten years, this revitalization dramatically changed the environment and atmosphere of downtown and brought back locals and tourists to the once desolate area. These renovations also caused havoc for poor residents by raising rents, resulting in the displacement of longtime dwellers.

The restoration of the downtown vicinity was a gamble for both Centre City Development Corporation (CCDC) and local entrepreneurs. Many critics said it would be impossible to lure people to the city from their safe, self-sufficient suburbs. CCDC was a public, nonprofit agency that was established in 1975 by the Redevelopment Agency of the City of San Diego, but it was not until the mid-1980s that it was apparent the organization had proven the skeptics wrong. The original redeveloped areas included Horton Plaza (initiated in 1972), the Marina (1976), the Columbia (1976), and the Gaslamp Quarter (1982).

In early 1980, the Gaslamp Quarter Historic District, which included some Asian buildings, was placed on the National Register of Historic Places. At this stage, neither members of the Chinese or Asian community nor their organizations were offered any official input in CCDC's decisions.[5] It was not until March 1986, after being requested to do so by some Chinese American leaders, that CCDC began a research, evaluation, and community-input process to acquire recommendations regarding buildings in the Marina Redevelopment Project associated with the Chinese heritage.[6] In 1986, CCDC formed a Chinese Community Ad Hoc Advisory Committee to gather information and receive feedback from the Chinese American community. In the early stages of seeking approval for the district, there were seven committee members.[7] The historical data collected by those hired by CCDC found more information on the Chinese community, and this augmented official historical reports by the city.[8] Additionally, the Chinese American community supported the efforts by word-of-mouth and advertisement in order to collect personal stories, photographs, records, and other mementos that tied Asians to the district. Within the year, the CCDC board approved in concept the idea of establishing a Chinese Thematic District, with incorporated buildings in the Marina District and additional buildings in the adjacent Gaslamp Quarter District.

Although there were other Asian Americans involved, support for the project came mainly from Chinese American leaders and organizations in the initial stages. The Chinese still had a visible attachment to the area, with estimates of about 200 Chinese residents, the San Diego Chinese Center, and two tong associations still there, so they were the first to feel the effects of the urban demolition and renewal. A number of longtime members of the Chinese American community, some of whom were descendants of original residents in the district, played a pivotal role in preserving the district. Aid came from a mixture of cultural, social, and religious groups, some of which focused on Chinese American issues, while others were more interested in Chinese cultural nationalism. Members of the House of China and the San Diego Chinese Center voiced their support for the district.[9] The Chinese Community Church was in favor of the district and urged the board to declare the Chinese Mission a historical building for preservation.[10] The Chinese Historical Society of Greater San Diego and Baja California led by Tom Hom, who was raised in the district, was active in gathering data from private individuals and organizations.[11] Hom's wife, Dorothy Hom, also active in the organization, was on the Historical Site Board, so she was familiar with the process of preservation. Gil Ontai, raised in Hawai'i but of mixed Asian ancestry, including Chinese, was the only Chinese or Asian on the CCDC Board of Directors, and he was instrumental in informing the Chinese community about strategies for preservation. The Japanese Historical Society was formed after these events occurred, so the Japanese American Citizens League, which had been active in keeping records of the Japanese experience in San Diego, provided preliminary information.

At this stage, the mobilization effort was Asian American as a matter of efficacy, not as a well-thought-out plan. Instead of listing the small number of buildings in separate ethnic clusters (i.e., Chinese, Japanese, Filipino) that might get lost in the shuffle, the agreed-upon practical strategy was to group the buildings thematically as part of the Chinese/Asian District. Different Asian groups had used many of the same buildings for residences and businesses, and the thematic group nomination indicated that these buildings included "a finite group of resources related to one another in a clearly distinguishable way."[12] In early 1987, along with the City Redevelopment Agency, the City Planning Department, the Historical Site Board, and the Chinese Community Ad Hoc Committee, CCDC recommended that the Chinese/Asian Thematic District be listed with the local and National Register of Historic Places, and it was officially approved by city council on 13 October 1987.

Although there were efforts to get more buildings listed, in the final decision, the district was comprised of twenty-two structures that have "strong ties to the Chinese/Asian community either through ownership, business or cultural use."[13] With the Regal and Anita buildings slated for demolition, there are actually twenty properties in the Chinese/Asian District—thirteen in the Gaslamp Quarter District and seven in the adjacent Marina District identified as part of the Asian District.[14] These remaining buildings became representative of those that could not be included in the district and also symbolic of ones no longer in existence, such as the Stingaree Bordello, which had been demolished, and the Woo Chee Chong Building, destroyed by fire.[15] Whereas some property owners saw the small buildings as historically or architecturally insignificant and wanted to redevelop these sites with new structures, city planners and Asian American activists were allied in the fight to preserve them.[16]

This alliance was short-lived as debates were waged over the contours of a racialized tourist site. CCDC was concerned primarily with architectural aspects of the redevelopment process, while Asian Americans saw the preservation project in much broader terms. The official reports on the district define the focus of city planners quite clearly: "The significant aspect or theme of the Chinese/Asian Thematic Historic District is that the structures involved are the remnant buildings which are directly related to the Chinese/Asian community and its role in the commercial, historical, architectural and cultural development of the city."[17] Throughout the official booklets about the district, there is mention of how unique ethnic adaptations of vernacular American architecture were made to the buildings in technique and design, such as clay-tiled roofs, ornate balconies, inscriptions, patterned glazed ceramic tiles, and bright colors that convey an "Oriental" feel or appearance.[18] Mike Stepner, the main city planner, argued:

The [Planning] Department believes that there is an opportunity to try better, be creative, and achieve a 'win-win' solution, much in the same manner CCDC did with the Horton Plaza project. This project's [the Plaza's] historical context and design is so unique and exhilarating, as to make it an architectural, economic, and social success. We propose that this opportunity not be lost in the Chinese/Asian Thematic Historic District.[19]

Planners thought that the "quaint Oriental" architecture of the buildings was worthy of preservation on its own merit, and they added that it could potentially attract more San Diegans and tourists to the downtown area, which would mean an increase in city revenue.

For Asian Americans, architectural integrity was only one component of retaining their Asian heritage. They supported CCDC's plan of "bringing people back to the city." However, Asian Americans defined "people" in slightly different terms: Their primary concern was to bring back Asian Americans residents and businesses, making the district an active cultural, social, and economic center for them. The planners' excitement over Asian architectural features illustrates mainstream society's acceptance of "Oriental" cultural artifacts and commodities, from rugs to fine porcelain in their homes and offices (Tchen 1999), but a rejection of or distancing from Asian Americans in their personal lives or community, except as servants, gardeners, caregivers, or other service-sector positions. A commitment to restore this area meant a validation of Asian architectural contributions and Asians' historical occupation of the buildings; however, the renovation project ignored Asian bodies and voices. CCDC did not take seriously the Asian activists' hopes to recreate this as a site for the Asian American "community."

The Struggle over the Lincoln Hotel

These differing perspectives were represented in the debate over the fate of the Lincoln Hotel, a building designated in the Chinese/Asian District. The events that followed were aptly described in the local press: "What began as a simple attempt to lease the Gaslamp Quarter's Lincoln Hotel has turned into a politically charged battle for the leadership of San Diego's Asian-American community in their attempt to secure significant influence in the redevelopment of downtown's Chinese/Asian Thematic (CAT) District" (Cronin 1992).

City planners saw the property as an opportunity to satisfy their low-income housing requirement, stipulated by law, and to fulfill their architectural renovation plans for the district. For Asian Americans, the hotel, a modest building sandwiched between two more distinguished structures, came to symbolize the lack of power Asian Americans could exert in the city, even on issues which affected them directly. It was their exclusion from the decision-making process that prompted Asian Americans to formally mobilize.

The Lincoln Hotel building at 536 Fifth Avenue is centrally located in the Gaslamp Quarter, so it is one of the more valuable pieces of property in the Chinese/Asian District. Built in 1913, the Lincoln is a narrow, four-story building with business space on the first level and forty-eight single-occupancy rooms and shared central facilities on the other three levels. The official description states that the hotel "features a distinctive Chinese architectural treatment conveyed through a red clay tile roof and decorative hollow clay tile on the facade." While the lower level once housed a wine business, the first tenant of the upper floors was A. K. Sakai, presumably of Japanese ancestry, who ran a hotel. (At one point, the lower part of the building had been a tinsmith shop and the upper floors were a brothel.) The Redevelopment Agency, under the guidance of CCDC, bought the unoccupied and dilapidated hotel in October 1990 from an Asian American owner for $600,000, with the intent of giving it a $1 million face-lift and leasing or selling it to a private or nonprofit corporation.

In 1991, CCDC put out a request for proposals (RFP) for the purchase or lease of the building, including rehabilitating the property. They asked respondents to consider low-income housing for the upper floors, to meet the requirements CCDC is obligated to fulfill by law, and a retail business or restaurant for the ground floor. After reviewing the offers, CCDC asked two groups, the San Diego Chinese Center and the Vista Hills Community Treatment Foundation, to send in requests for qualifications (RFQs), which involved preparing more detailed proposals.

The San Diego Chinese Center, a nonprofit social service agency in the district, planned to build eighteen low-income apartments to accommodate some of the displaced elderly Chinese. The agency proposed the lower level be reserved for an upscale Chinese enterprise, such as a Chinese gallery, gift shop, tea shop, or bookstore. The proposal included a statement describing the residential section as a culturally sensitive space for the Asian elderly, many of them immigrants: "This area would allow for socialization thereby encouraging a healthy and cohesive spirit. This is extremely important to the Chinese seniors, the need to be identified with a group and not feeling abandoned without family or friends." It also stated that the hotel is "an ideal location which holds for the older generations a sense of historic value which they wish to preserve and pass on to the future generations."[20] Although the agency was inexperienced in building low-income housing, organizers stated that it had been in existence since 1971 and was experienced in providing multilingual social services.[21] With a small staff of part-time employees and volunteers, the center in a year served over 200 clients, approximately 65 percent of whom were seniors and 95 percent of whom lived either below or very close to the poverty level.[22]

The other bidder, Vista Hills Community Treatment Foundation (VH), wanted to restore the hotel as single-room-occupancy (SRO) housing units for graduates of its mental health program who had completed alcohol and drug rehabilitation. VH would lease the first floor to the Writers' Gaslamp Haven Café and Bookstore, which would hire some of the occupants residing in the building. Neither the VH nor the potential owners of the café/bookstore were affiliated with the Asian American community. Asian Americans would not be targeted as clients of the facility, as patrons of the business, or as employees.

After reviewing both proposals, CCDC selected the VH plan and submitted it to the city council for final approval. The final CCDC vote was six to one, with Gil Ontai, the only Asian American on the board, dissenting. For him, the board's decision showed "grave cultural insensitivity" (Lau 1991a). The Gaslamp Quarter Committee, along with the president of the Gaslamp Quarter Planning Board, also supported the VH proposal by a majority vote, citing the proposal as "superior" and "excellent." Other than the Asian American community, the only groups who expressed concern about VH's proposal were business tenants near the Lincoln Hotel, who were worried that it might become a "halfway house."

While the Asian community considered the sociocultural aspects of the hotel, city developers tended to view it from merely an economic vantage point. One Asian American participant stated that "the Asian community views the hotel as an important historic and cultural site that once served as an informal Ellis Island and meeting place for Asian immigrants" (Rodgers 1992b). The proposal from the Chinese Center stated: "Considering the historical significance of the Chinese Community in San Diego's downtown since the 1860's, there must be a substantial increase in [Chinese] representation and presence in the area." As one activist would later explain to the mayor, the "Asian communities responded in favor of the Chinese Center as it was felt that the center, having roots in the area for generations should be the appropriate entity to develop the Lincoln for senior housing and to establish an Asian oriented commercial use for the ground floor."[23]

In contrast, an individual on the Gaslamp board who supported the VH plan explained that the Chinese Center's proposal could be potentially $440,000 more expensive to the Redevelopment Agency than VH's, and this extra money could be used to develop other projects downtown (not necessarily in the Asian American district). VH offered to provide $500,000 from loans and grants to renovate the hotel. The Chinese Center offered to give CCDC 50 percent of its net operating income, which amounted to $238,000. For CCDC representatives, VH offered less financial risk, since VH operated eight residential facilities and two outpatient clinics, and the café would be operated by an experienced restaurateur. Additionally, while the VH plan would accommodate thirty-six single-residential-occupancy units, the Chinese Center wanted to build apartments, so they could accommodate only eighteen units.

During one meeting, CCDC's executive vice president noted the Chinese community's failure to raise money to fulfill existing obligations. She was referring to the Chinese Historical Society, which at that time had not raised the money to move the old Chinese Mission building (which had been given to the society by CCDC) to a new location. The assumption was that if one Chinese organization could not fulfill its obligations, then the San Diego Chinese Center would not be able to either. In defense, Chinese American activists stated that although both are Chinese American organizations, one is a historical association and the other a social service organization. A member of the Chinese/Asian Thematic Historic District Advisory Committee stated that "they're lumping the Chinese as one group. We are separate bodies working on different projects." CCDC argued that as a public agency, it was instrumental in establishing the Chinese/Asian District, had already donated $450,000 of land to relocate the Chinese Mission for the Chinese Historical Society, and was considering donating some land to the Chinese Consolidated Benevolent Association for the construction of a senior housing project. CCDC felt that an additional project such as the Lincoln Hotel would only burden the Chinese American community.[24]

The RFP and RFQ written by CCDC failed to mention that the building was located in the Asian American Thematic District. The original proposal submitted by VH included the minimum requirement. Since it was a historical building, VH agreed to restore it, basically by maintaining the Chinese architectural features, but this was to be the extent of their responsibilities as stipulated by city requirements. According to CCDC this was normal procedure, since other buildings designated in the Chinese/Asian District had been architecturally restored. But those businesses were not Asian owned, nor did they have an Asian theme or cater to Asian Americans.

The Chinese American community, along with some other Asian American leaders, protested the decision to give the project to VH, stating that the building should go to the Asian American community, and took their petition to city hall. At the August 1991 hearing, the Redevelopment Agency/City Council overturned CCDC's recommendation to give the Lincoln contract to VH and selected the Chinese Center instead. By a vote of seven to two, the agency recommended that another site be found for the VH project and that an Asian-oriented use be established for the Lincoln Hotel.

This was the first time the city council had ever overturned a recommendation by the CCDC board since its establishment in the 1970s. To make an impact on city council members and to sway their votes, the Chinese Center had brought approximately thirty elderly Chinese who still lived in the downtown area to pack the room. A member of the Chinese Center board states: "We were told that if we want to get the ears of the city council, to load the audience with Asian faces, so we asked the seniors to go out there. . . . I didn't realize the importance of it or how effective it was until I was sitting there and we saw it happening. The city council was on their best behavior when they had all these senior citizens show up and they're sitting in the audience." There was an interpreter assigned to the seniors, and although the seniors did not provide any testimony, which was left to the younger generation, it was their physical presence that was essential.

After the vote, the current chair of the Chinese Center Advisory Board framed it as a victory not just for the Chinese Americans, but for Asian Americans: "This is Asian empowerment. When we come together to voice our concerns, we get the support we need" (Lau 1991b). A fourth-generation Chinese American, the former chair of the center, claimed it as "a symbolic victory for all the Asian communities having roots downtown." Neither of these individuals was related to the Chinese seniors or was a native San Diegan, but they were active in local ethnic Chinese and Asian organizations. They had moved to San Diego as adults and came from families with a long history of activism in their respective Chinese communities, the former in Tijuana, Mexico, and the latter in Sacramento, California. They felt that the struggles of the Asian population in San Diego were related to the struggles of their parents and earlier generations who had emigrated from China to create a better life for their families.

In January 1992, representatives from the Chinese Center announced that the restoration project was too expensive for it to manage.[25] The center could not obtain the necessary loans and the board members were unable to raise sufficient funds. When the Chinese Center rescinded its bid, CCDC reinstated VH as the main bidder for the hotel. The Asian American community felt that another RFP should be sent out and thought the project should go to another Asian American organization, since the Chinese Center was not the only Asian social service organization in San Diego. Instead, CCDC supported the VH project again and explained that everyone had been properly notified about the availability of the site in the original RFP. A CCDC board member who was a mayoral candidate at the time explained why he wanted to give the project to VH: "The entire Asian community was behind the Chinese Center proposal, and it fell through. From the very beginning I stated that I thought they would come up short of money. The process was followed correctly—everyone knew VH was the second choice. We cannot keep sitting on these properties" (Cronin 1992). Yet Asian Americans were infuriated and rallied for the Lincoln to be given to another Asian American organization.

The reason that Chinese and Asian American community leaders felt justified in defending their claims to the Lincoln Hotel was that this building represented the loss of other Asian American buildings and was a symbol of their history downtown and their contribution to the city. Many of the buildings associated with the Asian American community were not designated to be in the district for a variety of reasons; additionally, many of those designated had already been gentrified with non-Asian businesses and residences. From the perspective of the Asian American community, there were few viable buildings that might preserve their heritage, whereas there were numerous buildings in the downtown area, outside the Chinese/Asian District, that Vista Hills could purchase. For the Asian American community, the Lincoln Hotel presented a unique opportunity, because CCDC, a public institution, owned it, rather than it being privately owned, and since it was empty, it could be restored for any use. The business space and apartments above could potentially be owned and operated by Asian Americans for Asian Americans. It was the Chinese/Asian Thematic Historic District Advisory Committee, a pan-Asian organization that would be created within CCDC, which led the opposition to the reinstatement of the VH project.

The Chinese/Asian Thematic Historic District Advisory Committee

While a Chinese American ad hoc committee had been formed to establish the area as a historic district worthy of preservation, once the district was approved, the committee was relegated to the margins. In March 1991, Denise Leon, representing an ad hoc group called the Asian Thematic Design Review Committee, requested that the Chinese/Asian community be involved with the design review of projects in the "revitalization known as old Chinatown." In her letter, Leon recommended six members of the Chinese community active in Chinese organizations for the board (including herself), and three eventually became members. The one Asian American member of CCDC's board also supported the formation of this committee and said that it should have an "equal review and an equal voice" in the structural designs. An organizer states: "And it naturally evolved into a need that we saw for having a voice in the Chinese/Asian Thematic District as to how it should be, how the plans should be and how it should grow."

CCDC responded to this request by proposing the formation of a Chinese/Asian Thematic Historic District Design Review Committee to appease the community, never intending the committee to play a significant role. The draft proposal stated that the committee's task would be to review proposals of new renovation projects in the district, and their comments would be "taken into consideration." Yet the Gaslamp Quarter Planning Board voted against the formation of the committee, since the board, along with the Historic Site Board and the Resident Advisory Committee, already performed design reviews for the buildings in the Thematic District downtown. The board felt that approval of the design by the Asian American community members would be an overlap of duties and another unnecessary bureaucratic step for potential tenants and architects. As a result, CCDC altered the proposal, renaming the Chinese/Asian Thematic Historic District *Design Review* Committee the Chinese/Asian Thematic Historic District *Advisory* Committee, noting: "The purpose of the committee would be to advise CCDC staff and Board on issues which affect the Chinese/Asian Thematic Historic District." Inadvertently, this new proposal implied that the committee was responsible for more than just the design of the structures, allowing Asian Americans to ultimately broaden the range of the committee's duties.

After a couple of months, the executive director of CCDC wanted to rescind the proposal for the committee, based on a perceived lack of interest from the Asian American community, and stated that another advisory committee would burden CCDC with unnecessary work. For her, the community's input was unimportant, even bothersome. At a CCDC board meeting, an ad hoc group of Asian Americans challenged the withdrawal and complained about the marginal role of the proposed advisory committee. They sent a follow-up letter stating that "the community proposes to have a meaningful participation in what happens to the future of our property, our cultural activities, our organized senior citizens events, our jobs, our cultural landmarks, our residences, our businesses, and our community appearance, which should be Asian in character."[26] Confronted with opposition to their plans and the dismissive attitude of CCDC representatives, these Asian American leaders actually increased their demands, stating they wanted decision-making power in *all* future developments in the district.

This stage also saw the formal inclusion of other Asian American participants, although some Chinese Americans still preferred having exclusive control. If they wanted to substantiate their claim with mainstream agencies, however, these activists, mainly Chinese American, realized they would have to include other ethnic groups. They began to explicitly state that the committee should include members from all the Asian subgroups who had a history in the district. Up to this point, other Asian American organizational leaders were informed about the unfolding events, but they were not formally involved or affiliated with the process. Leaders knew that organizational support would give them more clout, and through their personal networks they were able to convince the Filipino-American Chamber of Commerce and other Asian American organizations, such as the Asian Business Association (ABA) and the Mayor's Asian Advisory Board, to officially support the formation of the advisory committee.[27]

Asian Americans gained approval for the committee, yet their efforts were again undermined when CCDC wanted to open the selection process for membership on the committee to non-Asians. Although the Chinese originally wanted to appoint all seven individuals, they conceded that CCDC should be given this task. Previously the application stated that "membership is open to anyone residing in the City of San

Diego," but after protests from Asian American activists, the revised application asked for the applicant's race or ethnicity. In the final draft, applicants had to specify their involvement in the Chinese/Asian District, "such as a member of a community organization, property owner, business owner, resident or active in promoting the District's culture, history or architecture." Basically the Chinese wanted to ensure that Asian Americans would be assigned to the committee, since non-Asians already dominated the other mainstream committees involved with making decisions in the district.

In September 1991, the first Chinese/Asian Thematic Historic District Advisory Board (CAT) committee was established and consisted of one Japanese, four Chinese, and two Filipinos who were involved with existing pan-Asian organizations or committees. It represented the formalization of the community's participation in the district, something many argued should have been instituted from the beginning. Given the misinterpretations that had occurred, CAT members defined their mission as follows: "Sensitize the San Diego public, City staff and legislators to the citywide benefits of conserving and enhancing the rich heritage of the multi-cultural Asian community" and encourage rehabilitation of structures and projects "by going beyond the traditional approach and framework that addresses strictly architectural and land use issues and considering social, economic and cultural aspects of the development."[28]

Even though Asians managed to expand CAT's tasks and had made a transition from a temporary, peripheral committee to a permanent one in the CCDC organizational hierarchy, they soon realized that they were being tokenized and marginalized again. At their third meeting, CAT members learned that the CCDC planned to give the bid back to VH and that the official vote would take place in one week. CAT members were upset with the plan to reinstate VH, but they were even more dismayed that they were not given any input or prior notice of the impending vote. A CCDC official explained that CAT was not officially informed of the vote because CAT was officially approved after CCDC had made the decision on the hotel—a response that further infuriated CAT members. A member of CAT, a Filipina, agreed to go to the CCDC board meeting, request a postponement on the vote until other bids by the Asian American community could be submitted, and ask that CAT have the opportunity to review all new proposals.

She confronted resistance from CCDC board members and was faced with an unexpected twist in the controversy. An official from Vista Hills present at the meeting was infuriated by CAT's requests and accused

CAT and the Asian American community of trying to prevent a treatment center for the mentally ill from occupying the building. Having already lost the building once, he stated: "Enough is enough. . . . We are trying to provide housing for the mentally ill and homeless. . . . The mentally ill are the niggers of the '90s!" (McClain 1992). He later justified his statement as made in defense of the mentally ill, not to denigrate a racial group. In his statement of apology, he explained that he "intended to illustrate the fact that the mentally ill are often devalued, dehumanized, and treated with a callous disrespect and insensitivity, as have been other minority groups. My use of the term 'nigger' was intended to be a generic example of that ugly mindless hate and prejudice."[29] The chair of the CCDC board supported the VH representative by also questioning the request for the delay, stating that CAT, which he referred to as a special-interest group, was being "obstructionist." The vote was not delayed and the final decision was five to two to recommend that VH be given the hotel again; the only Asian American on the CCDC board was one of the two who voted against the recommendation.

The Filipina representative from CAT was outraged that there was no intervention, particularly by the chair of CCDC, when unwarranted inflammatory language was interjected at the meeting. She states that the VH representative, who was "pitting one minority group against another and denigrating another with a racial slur (and himself in the process) no matter how well intentioned and contextual is hurtful to the entire community."[30] She added that allegations that the Asian American community harbored prejudice against the mentally ill were misinformed. It was rumored in the local media that Asian Americans were warning business owners near the hotel about a rehabilitation facility opening in the vicinity to drum up protest. In defense, she explained that she was a board member of the San Diego Fair Housing Council and a founding member of the Gaslamp Quarter Project Area Committee, which promotes low-income housing and had been a staunch advocate for the homeless. In 1987, as part of her job, she had arranged the meeting between Vista Hills and the San Diego Housing Commission in order to provide housing assistance to clients of Vista Hills's Semi-Supervised Living Project. She explained that another member of CAT is the landlord for some of the facilities for VH's programs and serves on the board of the Salvation Army. The Asian Business Association joined the protest and in addition to sending a letter of complaint to the San Diego Human Relations Commission asked the city council to investigate the chair of CCDC, who they stated needed to be more aware of cultural diversity within the city. They commented that he failed "to handle a culturally sensitive issue and to maintain an atmosphere of positive race relations. The chair of the board allowed a speaker from the public to denigrate African-Americans and to make it appear that Asians are biased against African-Americans and the mentally ill."

The accusations directed at the Asian community only intensified its mobilization efforts and brought more media attention to the issue, making it an embarrassment to CCDC, and when Asian Americans took the issue before the city council asking for a delay on the vote over the hotel, they had a stronger coalition. At that point, CAT recommended to CCDC that more time was needed to contact those in the Asian American community who had the potential to develop the property, residentially or commercially, before the final vote on the fate of the hotel could be fairly taken. The vice president of the Asian Business Association, a Filipino, testified that ABA supported CAT's request to reopen the RFP process, noting that "wording in the original RFP failed to mention that the Lincoln Building was located in the Asian Thematic District and failed to emphasize the importance of participation by the Asian community."

During informal discussions at a meeting for a pan-Asian business organization I attended, members complained about the misconception by CCDC representatives that one Chinese organization equals "all Chinese or all Asian" organizations. An Asian American involved with lobbying members of CCDC and local politicians commented that certain individuals on the CCDC board have no comprehension of the Asian American community or Asian Americans' histories and consider the groups interchangeable. She added that "they do not understand the Chinese Center, the Chinese Historical Society, and the Chinese Benevolent Association are separate entities, much less that there are differences among the Chinese, Japanese, or Filipinos." For them, the failure of the Chinese Center to refurbish the hotel did not necessarily represent the whole Asian American community, but simply one small faction and, therefore, another Asian American organization should be given the property.

A Second Bid for the Lincoln Hotel

Both parties, VH and CAT, along with members of the Asian American community, were given two weeks by the city council to discuss a compromise that would give VH control over the residential quarters and encourage them to incorporate "something of the Asian culture into the ground floor of the hotel."[31] The 25 February 1992 meeting between VH and CAT in an attempt to resolve the issue was held in a Chinese restaurant owned by a member of CAT. The other meetings I attended were in the sterile conference rooms of the CCDC office in a high-rise building downtown. The restaurant site near the district was identified with Asian American activism, since it was a place where numerous political and business meetings were organized by the Asian American community over the years, so they were on their own turf. Even the setup of the room reshaped power relations, with CAT members sitting prominently behind panel tables facing the audience of ABA members, VH representatives, CCDC employees, a reporter, and other Asian Americans, myself included. VH representatives were conciliatory and hoping for a compromise. Asian activists were not interested in negotiation and were either going to convince VH to forfeit pursuing the project or take the matter to the city council.

Following these requests, VH stated it could not forsake its agreement with the retailers but made "cultural" concessions to the Asian American community in its revised proposal, a proposal that only infuriated Asian Americans further. The revisions by VH read as follows:

1. To include space for a section on Asian Literature in the first floor Café/Bookstore/Writer's Haven (with CAT being involved in the selection of materials).
2. To open up all the available wall space in the café/bookstore to displays of Asian art and artifacts (which CAT could control).
3. To let CAT approve plans for developing an Asian motif for both the outdoor and indoor space.
4. To target persons of Asian descent as employees of the retail space.
5. To approach the Asian American social service organization (another mental health provider) to target rooms in the hotel for the mentally ill of Asian descent.
6. To let CAT rename the hotel.[32]

CAT felt that the first, second, third, and sixth suggestions treated Asians as exotic objects and conflated Asians and Asian Americans. CAT members expressed dismay that the revisions were merely cosmetic "token gestures," since Asian Americans ultimately would have no control over the residential or commercial aspects of the project.

The VH representative apologized for the racist language he had used at the previous meeting, but his approach only worsened matters. He explained repeatedly how he had served in the Peace Corps in the

Philippines for two years, so he was "culturally sensitive to Asian American needs." This only incensed the committee further, since he was treating Filipino nationals and Filipinos in the United States as interchangeable groups. His audience was filled with primarily Asian American professionals and business owners, as well as longtime community activists; his framing of Asians as "helpless natives" who needed the help of "white neocolonial masters" did not resonate well with them. The fourth and fifth revisions were reminiscent of this colonial benevolence, to hire Asians and admit Asians as patients, yet allow them to play only a subordinate role in running the business or the center for the mentally ill. Asian Americans at the meeting were noticeably making faces and shuffling uncomfortably in their seats while trying to ignore his statements, which he made repeatedly, seeming unaware of their implications or the reactions he was receiving.

Asian Americans objected to the revised proposal on the grounds it was not culturally sensitive to the impact of racism or cultural isolation experienced by many Asian immigrants, especially the elderly. They argued the proposal disregarded the social and racial incompatibility of the two tenant groups, Asians and non-Asians, the latter recovering drug and alcohol addicts. The VH proposal explained the need to create "a strong community living component" in order to develop "a community spirit" in which tenants who were being rehabilitated would share a community kitchen, laundries, bathrooms, halls, and other community living spaces.[33] Since the single-occupancy rooms would be small, the community space would be an essential component of the project, but VH had not contacted UPAC, the Asian American social service organization, nor did the VH representative seem cognizant of possible cultural and linguistic needs of Asian American mental health patients. Additionally, the Asian American community was more interested in housing for Asian American seniors, most of whom did not speak English or had limited English skills, and many of whom have had limited interaction with non-Asians.

Not surprisingly, after much heated debate, the parties could not come to an agreement to work on the project together, since VH stood by its final proposal and the Asian American community by theirs; the issue went before the city council. After hearing testimony from the various parties, the city council voted six to three on 17 March, directing CCDC to solicit new proposals, to specifically target advertisements for the project within the Asian American community, and to find another building downtown for VH (Carrier 1992b; Rodgers

1992a, b). RFPs were sent out a second time to the Asian American community, and this time CCDC consulted with CAT about which local Asian American newspapers to use to post public notices and which organizations to contact.[34]

Asian American leaders had convinced the city council that they wanted the Lincoln Hotel, yet at that point no one had committed to developing the business or residential components of the hotel. ABA leaders suggested that the upper levels could be used for SRO units in conjunction with an Asian American social service organization other than the Chinese American one, such as the Union of Pan Asian Communities, the Council of Pilipino-American Organizations, or the Indochinese Mutual Assistance Association (IMAA).[35] Other groups, such as the Filipino-American Chamber of Commerce, also stated their interest in the business and housing prospects in this new "Asiantown" and encouraged their membership to do the same, yet made no commitment to the hotel.[36] Therefore, Asian American leaders scrambled to get Asian American organizations to submit proposals to develop the residential units in the hotel. Such an organization would have to meet two criteria; its members needed to be respected by other Asian ethnic groups to gain their support, and the organization needed to be recognized by the mainstream society. As one activist stated, members of the social service organization must be "sophisticated and professional" enough to write the proposal and work with mainstream agencies.

In 1994, the San Diego Filipino-American Humanitarian Foundation, a nonprofit organization of doctors and professionals, met these two requirements and entered a negotiation agreement to develop the Lincoln Hotel for $1.5 million. The foundation proposed "to utilize the upper floors as a SRO for low income people with medical and/or mental needs. The lower levels would be utilized to accommodate the activities of general counseling and referral services including mental health services, a Filipino-Asian American library and museum, a language center for the various Asian groups and other minority groups as well."[37] In addition, the foundation proposed to have an international visitors bureau and a center for academic research and to encourage nonprofit Asian American organizations to use the center as a community forum, along with a Filipino business, possibly a restaurant. In 2003, the refurbished building was opened to low-income residents of all racial groups, with the San Diego Filipino-American Humanitarian Foundation office, the Philippine Library and Museum, and the San Diego Trading Company, a clothing store, located on the first level.

The Process of Politicization

Throughout the Lincoln Hotel debate, Asian American individuals in key political positions were allowed access to vital information, and they were instrumental in galvanizing other members of the community, disrupting business as usual in city politics. Behind the scenes, individual Asian Americans lobbied city council members and the mayor, as well as their aides, to sway the vote. The few Asian Americans with direct official political access—Yen Tu, a Chinese-Vietnamese American liaison for a city council member; Villa Mills, a Filipina who served as an assistant to the mayor; and another Filipina experienced in planning issues downtown—were intermediaries in lobbying politicians. Members of the Mayor's Asian Advisory Board were also involved in the process, and the chair, Romulo Sarno, would later become chair of CAT.[38] When Gil Ontai, who is a migrant to San Diego, left his position on the CCDC board, he was replaced by Joe Wong, a Chinese architect whose family has a long history in San Diego and who had worked on renovating another building in the district; he would later be replaced by a Filipino American.[39] As a Japanese American pointed out, the awareness level has been raised so that in the future, Asian Americans will be considered for these spots, something he wants to see established with other powerful boards in the city. Without Asian Americans in key political positions, a board member of CAT acknowledges, events would have taken a different course: "I don't know that it [CAT] would have ever happened."

The perception of Asian Americans as a potential economic and political asset was a definite bargaining chip as they negotiated with San Diego city planners and politicians. ABA, as a pan-Asian organization, was beginning to establish some political clout and used its leverage to support CAT, with the expectation that CAT could play an instrumental role in the development of Asian small businesses in the district.[40] As well as lobbying politicians personally for support, Asian Americans have continued to raise the Chinese/Asian District issue at political forums and fund-raisers sponsored by the Asian American community.[41] A Chinese American who chaired CAT previously states that "since then we've had successes after successes. . . . I can't emphasize how important for it to happen more often, for us to really pull together and lobby more and have strategic planning for it."[42]

Some Asian Americans have used this experience as a model to exert more influence on the political process and to sway the political vote in their favor with other development projects downtown. For example, a Japanese American who is a director for a nonprofit housing and employment agency and who was involved in the Lincoln Hotel controversy applied similar strategies to a low-income housing development which caters to many African Americans and Latinos. He explained to me:

> I got this project here approved [pointing to blueprint]. I had a $350,000 gap with a $6.5 million project. . . . I needed to get that money through the Centre City Development Corporation. And I was rejected by CCDC and I went over their heads and went to the city council and they overruled. That was only the second time that had been done in their history. The first time was when the city council overruled the CCDC on the Lincoln Hotel. . . . I spent a month and a half getting in the mayor's office, [City Council Member] Vargas's office, you know, [City Council Member] Stallings, et cetera.

He would build Hacienda Townhomes, affordable housing units for low-income residents, part of an effort to revitalize the crime-ridden and blighted East Village area downtown (Powell 1994). CCDC expanded its area from 360 acres to 1,398 acres, which basically covers all of the downtown area, making the group an even more powerful entity in the city (Carrier 1992a), so familiarizing oneself with this hierarchy is essential for doing business downtown.

During this redevelopment, Asian Americans continue to learn about the process of maintaining an ethnic balance, as another CAT member remarks: "I think in the mainstream, people tend to think of it as the Chinese historical experience in San Diego, but they tend to forget that there is also a Japanese influence and Filipino influence and so we, the committee, have always made a conscious effort to make sure that we are diversified . . . to be representative of all the other Asians that were in the downtown area." ABA also recommended that "a balanced approach toward incorporating participation by the various Asian communities with historical roots in the Asian Thematic District" be taken.[43] In the second year, a Filipino American—one of the highest-ranking county officials and the chair of the San Diego Mayor's Asian Advisory Board—became the chair of CAT.[44] The other members included three Chinese, one Taiwanese, one Japanese, and one individual of mixed Asian ancestry who was formerly the president of ABA and on the board of CCDC. The potential for interethnic conflict remains, as they continue to make decisions on the master plan and determine the fate of other buildings in the district.

Asian subgroups that had a history in the downtown area initially intervened in the designation of this district and became active participants in this controversy; however, other Asian Americans will also shape the development of this district and can benefit from the opportunities created within it. For example, a Thai restaurant replaced the closed Nanking Restaurant site, which had been occupied by either a Chinese or a Japanese restaurant since its construction in 1912.[45] The president of the Vietnamese Federation made public statements that the Vietnamese community is interested in possibly opening up businesses in the district to take advantage of the tourism industry (Lau 1994). So although these latter two groups have no direct attachment to the district's history, their current inclusion in the Asian American grouping allows them to partake of the resources of the district.

By 1995 the district was redesignated the Asian Pacific Thematic Historic District. This combining of grassroots activism and Pacific Rim investments has occurred in other cities and is a pragmatic alliance because projects often require substantial capital that is not always available locally (Shiroishi 1996). CAT stated they were seeking overseas Asian investors to assist them in developing projects in the district.[46] ABA leaders also pushed "to utilize the ground and basement levels for business, retail, office and community functions with a focus on Pacific Rim cultural activities and trade opportunities."[47] They wanted the district to have an international cosmopolitan flair, more reflective of the contemporary immigrant experience, contrary to the historic image of the district as a place of dark alleys filled with Asian laundries, gambling dens, and chop suey houses.

Organizers have been quite receptive to the involvement of Asian countries in the formation of the district. The Chinese Historical Society of Greater San Diego and Baja California moved the Chinese Mission Building, once used for religious training and education, to the corner of Third and J Streets with a $1.2 million restoration project and converted it into the Chinese Historical Museum, which opened on 13 January 1996 (Lau 1996). Taiwanese ambassador Mou-Shih Ding donated $250,000 as seed money for the project from the Republic of China's Council on Cultural Planning and Development, matching the amount raised locally. The building includes an Asian garden with an entry gate that honors Dr. Sun Yat-Sen, who led the 1911 revolution in China; a bridge which is a memorial to the late U.S. ambassador to the Republic of China Everett Drumright; and a seven-foot bronze statue of Confucius (a gift from Taiwan to San Diego). In addition to the pictorial and archeological displays of the Chinese experience in San Diego, part of the museum's permanent exhibit includes Chinese historical cultural artifacts from mainland China and Taiwan, such as art objects from the Ching Dynasty, maps and books from U.S. diplomatic personnel residing in China, and calligraphy and art by artists in China and Taiwan, along with coinciding cultural events.

Although Asian Americans are involved with the Asian Pacific Thematic Historic District, it is still controlled by non-Asians, since CCDC and ultimately the city council have final say on the residents, businesses, and aesthetics (streetscape, street furniture, lighting, and architecture) of the district. Installed on Third Street between Island and J are Asian-inspired lantern light posts, an effort to make the district more visible. For the most part, the ornamentation and businesses of other properties in the district demonstrate how city leaders want an Asian presence, but one that is not "too Asian." Like the Lincoln Hotel, many of the businesses in the buildings that are part of the district are not "Asian." Bordering the museum is the Quong Building, occupied by Candela's Restaurant, which offers "Mexican nouvelle cuisine"; the Ying-On Labor and Merchants Association Building houses a mainstream realty office. Also in this area, next to the historic building that now houses the Chinese Senior Citizen Association and the San Diego Chinese Center, is a $3.6 million four-story Chinese Consolidated Benevolent Association Senior Garden Housing Project with forty-two one-bedroom and three studio units, a project initiated in 1990 (Lau 1997). This building's exterior has a muted Chinese design, except for a small dragon mural. The six-story fifty-three-unit Pacific Terrace condominiums across the street, which will house an expansion of the Chinese Historical Museum, has pastel coloring with Chinese-like designs on the balcony.

This architectural "blending" policy is the same for all buildings in the district. Having a more elaborate Asian design along with Asian language–only signs would not be looked upon favorably. These aesthetic choices may appear justifiable, with the buildings historically used by Asian American businesses having simple Asian characteristics, and given the modest incomes of the occupants, since most were barred from owning the properties. Yet these limitations on the ornamentation of the buildings can be interpreted as making them "nonthreatening" or "less offensive" to non-Asians. Downtown buildings are supposed to be architecturally harmonious with the historical theme of the area. Yet Horton Plaza, an initially controversial shopping complex in the Gaslamp District, and many other buildings (not part of the Asian district) in the downtown area were allowed to break these rules with their modern European-influenced architectural designs. The few Asian Ameri-

can senior residents, along with a limited cluster of buildings with subdued Asian motifs, pose little threat to downtown institutions. In design-
ing the district, Asian Americans are trying to meet the demands of
their ethnic communities, of mainstream society, and of Asian nationals. Their attempts to please these varying constituents contributes to
their making contradictory and "safe" choices.

A Geography of Community: Residential, Commercial, and Cultural Spaces

The Lincoln Hotel case differs from other pan-Asian efforts in San
Diego, because participants were making claims on a public space. City
planners expressed skepticism about Asian Americans' willingness to
"come back" to downtown. At a meeting after the second rejection of
the VH proposal, CAT board members explained that each of the ethnic groups was distinct and should have its own cultural center. The
executive director of CCDC declared that the Chinese Mission would
be the cultural center of the district and questioned the viability and fea-
sibility of designating and building centers for the Japanese American
and Filipino American communities. Exasperated by the demands of
CAT, she sharply replied: "I don't know if we will ever make this the
focus of the Asian American community [again]."[48] In contrast, other
city planners seemed supportive of reviving the district and of including Asian Americans in the decision-making process, such as a CCDC
senior planner who, from my observations, had better relations with
CAT members and was more receptive to multiple sites. She expressed
hope that the community would "unite itself" downtown (Lau 1994).

CAT's objective was "to preserve Chinese/Asian history and promote
re-establishment of Asian presence/identity in both residential and
commercial areas." The plan of the main organizers is to make this a
central location for the Asian American community—a place where
they can have businesses and residences, hold community meetings,
gather for cultural celebrations, and maintain a permanent site for their
historical collections. The challenge is to encourage Asians who reside
in other parts of the county to make an economic and personal investment in the district.

Since World War II, Asians in San Diego have formed geographic
attachments elsewhere, particularly on the outskirts of city boundaries
or in the suburbs. The majority live, work, and socialize in other parts
of town, and this poses the greatest barrier to gaining support for the

district. With their museums and historical links, the Chinese, Japanese, and Filipinos can claim the space as their own. However, for other groups, such as Asian Indians, Cambodians, Koreans, Laotians, and Vietnamese, the connection must be "created." Some Asian Americans believe this is a sentimental project being carried out in honor of the older Asian immigrant population, and it is not aligned with their vision of the contemporary Asian American community, whose heart and soul lie elsewhere. Some consider it an impossibility to entice Asian Americans away from their residential clusters, while others consider it sociopolitically unwise for Asian Americans to resegregate themselves in the downtown district.

The downtown project also competes with established Asian business areas in other parts of the county, such as Kearny Mesa, where numerous Asian restaurants and businesses were established in the 1980s and 1990s. As one CAT board member comments: "I think Kearny Mesa area is probably the most diverse and most dynamic commercial area, Asian ethnic area. . . . I think Asians in general are comfortable there with other Asians." With numerous sites of commercial development for the Asian American community, downtown business developers have to compete for local and international capital, as well as for technical and entrepreneurial resources. For instance, from the early to mid-1990s, major new supermarkets, some of them part of larger chains, opened in locations throughout the county (Telles 1991). Many mom-and-pop businesses were already competing with these modernized, highly financed markets and restaurants for ethnic customers, so there was little incentive to support the project downtown. Asian Americans, particularly business owners, want to protect their investments in outlying areas of the city and in the suburbs. Providing an incentive to encourage Asian Americans to make investments in the district is difficult, and this explains why downtown projects rely on investments from abroad.

Given the difficulty of attracting Asian American residents and businesses, another strategy to lure Asian Americans downtown has been to make this district a permanent site for cultural celebrations—allowing the dispersed communities to congregate in one place where they can comfortably express pride in their cultural heritage. The locations of ethnic celebrations have varied over the years, sometimes based on where Asian Americans were concentrated or where space was available. The CAT-sponsored "Celebration of the Asian District, Its Past, Present, and Future" was a rededication of the Lincoln Hotel and a fund-raiser to create a nonprofit foundation to raise money for cultural events downtown.[49] One of the oldest annual festivals, the Chinese New Year Food and Cultural Faire sponsored by the San Diego Chinese Center, was held at the Del Mar Fairgrounds in North County, but has since moved to the downtown district. These were followed by the Fiesta Filipiana Street Faire to celebrate "Philippine History, Heritage, Culture, and Tradition," sponsored by the Philippine Library and Museum, which is based in the Lincoln Hotel building. There were plans to hold a multiethnic Asian festival to coincide with Asian American Heritage Month to promote the district further; however, in 2003 the second Asian Pacific Island Heritage Festival was held in the Balboa Park area instead. These festivals vary in the crowds they attract; for instance, the Chinese festival attracts the general public, whereas the Vietnamese one attracts mainly Vietnamese, so a downtown venue makes more sense for the Chinese. CCDC seems more supportive of "inclusive" efforts and since 1998 has sponsored an Annual Downtown San Diego Multicultural Festival, with one of the sponsors being the Asian Business Association, coordinating it with the Martin Luther King Jr. Parade, all taking place on King Promenade in the waterfront district. These downtown events conflict with multicultural, multi-Asian, and single-ethnic Asian festivals held in other parts of the county where communities of color, including Asian Americans, actually live, socialize, and work.

Downtown may be a thriving, bustling cosmopolitan area, yet on a pragmatic level, how welcoming is it to a large congregation of Asian Americans, many of whom are immigrants or refugees? The ability to bring Asian Americans to the district is dependent on making them feel comfortable in this space. In my interviews, some expressed preference for particular sites over others. For instance, an acculturated woman who is half Japanese and half Filipino remarked:

> When I miss seeing brown people, I go to Plaza Bonita [in South Bay] purposely. You see a lot of Filipinos, a lot of Chicanos, and it's one mall where you just see families. I don't think you see so many children in any other mall. People are friendlier. I think there's a dramatic difference from when I go shopping at North County Faire, the clerks aren't as friendly or trusting. And this isn't just at North County Faire, but at other malls too. I have sometimes been followed around like I'm gonna shoplift something or have somebody scrutinize my signature when I sign something even when I give them my picture ID, for crying out loud. You're treated more receptively at Plaza Bonita. More people of color work behind the register.

A number of immigrants may also feel more comfortable socially and linguistically with coethnics in places where they will not be ridiculed for the language they speak, the foods they eat, or any other cultural habits. This "safe space" is something that the gentrified sites downtown do not necessarily offer. In 2004 there are efforts to promote the developing "Filipino Village," an area south of downtown where Filipino Americans actually live and have commercial spaces. The chic new Chinese, Japanese, Indian, and Thai eateries that opened up downtown after redevelopment began were designed to cater mainly to the population at large, not to an Asian American clientele. A new informal organization, the Asian Pacific Historic Collaborative, has the goal of "encouraging the rebirth and growth of the Asian Pacific presence in downtown San Diego" and held an exhibit of Chinese, Japanese, and Filipino history at the Horton Grand Hotel in 2003 as part of this effort.

Conclusion

This story is about more than the role of Asian Americans in a gentrification or redevelopment project in the downtown vicinity. These events transformed power relations between the Asian American community and the larger one. As a result of their strategic organizing, Asian Americans managed to defeat CCDC twice at city hall, which was unprecedented, and they also became formally incorporated into the political structure. One of the former chairs of CAT, now known as the Asian Pacific Thematic Historic District Advisory Committee, optimistically explains:

> Reality in life is unless you speak up, you won't be acknowledged. And so, we learned that and that is the difference. I don't think that it had to do with prejudice or anything like that or that they didn't want to do it. It's just that they never thought of it, so it's just a matter of letting them know that this is what we wanted. We do exist and you need to take us into consideration in the overall planning.

A few members of this committee are working with CCDC on conducting research to assess the Black history of the area. The city benefits from these endeavors since the district can boost its tourism industry by claiming to be both a multicultural and an international city, fulfilling its slogan "America's Finest City." As the past president of ABA states: "There is definitely a need for Asian identity in San Diego" (Lau 1994), and Asian Americans are still struggling to come to terms with how they will reconstruct their shared history and redefine community space.

8

Ambiguities and Contradictions

Narratives of Identity and Community

There is little debate that the Asian American category is a constructed one; however, there is confusion as to what an Asian American identity is and what it means to those who are identified as such. Being identified as Asian American is not an abstract notion; we struggle with it daily, on a conscious and unconscious level (Kibria 2002; Tuan 1998). Asian American identities are nurtured and transformed over time among individuals, and I wanted to understand the ways in which this identity was being experienced, created, acted upon, and represented by Asian Americans.

This is not an exhaustive, systematic exploration of Asian American identities, since my contact was with a select group of Asian Americans, primarily those actively involved in Asian American organizations and events in one site during a particular time, and it is their perspectives that I have captured. These narratives may not be representative of the whole community or, for that matter, embraced by all members; nonetheless, I imagine aspects of these narratives would resonate with Asian Americans in general. My intention is to provide a sampling of recollections and personal experiences to illustrate the complexity of the formation of Asian American identities and communities, in addition to pointing out how this might affect Asian Americans' organizational participation. I want to show the experiences of these Asian American men and women as children, teens, and adults with their parents, families, friends, and romantic partners in their neighborhoods, schools, workplaces, and organizations. I was curious about their exposure to other Asian Americans and to other communities of color and how these experiences impact their sense of identity. The individual reflections address micro-level identity formations, but in the latter part of the chapter I link these formations more explicitly to their participation in macro-level organizational processes.

One of my Japanese American respondents, when asked what Asian Americans have in common, answered: "They're not Black, they're not Latino, they're not Caucasian, so they must be Asian." He is referring to an essentialized notion of race, that Asians share a distinctive set of physical characteristics. However, closer examination contradicts this biologically essentialist assumption. Asians tend not to have blonde hair and blue eyes, but they may, due to interracial mixing. Although many have straight hair, others have rather wavy or even kinky hair. Many are small and petite in stature when compared to the average "American," but others are quite tall or husky. Although they have been labeled "yellow" (they co-opted this terminology during the Yellow Power movement of the 1970s) or in some cases were identified as "brown," their skin shade covers all skin-color spectrums from very dark to very light. Racial constructs can belie visual realities, since those grouped in the Asian racial category differ physically, even if one uses skin color as a measure of racial identification; but the perception exists that they have the same phenotype. However, this is also not to say that racial indicators are irrelevant.

Identity work is embedded in relationships of power and in the social structure. Dominant societal constructions of "typical" racial characteristics popularized in a bygone era still determine how one is perceived and treated (Zia 2000). Primordial theories focus on biologically inherited characteristics, disregarding the dynamic aspects of ethnicity; however, situational ethnicity models account for levels of ethnic intensity in different periods, as well as its fluid, multilayered forms (Okamura 1981; Scott 1990). For many White ethnics, ethnicity is flexible, voluntary, and symbolic (Gans 1979). In contrast, for those who are racially identified, there are costs that affect the daily routines of their lives and their life chances (Waters 1990). In their racial formation model, Omi and Winant (1986) discuss how learned "racial etiquette" practices present us with a set of interpretative codes and racial meanings that inform our daily interactions. Racial markers can provide outsiders with identifiable, recognizable elements, which are then interpreted and acted upon, but they also become a form of self-definition (Du Bois 1990).

Earlier scholars have used assimilationist models to examine how rapidly immigrant groups melted into the U.S. mainstream (Gordon 1964; Kitano 1969; Park 1950; Sung 1967; Warner and Srole 1945), but these have been replaced with ethnic retention paradigms (Glazer and Moynihan 1963; Maira 2002). Although mainstream society often still dictates an assimilationist model, as their numbers have increased substantially in the 1980s and 1990s, Asian Americans have become more assertive in their ethnic and racial expressions, articulating that they belong to America on their own conditions. Identity work is shaped from the top down as well as from the bottom up; hence, racially identified groups can maneuver within the constraints placed upon them and generate their own meanings. Using their social agency, Asian Americans engage with identity work and reckon with it through their interactions in their neighborhoods, schools, workplaces, and organizations. They are attempting to figure out exactly how they "belong" in U.S. society, where many still consider them "foreigners."

I emphasize less whether the identity created is "real" than that it has real life consequences and that it does matter. My conception of racial and ethnic identity formation emphasizes nonessentialized notions of identity and is not based on a unilinear model of stages or levels of identity attainment, so it is in constant flux, involving dimensions of the past and present. Asian American culture is not monolithic and there is no "authentic" or "true" Asian American identity (Mura 1994). The racialized boundaries of a group are created and imposed upon the group for the convenience of outsiders and may not initially produce a sense of in-group commonality or a collective identity. In my *interactive identity model*, constructions of identity are shaped by interactions among individuals, groups, institutions, and community members; it is an evolving, negotiated process.

Indirect Racialization and the Shaping of Identity

Individuals I interviewed conveyed how they saw their parents negotiate personal and institutional racism. The children of immigrants, especially, saw how their parents faced the difficulties of adjusting to a new country. Asian immigrants and refugees may have experienced ethnic chauvinism, political persecution, and gender discrimination before their arrival, but these oppressions take a different form in the context of America's racial hierarchy. A U.S.-born Korean discloses that because of the racism his parents experienced as immigrants, they chose to protect their children by not teaching them Korean:

> I never learned it [Korean] when I was a kid. They didn't want me to have an English problem. Because my parents, at that time, they were suffering from discrimination and a lot of people were looking down on them because they had heavy accents. They couldn't speak English very well, so they didn't want their kids to have the same problem. And they felt it was so severe, they didn't even want me to learn the language. They made up their minds that, you know, this is so bad, the way we're being treated because of our language. . . . They don't want us to hit the same obstacles.

Both his parents went to the University of California, Los Angeles, as exchange students during the late 1950s and worked at menial jobs to support their education. His parents immigrated when there was only a small Korean population in Los Angeles, so the incentive to maintain the native language was not as strong as it is today.

Many interviewees also saw how the intersection of class, race, and gender limited the opportunities available to their parents. Raised in Hawai'i, a half-Filipino and half-Japanese woman who held a variety of jobs in public relations for nonprofit organizations speaks of her mother's struggles:

> She was the one who found the first job when they moved to Hawai'i. She got a job scrubbing taro [root vegetable] in a taro factory and then eventually the employer hired my dad to deliver poi [food made from taro] around the island. Then most of her years in Hawai'i, she was a seamstress in a garment factory in different Hawaiian wear companies. For a few years, she taught Japanese language school. She always fell back on sewing and it was like that's what she did at home, always. Have you ever seen the movie *Dim Sum*? Whenever I see that woman sitting at the sewing machine, that is my mother. . . . And that's why I'll never sit at my mother's sewing machine and sew anything either, cause it's, like, oppressive.

A number of individuals recounted incidents of racism experienced by their parents, and these moments can have a searing and lasting impact on the identity process of a child. A Filipino who was born in the Philippines and moved with his family to San Diego in 1965 after his father was recruited in the U.S. Navy as an inventory clerk recalls a bitter memory when he was a teenager at a family picnic at Shelter Island in San Diego:

> They [my family] got into a little argument with a White couple and the lady started saying something like, "Well, you foreigners, you don't own this state, you're only here, we were born here, blah, blah, blah." And my dad pointed

out to her, "Listen lady, I've been in this state before you were born." And she said something like, "You can't talk to me that way because my father's a captain on the San Diego Police Department."

In recalling their parents' experiences, these interviewees were talking about the valuable lessons they learned about survival in what can be hostile terrain for non-Whites, particularly for immigrants. As second-generation or 1.5-generation Asians, they had an easier time adjusting, since they learned English and acquired other cultural skills rather quickly, yet they too have to contend with being racialized. They are sensitized to the impact of racism by their parents' ordeals.

Direct Racialization and the Shaping of Identity

Asian children learn at an early age in experiential ways that they are racially and ethnically distinct, even if they are monolingual (English), monocultural, living in White suburbia, and eating only "American" foods. One fourth-generation Japanese American vividly recalls how a racial taunt reinforced that he was "different":

> In the third grade, I remember being on the playground at Encanto Ele-mentary school and I remember the guy's name to this day—Gary English—this guy who was in my class, for whatever reason, had come up to me and kind of from the side pushed me like this and did one of these numbers, "Ching-Chong Chinaman." And we kind of got into a pushing thing and then he ended up coming behind me and grabbing me behind the neck and throw-ing me down on the ground, and that's when the teacher came and broke us up. But it was real clear to me that I was different. You don't have to have that reinforced by your parents.

His father, who served in the segregated Japanese American 442nd Infantry during World War II had received two purple hearts and a bronze star for his valor.

A number of individuals spoke of sobering personal encounters as adults that reminded them of their race. For example, a number of women recounted incidents in which they had negative experiences when dating White males. A mixed-race woman comments: "I guess I realized that people saw me as Asian, but I really didn't think of myself as Asian. It wasn't at the top of my consciousness at the time." But then

> I had an experience when I was in college where it was brought on very clearly that I was Asian or Japanese. I had a boyfriend whose mother refused to meet me when she found out I was Japanese. I don't know whether she

had lost a relative or something during the war. When she found out I was Japanese she refused to meet me and of course I thought my boyfriend was a jerk for not telling her off and everything. He basically wouldn't go against her wishes and I dropped him. . . . Just the concept of a Japanese and an American being together at all even though she knew I was half Japanese just apparently made her sick or something, so she never wanted to meet me. That really struck home.

An Asian American male who is half Japanese and half Chinese reports his reaction to several occurrences in which others took his race into account:

I've had comments that came up to me rather recently that I just think is hilarious. I was at a bar and this White gal comes up to me and she asked me if I date Caucasians. She wanted to go out with me. I was in another bar, like a week later, and a buddy of mine was there and he was talking to this girl and this girl comes up to me and we were talking for a while. She said, "I wanted to tell you something but I don't want you to take it the wrong way. I just wanted to tell you that I think you're really attractive." I said, "Why would I get upset at something like that?" She said, "Well, because most Asian guys I'm not attracted to, but you seem very different." And I just thought that was a very unusual comment. I don't know why, but I couldn't understand why she thought it would offend me. That really intrigued me, but those types of comments really make me very conscious of being Asian.

In contrast to the experiences discussed earlier, this male's encounters with being racialized seem more "positive." But the experiences reinforce one's racial identity regardless of how one might attempt to distance oneself from one's racial markings.

Reinforcement of Identities: The Role of Family and Community

Perceptions of being "Asian" are externally reinforced, but they are also internally emphasized by family and community. The major difference is that external prompts are most likely to be based on negative racial experiences whereas internal ones are more often positive reminders of their ethnic history and culture. Some interviewees told me their parents and other family members explicitly made them conscious of their ethnicity, while others remembered this as an implicit process they learned through observation. A Chinese woman born and raised in Mexico whose father was a leader in Chinese organizations in Tijuana, Mexico states: "My father, he beat it into our head that we are Chinese before anything else, so I've always been very conscious of being Chinese [Mexican] American." Each weekday growing up, she crossed the border into San Diego to attend a Catholic school and as an adult moved to San Diego. An individual born in Havana, Cuba, and raised in Chinatown, Los Angeles, explains that "there was a definite influence or upbringing to influence us to remember our backgrounds, like Chinese, our language, our cultures and the foods.... In Cuba, ... we spoke almost exclusively Chinese in the house and Spanish outside the house. When we moved to the United States, again it was Chinese in the home and English outside." His parents encouraged their children to maintain the native dialect for cultural purposes and because the parents spoke limited English.

Often parents had their children participate in language schools, festivals, and other social activities sponsored by ethnic religious centers, even though they themselves were not religious. A Korean raised in Hawai'i remembers that ethnicity "was pretty strongly identified then because we went to a Korean church, Korean Methodist church, and we had the youth group, which was a pretty good organization." A third-generation Japanese American raised in Los Angeles recalled going to an exclusively Japanese Christian church and belonging to the Boy Scouts run by the Japanese Buddhist church, where he also attended an annual bazaar. He mentions that although his parents spoke English at home, they passed on Japanese ethnic traditions to their children: "It was not done as directly. But it would be sort of, oh, some of the books [I had] when I was growing up or some of the things I would see would be Japanese Samurai movies. Again, going to these picnics or other sorts of events. I mean let's start with food. I would have rice with breakfast, lunch, and dinner. And it would be eggs with rice for breakfast. And I'm going to say with lunch and dinner."

A second-generation Chinese American man comments that his "folks were not very well educated and they were just working people," conveying that his parents who worked long hours at their market did not have time for daily lessons on traditions, but through example provided him with a sense of his ethnicity. "It's an everyday thing with all Chinese parents that they remind you constantly, 'You're Chinese and you have to watch every aspect of your life. Don't bring shame to the family.'... But you constantly know what your folks have to go through, working every day. And a lot of times, you're working beside them and you appreciate that."

Having tangible connections to homelands and familiarity with the struggles of his predecessors was important for a fourth-generation Chinese American who discusses his first trip to China as an adult:

> That was pretty cool. Going back to your roots, it kind of makes you humble.... I still have relatives there. I have a great-aunt, my grandfather's sister is still living in the same house that they all were born in, basically doing the same thing. They were rice farmers. Oh God, it was great. I mean, a lot of times some of my other relatives go, "It's so backward there." But I didn't really mind it.... Just to have the opportunity to kind of see where you're, I mean, actually the bed where my parents were born—my father was born and my uncles. Just sitting there, it's amazing. So that was a good experience and actually throughout the years we've had a lot of our cousins from the village actually come to the States. My grandfather sponsored them.

Like other Chinese of their generation, because of restrictive immigration laws, they maintained transnational families, and some sons would eventually join their fathers in America.

Yet it is also clear to most Asians born in this country, and some immigrants as well, that although they may not be accepted as bona fide Americans, they ironically are not accepted as full Asians either—regardless of whether they look "Asian" or the ethnic traditions they practice. In some cases, the criticism came from other Asians, as one woman's comment of another Chinese shows: "He lost his whole identity, he's an ABC [American-born Chinese] or really Chinese American and he's too Americanized to be Chinese, but yet he tries so hard to be Chinese." Ironically, in contrast, my observations indicated that younger Asian American activists perceived this man as too Chinese and too politically conservative, essentially representative of the old guard. When an individual whose grandfather was the first in his family to arrive in this country from China went to Hong Kong on a visit in 1965, he explains that "the funny thing is that it was the first time I would step foot in a country, in a city that was dominated by Asians. And I was really looking forward to it. 'My God, it's the first time I'll be in the majority.' The funny thing is, ... I still felt as American as when I left."

The Collegiate Years and Identity Transformation

For those able to attend college, these formative years seem to have transformed many of the individuals I interviewed. Given the age group of those I studied, a number came of age during the period of the civil rights movement and the power movements of the 1960s and early 1970s. These historical times seemed to shape the experiences of what I term *generational cohorts*. The sociopolitical events transformed minority communities, giving them the opportunity to rearticulate the positive attributes of their racial groups, and provided them with a sense of ethnic pride. Additionally, this political climate allowed the admission of Asian Americans into universities; many were U.S.-born Asians who shared similar experiences growing up, and college provided them with a setting to interact with one another. For some it led to a positive, personal affirmation of who they were as ethnics, while for others, it helped to foster the development of a political consciousness that led to political activism.

Although they may be college educated and are involved with activities in the community, a number of these activists have limited knowledge of the historical experiences of Asian American groups and are not well informed about race relations in the United States beyond their own lived experiences, conversations with others, and traces of information from the general media. At that time there were few Asian American Studies or Ethnic Studies courses available, so it was not until they were older that they learned more about the history of Asian Americans.

A third-generation Chinese American man raised in a primarily White community in Sacramento recalls his transformation at the University of California, Berkeley, between 1958 and 1962. He became active in Chinese American organizations, which were mainly socially oriented during the pre–Asian American movement stage, while attending college:

> Whereas a lot of Chinese did grow up in a Chinese area, I grew up in the suburbs. In fact, I didn't have very many Chinese friends until I started going to college. I started to really get more active in the Asian society, so to speak, and culture and understanding the history, basically at the college level.... Those four years were kind of eye-awakening for me. "God, I'm Asian and I've got a lot of Asian friend." So again having not grown up with Asians, it wasn't like I was looking for it, but it was a different thing for me.

His nephew, also raised in the suburbs of Sacramento, explains that he participated in the Chinese community center and the Chinese church and was part of a Chinese Boy Scout troop, but because there were few Chinese in the suburbs, most of his interactions were with non-Asians. He did not have extensive contact with other Asian Americans until he went to the University of California, Los Angeles, during the early

1970s: "And one of the reasons I chose that school in Southern California was because I knew that there were a zillion Asians. That was a good experience for me, not only going to school, but socially it was the first time in my life that I had so much interaction with Chinese and Asians." Both uncle and nephew were raised surrounded by Chinese American relatives, and their lives revolved around the family-run Chinese restaurants their families owned (which catered primarily to the White population). Yet growing up, they were more absorbed with mainstream cultural influences and not until they went to college did they make a conscious choice to readily identify with being Asian American.

A Japanese American woman talks about her racial experience being raised primarily in San Diego and then during college in the early 1970s:

> I didn't really become very aware of my ethnicity until I went to Berkeley. I was brought up pretty much in a White neighborhood, White school, very few Asians there, so I identified with Whites. I didn't think of myself as Asian at all.... The Berkeley experience was so different. I met so many Asians in Berkeley. All my roommates were Asian. I became totally immersed in being Asian. It was the first time in my life. It was just wonderful in a lot of ways. It really opened my eyes. I really didn't have Asian friends when I was growing up. I had one friend who was Japanese American and we didn't talk about being Japanese or anything. It wasn't something you talked about.

At Berkeley she discovered "that there were a lot of good things about being Asian." This transformation occurred at a very personal level. She did not take Ethnic Studies courses, nor was she politically active on or off campus with the Asian American movement at the time.

A Japanese American describes Edison Uno as a model for him, "someone who would sort of stand up and articulate a different challenge or different sort of perspective and Edison was the one involved with the riot things [and] was considered a community maverick."[1] Concerned about him being away from home for the first time when he went to medical school in San Francisco, his parents introduced him to Uno, asking him to "look after" their son. He fondly recalls the mentoring he received from Uno:

> And part of Edison's sort of thing was sort of inviting me over after being over in the dorms for two or three weeks. I'd never gone that long without rice!... [I remember him] calling and saying, "Hi, why don't you come over for dinner?" And I think I ate probably three or four bowls of rice. And he similarly kind of invited me to JACL [Japanese American Citizens League] events, community this and that. And San Francisco—that was between '68 and '72—so it's a very politically active, socially active sort of time. And part of that then was to hear and see a variety of people in Berkeley, in San Fran-

cisco, other areas around the Bay Area as a consequence of Edison. By the way, he himself was a very active social political individual of the Japanese American community. I found it just very, very stimulating.

He explained that as a result of these collegiate experiences, when he first came to San Diego in the mid-1970s, he participated in the JACL and later was introduced to pan-Asian organizations through the JACL president.

The Vietnam War was also a crucial political marker for many Asians in this country, including college students. Asian Americans, primarily Chinese, Japanese, and Filipinos, who were involved in the Asian American movement at the time saw the war not just as a genocidal destruction of the Vietnamese people. They spoke out against what they perceived to be a racist war that also denigrated the lives of Asians in the United States (Wei 1993: 37–41). This was a racial war in which the "enemy," depicted in images through print and television news, looked like them. While some Asian Americans actively protested the war in Vietnam, arguing that it was an imperialist and racist war, others were supportive of the antiwar movement but did not directly participate. An ethnically mixed Asian who graduated from the University of Hawai'i in 1968 at the height of the war explains:

> I was against the war and I was against my peers. Most of my peers at that time were either neutral or for it. . . . I was vocally opposed to it, vehemently opposed to it, and in Hawai'i, too. They were pro–military base and all that. . . . I would attend rallies, stuff like that. Never got arrested though. . . . Number one, it [the war] just didn't make sense. . . . How can there be a civil war when obviously the southern part doesn't seem to support its leadership and we're supporting the southern part, and it appeared that we were just propping them up. . . . It struck me that we had our own interest there and we had a puppet government there. I was thinking along this line and we were dividing a culture, a people, and that we had no business there. . . . It did have a lot to do with that [the fact that they were Asians], because I understood Asian culture, and it was Asian faces. And it was Caucasian faces that were saying, painting a scenario that didn't fit, culturally didn't fit, it didn't make sense.

To please his parents and to avoid being drafted and sent for combat duty in Vietnam, he volunteered for the U.S. Air Force as a meteorologist:

> But that didn't go too well because of my personal views against the war. I ultimately ended up an objector even in the service. I joined the radical student group, which got these newspapers out in the military bases. . . . They [the military] . . . knew I was involved but they could never prove it. So finally one day, I remember my commander called me in. "Are you against the war?"

I said to him, "Yes." "Are you actively doing things on the base to oppose the war?" I told him "Yes." . . . So they kicked me out of the division, Air Services Division, and I ended up being placed in the shit list with all of the derelicts and rejects and everything from drug pusher to those being ready to be discharged.

For several months, he was assigned to pick up trash on the base and then instead of being discharged, much to his surprise, for the rest of his four-year term was reassigned as an assistant to the inspector general (who he believes was sympathetic to his political views on the war).

For one woman attending college during that time, there was a connection between the dehumanization of Asians during World War II, which led to the justification for dropping the atomic bomb on Japanese civilians, and the massacre of Vietnamese peasants:

At that point, I was starting to feel a little more identity with being Japanese, not even Japanese, it was sort of Asian in a general sense. I still resisted being Japanese because there were so many negative stereotypes of the Japanese— the internment, being defeated, being bombed, the only group ever to be bombed by the atomic bomb. To this day I feel it's a very strange feeling to know that people hated the Japanese so much. . . . There's something that really hurts about feeling that we were being treated as dogs or something, I don't know, "Jap dogs." And that carried over. It's interesting though that during the Vietnam War, for instance, it always jolted me when people called them "gooks." Even though I wasn't terrifically conscious of being Asian in college, that was one thing that sort of hit home for me. . . . It seems it makes it easier to kill people if you objectify them that way and call them these horrible names or that kind of thing, and so I think that's partly why I became antiwar at that point because I thought these people, they are treating them like they're not even human. . . . I could feel that connection because I felt that we all had a stake in it somehow, being Asian. So though even here, being Japanese and feeling that Japanese are no good, now all Asians are no good and that all Asians are "Other," not Americans, and therefore easy to kill, easier to fight and blow to pieces, whatever. So I think that made me more conscious and so I started to feel more Asian through that process.[2]

Although she did attend some antiwar rallies during college, she was not an active antiwar participant, partly because she was afraid of losing her academic scholarship.

For these individuals, college became a pivotal part of their transformation as Asian Americans, instilling in them a sense of pride in their ethnicity. As one woman explains: "I did get involved with the minority affairs office in college and I met some pretty radical Filipino friends of mine who kind of heightened my awareness of my being Filipino. I mean, we produced this musical about the migration of the Filipinos to

Seattle and how they kind of went through Hawai'i first." During these formative collegiate years, personal transformation helped many individuals to develop a political consciousness about racial discrimination, although only some were involved in public protest. However, many from this generational cohort are still uncomfortable using direct confrontational strategies and may be perceived by radicals as apolitical or politically conservative. These individuals prefer to mobilize using accommodationist strategies to bring about social change; in some cases, these seemingly more conventional tactics can be sustained longer and can garner the support of a more broad-based population.

The Process of "Minoritization"

Asians who originally came from places in the United States and in Asia where they were the majority experienced the *process of minoritization*, which means recognizing that they are not the dominant racial group in their new setting. Their identities are shaped by personal social interactions. For two individuals of mixed Asian ancestry raised in Hawai'i, venturing off to the mainland for college not only involved adjusting to a new environment (one in Berkeley and one in Seattle), but also involved recognizing for the first time what it felt like to be a "racial minority":

> And there and then I noticed the Caucasian community. For the first time in my life I was the minority. . . . But I was profoundly affected by the fact that I was a minority. It just never occurred to me. I mean, I always knew in the islands [that Asians were the minority on the mainland], but experiencing it emotionally made a big difference.

> That was like going through adolescence all over again in my freshman year; the awkwardness of adjusting and being in a different environment. And that was the first time I experienced being a minority. . . . I have just never been in a predominantly White society until then. And I noticed that we were dramatically different from the Asians who were born and raised on the mainland because from day one they accepted the fact that they were also minorities. I knew that I didn't have to think that way.

The former adds: "I grew up in a multiethnic culture where differences were accepted, differences were tolerated, differences were like a tree and the leaves, it was just there." Raised in ethnically mixed neighborhoods in Hawai'i, they were used to Asians being the majority and part of mainstream life, although they noticed the ethnic and class tensions that existed among native Hawaiians, Filipinos, Koreans, and Japanese. Those raised on the mainland, even if they grew up in insular Asian

American communities, realize their minority status as children and may be affected by the constraints this label imposes upon them.

For immigrants coming here from Asian countries, being a racial minority is also a novel concept; however, being socialized in an environment as part of the majority seems to have a positive impact. An ethnic Chinese woman who lived in the Philippines told me during an informal discussion that being raised as part of the majority population at an early age gave her a sense of self-esteem in her racialized identity. This confidence helped her adjust after moving to Canada as a teenager and interacting primarily with Whites:

> I'm comfortable working with the Anglo [population]. I guess again through my background. From thirteen on, when I was in Vancouver, I've always dealt with Anglos. At that point, I really don't feel like a minority even though I am a minority. That I can't change. But inside me, my self-confidence, I don't feel I am. Or maybe it's information that I blocked out. Because I feel that people react on how you perceive yourself. And so I never perceive myself any less than they are.

Although she realized that she was part of the minority group in terms of numbers, she refused to think that this imposed limitations on her. Her father was an international businessman, so her family's class status also augmented her sense of self-worth. All these factors contributed to her ability to deal with non-Asians with ease and were an asset for her as an accountant, a profession in San Diego in which "outsiders" are disadvantaged and in which there are few minorities and few women.

Repeated incidents of outsiders pointing out that one is "Asian" can make an individual aware of the racial category. As newcomers interact with non-Asians and, in varying degrees, with segments of the Asian American group, their identities are reconfigured. As a Singaporean who considered herself an international student while at the University of Southern California (USC) explains: "That was when I was aware . . . that I am an Asian and being classified and termed as one. Prior to that I always just thought of myself as a foreigner from Singapore. . . . Nowadays, instead of going around saying, 'I'm Singaporean,' I do say, 'I'm Asian.'" She also states: "I was definitely surprised by the racial tension and I think through my years at USC, I got a deeper understanding about the discrimination that existed between races and within the races." She compared the clashes of her African international student friends with African Americans to her experiences as an Asian international student with Asian Americans. Although she experienced misunderstandings with other Asian Americans, her marriage to a Chinese American and her involvement with Asian American affairs made her conscious of the racialization that occurs, regardless of one's self-perception.

Differentially Situated Immigrants

New immigrants challenge the general understanding of identities as discretely formed entities within nation-states. With the global capitalist system and cultural transmissions facilitated by technological advancements, countries are more interconnected (Basch, Schiller, and Blanc 1995; Hu-DeHart 1999; Rouse 1991; Wallerstein 1974). Although much is made of transnationalism, transmigration, and diaspora marking the experiences of contemporary immigrants, these concepts have always been integral to Asian immigrant history. Asians have migrated within the Asian continent and beyond to Africa, Europe, and the Americas. In addition, migration patterns are more complicated; for example, one Chinese activist immigrated from Peru to the United States to attend high school and college, identifies as Chinese Peruvian American, and is trilingual. In Asia, having foreigners and their traditions entering their territorial and social spaces, forcibly in many cases, has influenced Asian identities. Thus the formation of Asian cultural identities has not been the result of isolated or immutable processes; it has involved constant interaction and reformulation across geographic borders.

The "uprooted" immigrant model is no longer appropriate, given global political, economic, and cultural interconnections. Unlike their earlier counterparts, contemporary Asian immigrants are coming not only from rural regions, but also from cosmopolitan areas, where they are familiar with Western culture before their arrival in this country. An individual who came from Hong Kong and was educated in a British Christian school discusses her experience: "I have an idea of what the United States is like because we were so cultivated in [the] American way of life through the music. . . . Actually, I was more Westernized when I was at home. I knew all the songs. . . . It's something about going to English school. . . . The kids, you know, they want to act Americanized." These Asians have a common cultural currency—exposure to Westernized modernity, along with fluency in the English language, often from being educated in colonial or postcolonial educational systems—which enables them to adapt with greater ease. A male counterpart concurs. "It's not foreign to me, English and American culture. We see cowboy movies. In the sixties a lot of the programs on television in

Hong Kong are American. They dub it in Chinese and sometimes they don't. So there's a direct link. So a lot of the people who grew up in Hong Kong, we have no problem adjusting."

I learned the difficulties of deciphering the generational classifications (first, 1.5, second, third, etc.) of Asian Americans I interviewed, since many had complicated stories from both sides of their family about their ancestral connections to America. Outsiders may perceive these individuals as newcomers, since they essentially came to the United States as immigrants, yet a number were preceded by relatives. A Singaporean woman was born in Malaysia and as a child immigrated to Singapore with her family. Her paternal grandmother was born in San Francisco during the Gold Rush but returned to China and then, after marrying, moved to Malaysia. Her granddaughter, who came to America for college, is the only one in her immediate family "to return" to America and referred to her immigration to the United States as coming "full circle." Another individual was born in China; because of the political turmoil, his parents sent him to Hong Kong as a young boy to live with his grandmother. His great-grandfather farmed in the Sacramento area of California but returned to China, and his grandfather worked in the grocery business in California, where he remained. His grandfather and uncle, who resided in the United States, supported him financially while he lived in Hong Kong and later helped him adjust when he went to college at the University of Nevada, Las Vegas.

Although the "Asian" concept is most often regarded as unique to the United States, further investigation shows that this is hardly the case. The depictions of interactions between Asian countries focus on the conflicts between Asian groups, such as the colonization of Korea and the Philippines by Japan, the invasion of China by Japan, and the long-standing feud between China and Vietnam. In addition to memories of such antagonism that Asians bring with them as immigrants, these experiences also exposed them to other cultures and groups. Their previous contact with other Asian groups and cultures can be useful for coalition building, showing that the "Asian" concept does not start anew in this country. The experience in Singapore of the Singaporean woman mentioned in the previous section showed her the possibilities of collaborating with other Asian ethnicities. She elaborates on why she felt that "Singapore is actually more of a melting pot, I think, than even California or the States":

Singapore would not be as successful as it is today if the island wasn't united. If the people weren't united, if we have racial tensions the way Malaysia has,

Malaysia's our neighboring country . . . we would not have been able to survive. . . Singapore has no natural resources. None. We do not have rubber trees, we do not have palm trees, we do not have agriculture. . . The only resource that Singapore has is people. And it was then very important that we all be united as one and because of that Singapore is where it is today.

She goes on to explain that although the prime minister has always been Chinese, Singapore has had an Indian, a Eurasian (mixed-race European and Asian), and a Chinese president along with Chinese, Indian, and Malaysian cabinet ministers. The migration of individuals within the Asian continent and the colonization of Asian territories by other Asian groups have left an indelible impact on each country. There has been to some extent a blending of traditions, in some cases forcibly imposed, in cultural practices, foods, religious customs, and languages among Asian peoples.

Distancing and Subversion: Strategies of Survival

When the racial dominant model is Black or White, it is especially difficult for Asian Americans to negotiate a distinct identity. This model dictates that Asian Americans need to emulate either the "majority = White" or the "minority = Black" group, when they fit neither of these categories neatly (Okihiro 2001, 1994). It also is particularly difficult to be proud of a heritage that is ignored in the educational system and in the public discourse. Incidents of racial discrimination in which individuals are ridiculed or denigrated because of their ethnic or racial identity can have drastic effects. These incidents can lead one to reject one's ethnic identity, and in some cases, attempt to alter it as much as possible. An individual raised on the sugar plantations in Hawai'i finally was able to discuss with her father, a second-generation Filipino American, when he was in his late seventies the denial of his ethnicity: "My dad, I always thought that he wasn't proud of his background, because he never spoke [Tagalog] at home. We never really had Filipino food in the house. It wasn't until a couple of years ago that we talked about it, being Filipino, and I think it shamed him."

Others tell of rejecting their ethnicity and attempting to be more "American." For instance, a woman discusses her desire to be accepted by her elementary school classmates:

The thing that really stands out is that when I remember clearly being in Berkeley and playing a game of red rover, red rover, and hearing kids' names being called out, but never Mariko, which is the name I was born with. Never was I called for these games. I think that's part of the reason I changed my name to Sally. . . . I identify with the name Sally partly because of the Dick and Jane books where they have the little girl named Sally. Such an all-American name, a little blond girl. I wanted to be accepted so much, so I picked Sally.

It was only later in life that she was able to reconcile her Asian heritage, and when given the choice to select a category, she chose Japanese or Asian.

Before finally accepting their ethnic backgrounds, several individuals tried to pass as Hawaiian, which they thought was more highly regarded or exotic than Asian ancestry. An individual whose mother was a Japanese national and whose father was a second-generation Filipino describes his feelings: "You know, I think there was a lot of self-hate. There was a lot of anti-Asian feeling within myself growing up because we were different. I mean, we were called 'Jap,' we were called 'Chink.'. . . But back then it was like, don't even tell anybody that we're part Filipino or Japanese. Say we're Hawaiian." Regrettably, he also recalls how he rejected cultural aspects of his identity:

My mother was a member of the JACL and she used to attend the functions and she used to like to have to drag us to these functions. And she wanted us to go to Japanese school and it was like, "No way, Mom!" You know, why do we have to learn Japanese? You know, we could, like, kill ourselves now, it's like, we should have listened to Mother. No, we would have been kicking and screaming the whole way.

The following episode, in which a mother tells of her daughter's experience, illustrates how negative encounters can shape the formation of an ethnic identity:

My daughter was ashamed to be Filipino because my daughter encountered racial prejudice. She was at Community High School and there was a son of a German doctor who wanted to take her out in his Beemer [BMW car] for prom night and she was so broken-hearted and that's when she started acting out. The old man said, "No, you can't take her to the prom. She's fresh off the boat." And my daughter said, "Why, Mom, why?" . . . She was so upset. She says, "I'm not Vietnamese." I said, "It has nothing to do with being Vietnamese." She said, "I don't want to be Filipino either because Filipinos eat dogs." . . . She says, "I am an American." I said, "Yes you are, but you see, you look different." So she passed herself as Hawaiian. And it's only now that she's proud again that she's Filipino.

Gender and ethnic identities overlap, revealing the complexity of ways in which Asian American women negotiate their identities. As one woman conveys:

When I was growing up, I thought of myself as being White and I resisted the notion that I had black hair. I said it was dark brown because of the stereotype. In some ways I wanted to say I had black hair because there were some positive aspects of that, of being beautiful, that Oriental look and that kind of thing. On the other hand it sort of stereotypes you, and I didn't want to be this Susie Wong–type character, so that everybody would think I was a prostitute or anything. You had to walk that fine line.[3]

Another woman speaks of her feelings about some of the gendered cultural traditions she simply cannot accept:

I think the reason I rejected speaking Japanese is not only do you have to learn to speak it, you have to take on the demeanor of a Japanese woman and I fight that. . . . I just talked about this recently with another friend of mine who is from Japan. We have a mutual friend who dances in the Oban festival every summer and I love to go and watch, but I have never to this day gone and danced also. And this other friend of mine said that it's this whole costume you put on, the kimono [dress] and the obi [sash]. It's so binding. You have to walk, you know, inching your way. And you have to take on the [submissive] demeanor and it's too oppressive for her to do. It's the same feeling I have. In fact, I can't do it.

Resisting racist and sexist constructions, these women tried to distance themselves from the negative images and define their own identities as Asian American women.

In some instances, Asian Americans rejected their ethnicity in order to survive in the mainstream world. An individual of mixed Asian ancestry presents the following narrative of his experience in a city with few other Asian Americans at the time:

When I got here [San Diego] in 1977, I didn't know anybody and there was hardly any Asian presence that I knew of. I worked for a [small] firm . . . for a year and then I switched to a large firm. . . . So in that world, in the corporate world, there were very few Asian faces. Very few. It's a very Caucasian world. And to me, the rest of San Diego was like that and so, you know, I think Asians are very adaptive. We jump into or through hoops and we do it well and we concentrate and we do it to such a point that we forget who we are—that we're Asian. We almost become Caucasian ourselves and we don't know it until we look in the mirror. To assimilate and to adapt and to become effective, we have to do that. But we don't do that consciously, I think we just do it as a matter of survival. . . . I was thinking as a Caucasian. I was thinking Anglo. I was wrapped up in that world. . . . So I was a banana [Yellow outside, White inside] at that time.

He had lived in Hawai'i and Berkeley previously, two sites with a substantial number of Asians. In moving to San Diego and working in a profession with few minorities then, he was forced to make adjustments to adapt.

These individuals attribute these changes partly to the Asian American movement, which created a sense of ethnic pride, and to an increase in the Asian American population, which substantiated their presence. The stories of survival in this section convey the transitions that occurred for individual Asian Americans, as well as for Asian Americans as a group, and eventually led to their political activism. They worked to counteract the negative associations of "difference" with inferiority, replacing them with celebratory expressions of cultural pride, self-respect, and self-love. These strategies of subverting dominant racial constructions continue to be instrumental for peoples of color who live in a society in which "whiteness" is treated as normative and superior.

Levels of Contact and Comfort

The kinds of groups Asian Americans feel more comfortable around determine their close associates as well as their identity. There is not a consensus about this among Asian Americans; rather the racial backgrounds of these associates, Asian and non-Asian, varied according to where they lived, how they were socialized, and what conscious choices they made. Many spoke about having personal interactions with Asians from other subgroups, even before participating in Asian American organizations. Those who interacted with non-Asians at a younger age felt at ease with them later in life as well.

A number of individuals revealed having close relationships with Asians from other ethnic groups. A woman raised in Hawai'i states that "all through childhood and high school, I had Japanese, Chinese, Filipino, Hawaiian friends." A Chinese immigrant from Hong Kong states that while in college in Nevada, "I had a real good friend who's Korean. During the Korean War, he was an orphan and was adopted by an American family. He helped me a lot in English and we were in the same civil engineering classes." A Japanese American was part of a car pool from his neighborhood in South Central Los Angeles to the University of California, Los Angeles, with two other Japanese Americans and one Chinese American. A Korean American who grew up in West Los Angeles had a number of close Japanese American friends and in San Diego spent a lot of time with his Filipino American girlfriend and her family. Asked if he had any Asian American role models growing up, this Korean American remarked he wanted to be like Bruce Lee, a Chinese American, and he admired a Japanese actor who starred primarily in samurai movies. In contrast to his parents, who felt more comfortable speaking Korean and socializing with other Korean Americans, he interacted with individuals from a variety of Asian American groups. Although these interethnic contacts were problematic, at times, for their parents, they posed no personal conflicts for these individuals and were not seen as atypical events in their lives.

Another woman whose parents provided her with a strong sense of ethnicity and who was active in the Chinese American community acknowledges:

> I'm one of those who tends to stay with Asians and minorities. I'm more comfortable in that. I don't know if I feel intimidation being with the nonethnic, nonminority groups, but I know that I feel more comfortable with other minorities versus when I'm with an all-White crowd. I just don't feel as comfortable.... It may be just that I'm over self-conscious about it because I feel that I'm a minority.... Most of my friends are either Asians or other minorities. I don't have that many Caucasian friends.... Probably it has to do with who I am and being so ethnically minded that I tend to probably set myself apart. My consciousness is always that I'm Asian or that I am Chinese.

Although she felt comfortable around other Asian Americans, she was also quite cognizant of the distinctions between herself and individuals from other Asian ethnic groups.

This Chinese American woman met her Korean American husband while they were both students at California State University, Long Beach, and she remembers how difficult it was for their family members to accept their relationship:

> My husband and I, we dated for almost ten years before we got married, and the main reason was because . . . my father-in-law had the hardest time having a Chinese daughter-in-law.... But when I tell non-Asians that the reason we dated so long was because of the Korean-Chinese experience, most people say, "What's the big deal, you both look the same." And we hear that over and over. Well maybe Asians have the same look, but there are very big differences and it is a totally different culture even though we're both from the same region.

Her father disapproved of her relationship with a Korean American as well. Although in an interethnic marriage, she maintains a strong Chinese identity and her husband maintains a strong Korean identity, often traveling to Korea to visit his parents and for business. She participates in Chinese American organizations and in pan-Asian ones too, but her husband does not. Because her Chinese family members live with her and help to raise her daughters, she is able to pass along Chinese traditions to them, but she expressed concern that her children will not have a strong sense of their Korean identity.

A Chinese American man who grew up in Chinatown explains that through high school sports programs he had positive contact with other racial groups, which led to his openness to them later in life:

> Growing up, because of the diversity and my neighborhood, growing up with Blacks and Mexicans and even Caucasians later on in high school, and I think I attribute a lot to, quite frankly, to a lot of my activeness in sports because when you played sports, you didn't know any colors. You functioned as a team and you learned to work together and that helped me through a lot of the hard times growing up in an ethnic neighborhood where there was a lot of potential for ethnic separation. Whenever there were the gang fights, for example, when you had the Blacks against the Mexicans or the Mexicans against the, you know, the Asian or Chinese gangs, or whatever, and I would never be singled out as being Chinese because I knew all of them. I played sports with all of them. And I never felt that. In fact, if any threat, I felt, when I was in L.A., came from the Chinese—let's say, undesirables, the gangs and what have you.

While a college student in San Diego, he met and married a Caucasian woman. His coworkers are primarily White. He had minimal contact with the Chinese or Asian American community in San Diego until his involvement with pan-Asian organizations.

Another individual who was provided with a solid ethnic foundation by his family but was raised in a White suburb describes his level of comfort:

> I've always managed to get along, being accepted by anybody whether you're Chinese, Japanese, White, Black. I really don't think about it in my everyday life. . . . I don't know if that makes me a banana [Yellow outside, White inside]. The one thing that I've always tried to do is that I'm always pretty close to my ethnic ties, as far as community and friends and things like that. But on the other hand, I think I work pretty well with the White community.

His family owned restaurants that catered to a non-Asian clientele, one of which he ran in San Diego, so he felt at ease surrounded by non-Asians, but he was also very active in Asian American organizations.

An individual of Japanese and Chinese ancestry discusses his influences during his formative years on a U.S. military base in Okinawa, Japan:

> I never saw racial lines, growing up. I just noticed that some people looked different but I never classified anyone as being less than anyone else. That was just the environment that I grew up in. On a military base the only caste system that I saw existing was those based on your father's rank. You're either an officer's kid or you're not. And the officers' kids tended to hang out with each other and they tended to think that they were a little bit better than the

enlisted officers' kids, but even that was really vague. I mean, that was the only differentiation I saw. Blacks played with the Whites, played with Asians. I never saw those racial lines. But it was in an environment where everyone was forced to get along, you know, in the military system, all colors work together.

His father, a Chinese national, worked as an interpreter for the U.S. government and was stationed in Tokyo, where he met his Japanese wife. Interestingly enough, his mother, who was full Japanese, was raised by a White Canadian stepfather in Japan. His understandings of race relations are based on his mixed ethnic ancestry, along with being raised around an international community employed by the U.S. government and living under the colonizing influence of the U.S. military base in Asia.

Some individuals were exposed to the experiences of other racial groups in college courses, providing them with an opportunity to learn about the groups they knew little about and with whom they may have minimal contact. When I went to interview a first-generation Vietnamese American (a community leader who participated in pan-Asian affairs) in the office of his electronics company, I noticed a bookshelf of social science books. I recognized a number of classic titles on race relations in the United States and on the African American experience. During the interview I discovered he had acquired these books from his college courses and he spoke of them favorably, recounting how much he had learned about America's treatment of minorities at courses he had taken at San Diego State University over a ten-year period. He still feels uncomfortable around non-Vietnamese, partly because of his limited English-language ability, but unlike many of his compatriots, he has some appreciation of the experiences of other groups.

A Japanese American woman recalls how her understanding of the conditions of Asian Americans and other racial groups came from law school:

> We were forced to read a lot about American history through legal cases and it teaches you a lot about how really horrible this country has been to minorities. I mean just atrocious! We were just treated as bad as you can imagine. It's all there, so you learn a lot more and you become a lot more conscious about being a minority. Even if it hasn't impacted you directly, it has impacted your family, people you know, and so you can empathize with that. It also helps you to empathize with other minority groups, because you can see that if you feel that way about your own feelings and your own family and friends, then imagine what it's like for those who have suffered greater discrimination and for a greater period of time. That's how I have made my peace with

Blacks. Because for the longest time I had a lot of prejudices. I had pretty much adopted the White attitudes towards Black people and always thought of them as not quite good, not really deserving much attention or trying to distance myself from them. . . . [Now] I really appreciate what they had to go through and what they had to fight against for so long.

Clearly, personal contact during the formative years affects Asian Americans' perceptions of ethnic and racial groups, and also their level of comfort interacting with them. However, others made conscious choices later in life that gave them opportunities to interact with or learn about those of differing ethnic and racial backgrounds, making them more open to building relations with other people from varying ethnic and racial backgrounds.

Mixed Ethnic/Racial Asian Identities and Experiences

Individuals who are of mixed Asian ancestry or Asian mixed with other racial groups have more complicated racial identity issues to negotiate. Their stories indicate that "Asian Americanness" is not easily quantifiable merely by one's biology and shows how the role of cultural environment impacts identity work. The Asian American population has intermixed with one another and mixed with other racial groups globally and nationally for centuries; however, the literature on this issue is only beginning to emerge (Houston and Williams 1997; Leonard 1992; Williams-Léon and Nakashima 2001).

A number of multiethnic Asian Americans discussed how they negotiate the cultural influences of both sides of their families. As one individual raised in Hawai'i explains:

People always ask me who do I relate to more, the Filipino side or the Japanese? I think while I was growing up, it was the Japanese because my mother was from Japan and that's mostly what she spoke at home. . . . It was pretty much the dominant culture in my household. . . . I have an aunt and uncle that played a significant role in my upbringing. They were like my grandparents that I never had. And they were on my dad's side, very Filipino. I'd hear them speak, I guess it was Tagalog, and so I grew up with that cooking and everything too, so I'm comfortable in that culture as well.

Yet she is also sensitive to the prejudice she experiences as a multiethnic Asian American:

I remember there were times when running across Japanese nationals who had a problem with me being half. That really was a sobering experience for me, experiencing prejudice from my own people. But I never experienced it from Filipinos when they find out I'm half Japanese and that's pretty interesting.... You know, I look very Japanese, so people tend to forget I'm Filipino. In both incidences [of discrimination], they were both Chinese. I know they are very anti-Filipino and they would say these remarks about Filipinos. And it hurts when you hear this from another Asian. There are still some negative perceptions of Filipinos.

Those of multiracial backgrounds have had to negotiate their identities with both Asians and non-Asians. A Filipina who is of mixed Filipino and Spanish ancestry discusses how Asians and non-Asians alike have a difficult time identifying her:

I'm different because nobody can tell what I am. They cannot tell whether I am Filipino. They always mistakened me in New York as a Puerto Rican. Here in San Diego, they think I'm South American or Mexican. I used to be riding in the subways and Filipinos would talk about me. And I used to have fun when the subway doors open and we would get to the stop and I would say a Filipino word to them to let them know that I understood what they were talking about, you know. I have an advantage because I can speak Filipino, four dialects, and I can speak Spanish.

Even before she came to the United States, her elite class background exposed her to Filipino, Spanish, and U.S. cultures. Her interactions with the Filipino American community have been limited, and for the most part, she has participated in pan-Asian causes.

Another woman was born to an unmarried Japanese woman and a European American soldier (who does not know of his daughter's birth) and lived with her Japanese aunt until she went to live with her mother and her new European American husband:

When I was younger, I just felt that other Japanese would not accept me because I was half.... I just knew that it wasn't acceptable in Japan.... I also say this from the American perspective, since I wasn't all White, I wasn't accepted either, although less so with Whites than with other Asians probably. I haven't felt directly discriminated by other Asians recently. Sometimes it does come up. When I was working for a law firm, they weren't sure if they should include me as an Asian or not because I'm exactly fifty-fifty. I always put down Japanese, but it's something I'll always grapple with all my life—what am I, who am I?

Although she admitted an initial hesitation at participating because she was racially mixed, she has served as an officer in both Japanese and Asian American organizations. She wonders how her three children, who are one-quarter Japanese, will identify themselves once they are of age.

The hybridity of the Asian American population challenges the essentialist notions of ethnicity and race (Houston and Williams 1997). Identification is not directly connected to physical appearance, but rather to how one is socialized, since one can "look" more Japanese than Filipino but feel more connected to being Filipino, or "appear" more White than Japanese but identify as Japanese. From my observations, it seems that the pan-Asian organizational setting, with its already eclectic mixture of individuals, is more inviting for multiethnic and multiracial Asians, in which a number held prominent positions, than are single-ethnic organizations.

Organizational Participation and the Formation of Identities

Originally, I theorized that participants of pan-Asian organizations had a strong sense of ethnic or racial identity, yet I discovered through my fieldwork that this identity was not at the forefront of their consciousness nor was it the driving force that led to their participation. Joining an organization was not a deliberate or self-conscious act but happened by chance or accident. For example, when asked why they came to an organizational meeting or event, some individuals explained that a friend dragged them to a meeting. In other cases, unattached individuals admitted they came hoping to meet other single people and were surprised to find themselves intrigued by the dynamics of an organization and its mobilization efforts. Participating in pan-Asian organizations allows individuals and groups who are lumped together politically, but who in the past had little personal contact, to interact with one another—in many instances for the first time. The formation of these organizations led to face-to-face encounters and to the shaping of identities that have restructured the ways in which individuals think of themselves and their society—contributing to a process of *identity resocialization*.

How strongly an individual identifies as an ethnic is not an accurate predictor of whether or not that individual will actively engage in single-ethnic or pan-Asian organizations. There are individuals who have a weak ethnic attachment yet are active in organizational activities, whereas others who identify quite strongly with their ethnic group do not participate in ethnic organizations. Thus, the assumption that the greater the ethnic affiliation, the greater the ethnic participation is faulty. While unified action and organization can create pan-Asian consciousness (Espiritu 1992), there are variances in the level of consciousness and self-identification among participants. However, what can be tracked are the discernible patterns that many activists adopt in their organizational involvement: single-ethnic to single-ethnic; single-ethnic to pan-Asian; pan-Asian to single-ethnic; and pan-Asian to pan-Asian.

Many recounted scenarios in which their connection with an individual or organization led to further contacts and involvement. A fourth-generation Japanese American comments when asked if he was involved with ethnic organizations previously: "No, I didn't have any Asian friends in college. When I came to San Diego, I joined the church [Japanese Oceanview Church of Christ] and this was my first immersion in the Asian community per se." Through this participation, they developed a stronger sense of their ethnic identities. A Japanese woman who grew up primarily in all-White communities in California made a conscious decision as an adult to be more involved with the Japanese community, commenting: "I guess I want to connect more to my being Japanese. I feel having that certain sense of community is important to me, because I didn't have it while I was growing up."

An individual whose father was a second-generation Filipino American who met his Japanese mother while stationed in Japan during the Korean War reports a similar experience. In adulthood when he began working for a Filipino American community newspaper and as the executive director for a local Filipino umbrella organization (along with volunteering for the Filipino Democrats), he began identifying with being Filipino. He explains: "I'm finding that out now [what it means to be Filipino], you know, because of my involvement in the community." He further comments on how organizational participation facilitated his self-image:

> There was no foundation there. Nothing in education, nothing in family really helped foster a self-love of being Asian. I think I first started loving myself as an Asian when I founded the group, the gay and lesbian Asian Pacifics. And there was a young Filipino kid, we were out dancing and one of the bars is known for having Asians there. And he was in the group and he just gave me this real big smile and he goes, "Look, there are so many Asians here and we're all so beautiful," and that was when it hit me. Yeah, we're Asian Pacifics, we may not meet the standards of beauty that Wall Street puts out for us but, you know, we are a beautiful people.

Interaction with other Asian Americans in a pan-Asian organization provided a context for them to develop a pan-Asian consciousness. A Singaporean spoke of her involvement in an Asian-based organization, Leadership Education for Asian Pacifics (LEAP) in Los Angeles, which gave her the opportunity to work with other Asian Americans (many of whom were of Japanese ancestry) and made her more aware of her Asian identity. In addition to her involvement with pan-Asian organizations, she was active with the ethnic Chinese Vietnamese language school, the Laotian Scholarship Fund, and the Korean American Professional Association. One multiethnic male became more conscious of his identity after his involvement with Asian American organizations:

> I really didn't identify myself with the Asian community until about four or five years ago, just because I was immersed very much in the American community. . . . [Previously] I've thought of myself more as being American, you know, I just happen to have Asian features. But today I identify myself as being more Asian, and it's probably because I'm more involved with the Asian community [and organizations]. . . . So, my own personal consciousness is higher.

It is important to note that Asian Americans active in pan-Asian affairs were raised with single-ethnic cultures, rather than a conglomerate "Asian" culture. Asian Americans recognize there are significant differences among their ethnic practices but are cognizant of how these practices differ from what are considered mainstream American cultural practices. Along with recognizing that they share a common history (Lowe 1996), there is also a sharing of "difference"—of parents who speak foreign tongues, of eating treasured delicacies, and of engaging in "strange" rituals—all avenues for commonalties. The individualized emotions of both embarrassment and pride of "difference" become shared memories among Asian Americans, encouraging them to embrace and even celebrate their "differences."

The Maintenance of Single-Ethnic and Pan-Asian Identities

Asian American individuals in general, and those who participate in pan-Asian organizations, can differ in their viewpoints about ethnic affiliation. There are ethnics who do not support pan-Asian efforts, since they believe such involvement means forsaking the customs and cultures of their distinctive ethnic group. In other words, they consider supporting the pan-Asian model an assimilationist orientation that is counterproductive to maintaining ethnic cultural practices. This criticism against pan-Asian activists is not new. What is interesting, however, is that it is directed not only at the U.S.-born population, but also at the foreign-born population who are involved in pan-Asian affairs. Pan-Asian activists contend that pan-Asian identity does not supersede a single-ethnic identity but augments it. In working for pan-Asian causes, they argue they are also working to preserve single-ethnic Asian cultures and histories. Individuals may have multiple ethnic identities, but these identities are salient according to constantly shifting circumstances.

Although it is assumed by some that when Asian Americans participate in a pan-Asian organization, they forfeit their own single-ethnic identities, this is not necessarily the case. As an individual from Hong Kong involved with multiple pan-Asian organizations explains: "I tell people I'm Chinese. It's just that it's a more specific identification. . . . We're perceived as Asian American. But I don't tell people that I'm Asian. They know you're Asian." In contrast, an ethnic Chinese woman from Vietnam, active in pan-Asian activism, made the following comments: "Sometime in different contexts, I would say I'm Asian American. When I want to be more specific, I would say I'm Chinese American. . . . Some of my best friends are Japanese and Korean, and I consider us Asian first and then she's Japanese, she's Korean." Although they may have different approaches to identifying themselves, they both work with the assumption that they have a single-ethnic as well as an Asian American identity.

Although Asian Americans are involved in pan-Asian organizations, for many, their personal affiliation is rooted in single-ethnic terms, and they continue to live their lives within the boundaries of single-ethnic communities. An individual born in Taiwan and raised in Alaska was active in pan-Asian organizations but also in single-ethnic activities. He strongly identified with his own ethnic group: "I guess I have to confess I'm kind of discriminatory because I classify myself not as Chinese American, but as Taiwanese American. . . . That's not in any way saying that I'm against Chinese or people from Hong Kong, but I identify myself as Taiwanese. I want my heritage as a Taiwanese." Many of these individuals are quite active in their own ethnic organization as well as in pan-Asian ones. A typical example is a Chinese American restauranteur who was chair of the Chinese Social Service Center, chair of the annual dinner committee for the Union of Pan Asian Communities, and also a member of the Chinese/Asian Historic Thematic District. Some activists have little contact with other ethnics in their daily lives, since they do not live in an ethnic enclave or work with other ethnics. For them, organizations provide their only interactions and activities with co-ethnics.

A Chinese American lawyer who worked for San Diego County on gender and race discrimination cases said he did not identify himself as an Asian American. However, later during the interview, he complained that at the county level there were few high-ranking Asian American officials, and he went on to name a Filipino American coworker who was the highest-ranking Asian American. He also described how he had worked on Southeast Asian refugee issues and had helped to write a policy report for them to receive social service funding. He was sensitive to immigrant issues, since he emigrated from China to join his father as a teenager. Although he may have identified himself as Chinese American rather than Asian American, he was quite aware of this larger category. He was active with Chinese American organizations composed primarily of first-generation Chinese; for example, he was chair of the Chinese Consolidated Benevolent Association Housing Project Committee but had difficulty attaining some of the other leadership positions, because his spoken and written Cantonese was insufficient to communicate with the members.

Discussions of identity are often connected to one's biology, but this limits our understanding of the processes of identity switching. As one Korean American pragmatically points out: "I am Asian but I'm also American. I can go to Africa and be African. . . . I know I look Asian and I'll capitalize on that if necessary." The way in which Asian Americans can adopt another single-ethnic Asian identity shows how ethnicity involves some choice. For example, a woman who is Japanese and Filipino, raised in Hawai'i, participated in various Japanese, Chinese, Filipino, and pan-Asian organizations. She mentioned that in the late 1970s in San Diego, "in order to feel Asian, you had to become Chinese, [since] that was the most active community," so she became "Chinese" and helped to organize the Chinese Cultural Faire. These examples show the fluidity of ethnic identities, yet we cannot dismiss the ways in which racial constructions restrict how we can define ourselves and, particularly, how others define us. A racialized Asian may have an easier time being accepted as Hawaiian or Chinese than as Latino, European, African, or even "American."

Multiple Organizations, Multiple Identities

Asian American identities are based on racial factors; however, their lives are also shaped by multiple and intersecting interests beyond race, such as class, gender, and sexuality. In addition to being involved in ethnic organizations, given that their lives are embedded in a range of histories, they are active with numerous mainstream social, political, professional, and civic organizations. They participate for reasons of professional credibility, feeling a personal attachment to an issue, or because they consider it part of their civic responsibility to participate. The experience of a woman lawyer who is half Japanese and half Caucasian exemplifies the multiple and simultaneous identities Asian Americans have and how these identities can shape their organizational involvement. She participates with a variety of professional organizations, such as mainstream bar associations, but is also active with ethnic law organizations at the local and state levels. She explains her need to be involved:

> I find it useful to meet other attorneys that do the same type of work.... Whereas with the Asian [Pacific] Bar [Association] or Pan Asian Lawyers Association, it's very much an emotional thing. It's connecting with other people of similar backgrounds, whether from San Diego or elsewhere, who have been through the same kinds of experiences that I have. I think that it's something that you don't get from any other group. We've all pretty much experienced the same kind of prejudices, the same kind of obstacles, the same kind of whatever. It's very much a support group. To me it's very important. I don't know how to function without it. It's just necessary. I just have to go interact with people like that.

Additionally, she participates in law organizations based on her gender, such as the Lawyers Club, a women's bar association. She explains: "They were like a contact point for me while I was studying for the bar and having my babies and knowing other professional women who were going through some of the same things I was going through, ... kind of balancing my family against my profession, so that was a very good support group." She participated in the first luncheon for women lawyers of color in San Diego. She has also been active with the Asian American social service organization, the Union of Pan Asian Communities, organizing a free legal clinic for victims of domestic violence, many of whom were refugees. In the past, she has been a board member of the Japanese American Citizens League as well as of the Asian Business Association and the Legal Aid Society. In 2000, she became the founding executive director of the Southwest Center for Asian Pacific American Law (SCAPAL), part of the National Asian Pacific American Legal Consortium. These formal organizations, based on professional, ethnic, and gender affiliations, overlapped and provided her with multilevel networks of professional and personal support.

Conclusion

Cultural identities are useful in explaining the emotional attachments that allow people to reaffirm who they are in a highly complex society. It is often assumed that those choosing to retain their ethnic or racial identity are anti-American or unpatriotic; however, in many cases they want to retain their ethnicity at the same time they want to be "American." For example, a Vietnamese American leader said of his reasons for participating in ethnic organizations: "First of all we help each other to integrate into American society, but also figure out how we can keep the [Vietnamese] culture, language, and traditions." Ethnic particularism is not the sentiment of those I interviewed. In fact, the opposite is more likely—that Asians had tried to become "American," but because they were racialized, they realized they were not perceived as such by others. As a Filipino so aptly states: "[We're] so much easier to distinguish because of color or facial features, . . . so you can't just melt in. It's nice to have a melting pot, but you can't just blend in when your face looks different from everybody else's." The continuing significance of individual and institutional racism is a point that proponents of a color-blind society dismiss when they so blithely recommend that minorities drop the hyphenation and call themselves simply "Americans" (Hing 1993; Takagi 1992).

Race is not an abstraction that can be discarded—it affects all Americans, regardless of whether they choose to deny, suppress, or embrace their racial heritage. In this *interactive identity model*, individuals have to negotiate for themselves their own configuration of identity. There is no single approach to understanding how individuals become ethnicized or racialized. Although racialized peoples of color have social agency in determining their identity choices, they make these selections within the imposed power structure of the society. The collected memories in this chapter are selective renderings of the crucial factors that affect the process of identity formation. These are the private memories that can lead to public action, giving individuals an incentive to work toward changing racial inequities. Rather than seek a single or uniform voice, I have sought to analyze the multivocal, multifaceted, and dynamic representations of Asian America and its simultaneous role in remaking and reimagining community as well.

9

Conclusion

Milestones and Crossroads for
Asian Americans

I n the late 1960s when the Asian American movement began, Asians in this country demanded a voice in the issues affecting their community. Since then, sociopolitical circumstances have changed, the composition of the group has become remarkably more diverse, and the organizational capacity of the group has been reconfigured, along with the resources available to it. Although mobilization may not be a real force in the everyday lives of the general Asian American population, the actions of the organizers affect, directly and indirectly, the way the community is represented, perceived, and treated. San Diego Asian Americans organized for social, cultural, economic, and political reasons to improve their lives and those of future generations. Mobilizing on multiple agendas over three decades, participants recognized that their lives are interwoven and that their organizational efforts are interlinked. In the process of engaging in these interventions and emergent practices, they worked on creating identities, sustaining organizations, and forming communities.

Constructing Organizations, Communities, and Identities

It is through organizations that networks are formalized, leaders emerge, coalitions are forged, and political consciousness is transformed (Abraham 2000). The activists, through their organizational efforts, learned about the efficacy of different mobilization strategies and the viability of short-term and long-term goals. The ethnic and socioeconomic changes in the Asian American population, along with transformations in the larger political climate and economic conditions, have led to organizational shifts in priorities and agendas. Given their limited albeit expanding resources, Asian American organizations in San Diego have survived and thrived by engaging in a *politics of resistance* and a *politics of accommodation*.

I have learned a great deal from my research with community leaders and organizations in San Diego. Although I did not always agree with them, I respect and admire those I observed and interacted with for their courage, commitment, and dedication. I became keenly aware of the difficulties of sustaining organizations, even when leaders and members are sincere and earnest. Personality conflicts and the quest for personal glory or greed can displace the work of talented, well-intentioned individuals. All of these factors can destroy trust, desire to contribute, and enthusiasm for cooperation—all extremely difficult to rebuild or replace, especially in such a "small" community. And these components are even more challenging to recreate when external factors work to fractionalize fragile coalitions or whittle away a community's hard-won victories. Through my ethnographic research, I became acutely aware that struggling over the *discourse of oppositional politics* is exceedingly different from *doing oppositional politics*, especially in community organizing, where resources are limited, obstacles are overwhelming, and victories are incremental. What is plentiful are the differences of personalities, strategies, and ideologies.

I observed during my fieldwork a number of individuals focusing an inordinate amount of energy on voluntary activities, sacrificing time from their paid employment or businesses, and sometimes neglecting their personal relationships. The dedication of some stems from desiring a diversion from unfulfilling jobs or personal lives, while others were motivated simply by their enthusiasm for a project and their passionate belief in social justice. Activism can be stressful and time consuming, and the rewards are often intangible, which can take a toll on an individual's physical and mental health. The majority of the leadership positions in these organizations were voluntary, and leaders seldom received direct remuneration. I also saw how individuals originally intent on participating purely for self-interest and materialism could be transformed from casual participants to motivated activists working for the collective good.

Ethnic mobilization is often regarded as primarily serving utilitarian or instrumental purposes, essentially for obtaining calculated, tangible political or economic gain (Glazer and Moynihan 1963); however, this fails to capture feelings of group belonging (Gold 1992; Hing 1993). While Asian Americans may come together initially with utilitarian intentions, in the process of organizing together, they have also fostered a sense of a "social community" that at moments can cross ethnic, professional, class, sexual, generational, and gender lines. Through the formation of these organizations, spatially dispersed individuals were given the opportunity to interact with one another and build networks. A Chinese American who moved to San Diego in the 1970s explained that his involvement with community organizations changed his perception: "The term 'Asian American' was relatively new and it's still kind of new. . . . I'm now experiencing the newer cultures for me—the Filipino, you know, Vietnamese, Laotian. I didn't even know what a Hmong was until I heard it for the first time last year." He adds that he "kind of suspected there might be an ethnic community, but not an organized ethnic community." A longtime participant in both the Japanese and Asian community also remarks on the camaraderie: "My friends are in it. It's become kind of a community." They were able to articulate commonalities within difference and forge a sense of belonging to nonterritorialized communities.

Individuals can obtain intangible benefits from organizational activities at the personal level. One noticeable manifestation of this is the socialization that I noticed occurring among Asian Americans outside formal organizational events. Interviewees often stated that the camaraderie—and in some cases lifelong friendships—they developed with other Asian Americans was the main reward they received from their participation in community activities. An Asian American boundary is a political and economic tool that has become an essential basis for collective action, but it also fosters a sense of communal solidarity among divergent groups and provides them a sense of ethnic or racial pride. It is through group interaction that the ideology of community is transformed from an abstraction into the reality of people acting together who define their own political meaning or emotional comfort from it.

Race-based organizations provide a comfortable environment for Asian Americans to gain experience and allow them a circuitous or indirect route to participate in mainstream organizations. Rather than isolating or marginalizing them further from the mainstream, participating in these organizations allows them to gain leadership experience and to learn how organizations operate (Fugita and O'Brien 1985). Those I interacted with constantly repeated similar sentiments about how these organizations educated them about organizational functions as well as politicized them, essentially encouraging them to become further engaged with civic and political issues in San Diego. Being leaders of ethnic and race-based organizations allowed them to make the transition into mainstream economic and political positions. A Chinese American restaurateur who has been involved with the Chinese Center, the Union of Pan Asian Communities, and the Asian Business Association believes that his appointments on several mainstream boards "came from my leadership in the [Asian] community." In turn, lessons acquired from their involvement in mainstream organizations are used to help their communities, although this is a more difficult transition since many of the mainstream groups still "exclude" Asian Americans.

Paradoxically, while Asian Americans want to be integrated into the mainstream society, they are highlighting a factor that differentiates them from the mainstream society—the constructed Asian American racial boundary. They are criticized for promoting their own marginalization and isolation, in essence perpetuating their own status as "foreigners" or "segregationists." Yet given their continued exclusion from mainstream society, it should not be surprising that they have adopted this as a strategic organizing mechanism. Additionally, critics note that regardless of their usage of the term, by using the "Asian American" category to challenge the system, they are actually reifying their racialization. They argue that by promoting the idea of Asian Americans as a monolithic or uniform group, they are perpetuating the prevalent misperception that they *are* alike, inadvertently reessentializing or homogenizing their identity (Lowe 1991). While Asian Americans have politicized the racial categorization for their own purposes, they have not fully examined the racial classification that often subsumes, excludes, or silences individuals and groups. While organizing along racial lines provides new possibilities and opportunities for resistance and can be an effective strategy for mobilization, they are still working within the constraints of the racial model imposed upon them.

"Americans" of Asian ancestry may not embrace or accept the term "Asian American"; nevertheless, this label confronts them at both the individual and institutional levels. Often newcomers are unaware of the early experiences of Asians in this country, yet their lives are intrinsically linked to the historical and present-day circumstances of Asians already in the United States. The civil rights movement may have resolved, to a certain extent, de jure discrimination for racial groups, but de facto discrimination persists. Despite their long history in the United States, Asian Americans' status as U.S. citizens by birth or by naturalization does not prevent them from being treated as "foreigners." Asian Americans, native- and foreign-born, may feel ambivalent about the racial category, yet regardless of whether or not they acknowledge the dominating impact of race, they live racially structured lives. The choice not to personally involve oneself with Asian American organizations, not to interact with other Asian Americans, or not to consider oneself Asian American does not mean one can disidentify with the external racial label placed upon one.

Critical Transformations and Alliances

One of the major changes since I completed my fieldwork has been the role of technology in transforming both community building and mobilization. In the 1990s, phones, answering machines, and fax machines were essential for communication between spatially dispersed individuals, but by the late 1990s new communication technologies, for example, cell phones and Internet services such as e-mail and World Wide Web pages, facilitate mobilization efforts. As technological innovations change and become more commonplace, they also allow innovative methods of communications and creative group formation. Yet while technology may facilitate mobilization, it cannot dissolve the tangible difficulties of bringing together disparate individuals and groups.

New populations revitalize the community, enlarge the foundation of support, and bring improved resources and different perspectives on possibilities for mobilization. The 2000 U.S. census reports that of almost three million San Diego residents, approximately 300,000 are Asian Americans, 11 percent of the population. Future projections indicate that the Asian American population will grow substantially, and that by 2050 it will comprise 10 percent of the U.S. population (Shinagawa and Jang 1998). Both the U.S.-born and foreign-born populations will increase and both will play a central role in organizing, which means that they must continue to learn how to overcome linguistic, personality, and cultural differences.

Some ethnic subgroups will increase, while others will decrease proportionally, and this will affect leadership dynamics. In 1970, the Chinese and Japanese groups composed a two-thirds majority in San Diego and had more influence on the organizations. In 2000 in San Diego, the largest group was Filipinos, with Vietnamese a far second; however, having a numerically large population does not translate to equivalent representation in activism. There are complaints by other Asian groups that the Chinese, both American-born and foreign-born, still control many of the leadership roles, disproportionate to their percentage in the population. As Filipinos, Koreans, Southeast Asians, and South Asians, along with other previously smaller ethnic groups, gain numbers and prominence, they will bring in their personal histories and politics to restructure the organizations and can be expected to make demands for a redistribution of power in exchange for their cooperation and support. The ability of established Asian American groups to confront the ethnic shifts and to share power with growing factions will determine whether or not conflicts can be resolved amicably.

The advantages of class privilege, such as educational and professional status, do not necessarily protect one from experiencing racial discrimination in the workplace or in social settings, so we cannot assume that class mobility will erase racism. The case of Los Alamos National Laboratory scientist Wen Ho Lee, a naturalized U.S. citizen originally from Taiwan, who was falsely accused and imprisoned for being a spy for China, represents how racialization impacts Asian Americans (W. Lee 2002). Furthermore, mainstream cultural institutions of power are still exclusively White and are representative of the power brokers in America. As one activist states: "The collective cultural aspect of the city, which traditionally in large cities that's where the gentry is, that's where the money is, traditionally you'll find the old families, and traditions are hard to change and that's where racism still exists." In reality, there are always multiple intersecting variables such as class, ethnicity, race, sexuality, gender, generation, and citizenship status that affect the levels of discrimination Asian Americans experience and the kinds of resistance that will take shape. Whatever Asian Americans define to be the critical axis of inequality can become the salient basis for mobilization and can be modified according to the circumstances.

Social scientists often focus on the impact dominant groups have on subordinate groups, neglecting to observe the influence that communities of color have on one another (Stanfield 1993). These coalitions rarely garner media headlines; racial conflicts receive attention instead of the routine processes of negotiation and collaboration between racial groups. If communities of color in San Diego work together, they can claim to represent approximately 50 percent of the population, and this is a powerful inducement to form such alliances. Following the pattern in California, the White and Black populations will continue to decline in San Diego, and the Latino and Asian population will increase significantly, which will mean a reconfiguration in power sharing. The University of Michigan's Population Studies Center ranked San Diego the fourth least-segregated city among the nation's twenty largest metropolitan areas, so there is potential for stronger coalitions.

The transformations within each of the racialized groups can contribute to increasing tensions and erode any common basis for solidarity. As examples in this book point to, factors such as variations in class status, areas of residence, acceptance of racialized stereotypes, and inability to speak the same language can lead to conflict. In addition, competition between groups for scarce resources for jobs, electoral seats, college admissions slots, or social programs may lead to further divisions. These fragile multiracial coalitions may be limited and short-lived, but that such coalitions have occurred in San Diego and in other sites and times attests to the possibility for these groups to forge consistent cross-racial dialogues. It is imperative that Asian Americans actively engage in eliminating social injustices and building alliances with other individuals and groups, recognizing when and how their lives are interlinked.

Beyond the San Diego Case

There are noticeable regional differences in how Asian Americans decide to forge alliances. In sites where there are fewer Asian Americans and higher levels of racial animosity, there is more incentive to form alliances; however, in areas with large populations and relatively low perceived levels of racial discrimination, critical issues can bring together otherwise isolated, autonomous groups. Additionally, Asian Indians, Cambodians, Filipinos, and Koreans have gained prominent leadership roles in Asian American organizations. In some cases, even much smaller groups such as Thai, Indonesian, Malaysian, Singaporean, Bangladeshi, Pakistani, or Hmong are taking the lead, which forces us to rethink how we are to reconstruct "Asian American" in sites nationwide, particularly in the Midwest and the South, where Asian populations are increasing; however, there is limited documentation of these community developments. I was reminded of this lack of knowledge of regional developments at a recent meeting in Boston for Asian American scholars and nonprofit advocates. I met a Korean immigrant from Atlanta, Georgia, who was president of the Asian American Coalition in Georgia and was seeking advice on how, as a smaller and dispersed population, they could organize effectively at the state level.

A multitude of organizations, some single-ethnic, some pan-Asian, exist outside what have been considered the traditional sites of Asian American activism that have not been studied extensively. We must be cautious of privileging Los Angeles, New York City, and San Francisco as symbolic sites for all Asian American activism (Abelman and Lie 1995; Kwong 1987). Relying solely on these sites as models to understand Asian American mobilization presents an unbalanced picture of social transformation. The San Diego efforts, although influenced by activism in these other sites, did not employ the same strategies of resistance. It is crucial to acknowledge that Asian Americans living in sites across the country engage in activism every day that is just as important to understand. If we limit our research to major cities or defining moments such as the aftermath of the Los Angeles Rebellion to understand activism in Asian American communities, then we present an image of Asian Americans as rarely engaged in social change. Additionally, the image we present under these narrowly defined circumstances is that social change is important only for those who live in these select metropolitan areas and who engage in "radical" forms of activism. Social movement scholars have aided the evolution of this misconception by their inclination to focus on events that capture national headlines, while neglecting the daily struggles of groups working for social change. One can visit sites across the country and find Asian Americans facing challenges similar to those I discovered in San Diego, such as finding adequate social services, preserving historic sites, fighting anti-Asian images, creating job opportunities, and gaining political power. By neglecting important areas of Asian American social engagement such as San Diego, and dismissing the social problems Asian Americans face or even the ways they attempt to engage in activism as irrelevant, seems limiting, given the kinds of developments that have been occurring and are occurring in Asian American communities across the country.

Since completing my research in San Diego, I have talked to Asian Americans in various parts of the country and have lived in the Midwest and the Pacific Northwest, where I observed scenarios similar to those I found in San Diego—Asian American activists gathering, discussing, debating, and planning. Currently, in Orange County, California, as I talk to Asian American social, political, cultural, and economic community leaders, participate in their organizations, and begin a new research project, I have a feeling of déjà vu. As a board member of the Orange County Asian and Pacific Islander Community Alliance, a nonprofit organization started in 1997, I am taking a tour with the designers of Delhi Community Center, a Latino-based center in Santa Ana which serves the low-income neighborhood, to learn how we can build a similar one for the Asian American community. To build this multimillion-dollar facility that will offer English-language and job training, have health care and child care services, provide space for youth and elderly activities, and be a site for political organizing, we have to garner the support of politicians, apply for federal grants, solicit in-kind services at the local level, and, of course, get community input.

Asian Americans in the Post-9/11 Era

As a heterogeneous population, Asians Americans continue to be marked by animosities, distancing, and disidentifications; yet there are still pragmatic incentives for them to find common ground. They are still a racialized population and an easy target for anti-immigrant and anti-Asian sentiments, as well as being victims of U.S. nationalism. While conditions have improved, however, San Diego local Moto Asakawa is cautious, stating that "the current situation is nothing like the widespread and blatant discrimination felt during the 1930s and 1940s by American citizens of Japanese descent all along the Pacific coast. It's just a feeling right now, but it's there. . . . It's an undertone. But it could change overnight" (quoted in Clifford 1990a). He was on former Mayor O'Connor's Pan Asian Advisory Board, active in the JACL and the Union of Pan Asian Communities. The incarceration of approximately 120,000 innocent Japanese Americans, 60 percent of whom were U.S. citizens by birth in this country and their immigrant parents who at that time were forbidden by law to become U.S. citizens because of their racial ancestry, is a lesson about how global political events, in this case, the bombing of Pearl Harbor on 7 December 1941, can impact a racialized community. U.S. foreign policy, particularly economic and political interventions in Asia, and Western imperialism shape the daily lives of Asians in America, as well as their ability to mobilize.

We are living in another historical moment when it all "changed overnight" with the terrorist attacks on the World Trade Center buildings and the Pentagon on 11 September 2001. The earlier Persian Gulf War had fueled anti-Iraqi sentiments and actions in this country, complicated by the fact that we were protecting oil-rich Kuwait and allied with Saudi Arabia, so racialized images of the "enemy" were blurred. The expansion of British and U.S. imperialism in the Middle East, most notably the invasion of Iraq in 2003, was dubiously justified in the post-9/11 era, complicating matters. Previously, hate-crime reports on Middle Easterners had been minimal, with some increase during the earlier tensions; however, the post-9/11 period raises the animosities to another level. Americans perceived to be Arab or Muslim have become victims of violence and of state-sponsored detainment and harassment because of their race, often justified by slogans of American patriotism or protection against terrorism.

Alarming acts of racial harassment and violence are being committed against South Asian Americans and Asian Americans who are Muslims. Practitioners of the Sikh faith are mistaken targets because of their clothing, particularly their turbans, and beards that are perceived to be similar to those worn by Middle Easterners. Comparable to instances when Asian Americans looked like the "enemy" during World War II and Japanese Americans were treated as "enemy aliens" and interned in concentration camps, whole groups, regardless of their U.S. citizenship status, are becoming targets of racist sentiments and ignorance embedded within our educational, political, economic, religious, and cultural systems. This case also shows the complexities of racialization in this country. The 2000 U.S. census classifies those from the Middle East as "White" and categorizes South Asians originally from India, Pakistan, Bangladesh, Nepal, and so on as "Asian Americans"; however, in de facto racialization practices, both these groups are lumped together as "non-White foreigners." Overall, the Asian American response has been extremely supportive because many consider South Asians as Asian Americans and are empathetic toward Middle Easterners and Muslims, since they understand what it means to be victims of misplaced racial hatred and hysteria. The U.S. Patriot Act of 2001 and the transfer of the Immigration and Naturalization Service to the U.S. Department of Homeland Security on 1 March 2003 have impacted the admittance of immigrants into this country and led to the questionable detention of Asian Americans, as well as their inhumane deportation.

Depictions, whether of Muslim extremists in the Philippines, nuclear threats from North Korea and Pakistan, or Communism from China, work to construct Asia and its people as a threat to the moral and social order of the West and its empire building. These portrayals of Asians as the "Yellow Peril" are evident during wartime (Marchetti 1993), but also in times of relative peace with Asia when these narratives manifest themselves in maneuvers of "economic warfare." The United States is attempting to (re)gain its position of economic dominance in this postindustrial, post-Fordist global economic marketplace. Racist stereotypes of Asians are a way for the Western empire to reassert its dominance in a period of economic competition from restructuring Latin American and Asian countries. In this postcolonial era, more appropriately regarded as the neocolonial era, and post-cold-war era, Western powers are also attempting to regain their political position in this "New World Order." The dehumanizing discourse and portrayals of Asians are an outcome of America's anxiety about the loss of its economic and political dominance and works to further feed its apprehension. As Asians in America position themselves as transnational "citizens" in an age of globalization or focus on domestic agendas in an age of revived nationalism, they have to weigh the costs and benefits of such strategies.

Conclusion

In the early twenty-first century, Asian Americans are at several critical crossroads. Debates regarding such controversial issues as welfare, affirmative action, immigration, racial profiling, multicultural education, hate crimes, and collection of racial data, as well as more general policies such as housing, policing, education, and employment, will intensify as the gap widens between the wealthy and poor, as the racial composition of the country shifts, and as America's position in the global political economy is altered. Asian Americans will continue to grapple with internal political, generational, ethnic, religious, sexual, gender, linguistic, geographic, citizenship, and class distinctions. They can work toward addressing the needs of various constituents or they can decide that these differences will make it impossible for them to work together. They need to determine if and how race still counts in the issues that matter—their life opportunities and experiences.

The Asian American identity is not fixed and must be open to dialogue and debate from multiple perspectives and voices. It is not enough to articulate their positions as victims that are still marginalized from the uneven structures of power and whose lives are made invisible or less valuable. As a population, Asian Americans have varying interests and multiple agendas, yet as an activist optimistically concludes, "There's a lot more areas of commonality than areas of conflict." An individual born in Taiwan and raised in Alaska states: "People see disintegration among the Asian groups. We don't have a common theme that we are trying to promote, but coming together, working together, we can come up with a common theme." In acting and organizing together they need to figure out what it means to construct *solidarities of difference* and what it means to build oppositional strategies. Those engaged in building community recognize that it is unnecessary to form coalitions on all issues or to always be inclusive. This should be a selective process in which participants understand that it is possible for Asian Americans to be engaged in multiple alliances or to be engaged in alliances at particular periods on specific issues only.

They need to consider how to improve communication and coordination between groups at the local, state, regional, and national levels if they want to become a political force. Mobilization is based on the aggregate of emergent processes from the top-down as well as the bottom-up model, with an understanding that change can be stimulated from the top but cannot be sustained without a grassroots foundation at the community level. There are few nationally based Asian American organizations which can provide local organizations with a concrete model or framework for mobilization, unlike, for example, the San Diego African American community, which can rely on support, guidance, and funding from well-established and comparatively well-funded national organizations. Asian Americans need to recognize the multiplicity of sites where activism has occurred and to learn from these examples. Organizations such as the National Asian Pacific American Legal Consortium, the Asian Pacific American Legal Center, Asian Pacific American Labor Alliance, Leadership Education for Asian Pacifics, Inc., Media Action Network for Asian Americans, Asian American Legal Defense and Education Fund, Asian and Pacific Islander American Health Forum, and National Coalition for Asian Pacific American Community Development are gaining greater recognition and are working on capacity-building at the local level, yet they do not have the ability to adequately coordinate numerous local communities nationally.

This is by no means an exhaustive study of Asian American mobilization; rather it introduces examples of processes of mobilization to present a picture of the possibilities. Admittedly, I was motivated to conduct this study to contest misconceptions about Asian Americans as apathetic and apolitical. It is the lack of documentation of activist activities rather than the absence of action that contributes to these misperceptions. When circumstances become available and when issues demand it, Asians in San Diego have acted, not always successfully and not necessarily in unison with a clear vision; however, their efforts have given them a sense that they have more control over their lives. In the 1970s, Asian Americans were given a token piece of the pie. In the 1990s, distributive issues were still central; however, Asian Americans reached a new milestone—this time they were in a position to define the shape and size of this pie.

I have changed personally and intellectually since I conducted my fieldwork. I continue to struggle with making sense of the history of racism that has plagued this country and tarnished its democratic ideals. It has left an immense legacy for us today that permeates every aspect of American society. I learned that as Asian Americans, we have a lot at stake in the struggle for social justice and equity. We cannot remain silent. These lessons have made me question how I position myself, how I construct an identity, and how I engage in this struggle. Regrettably, there are daunting challenges ahead for us. Although I do not know exactly what will confront us, I can say with certainty that in the foreseeable future, Asian Americans will continue to work on improving our society and will continue to challenge those who have a vested interest in maintaining the status quo.

List of Interviewees

Teresita "Ching" Bacini	2 July 1993
Agustin Chang	11 June 1993
Winifreda Chang	9 July 1993
J. R. Chantengco	29 June 1993
Diana Chuh	14 June 1993
Jim Cua	24 June 1993
Dien Do	2 August 1993
Collin Fat	2 July 1993
Tom Fat	29 July 1993
Lambert Hsu	11 June 1993
Robert Ito	21 June 1993
Margaret Iwanaga-Penrose	23 and 25 July 1993
Edward Lee	17 June 1993
Johnny Lee	10 June 1993
Dee Lew	26 June 1993
Susan Lew	23 June 1993
Sally Lorang	10 and 21 June 1993
Robin Low	28 July 1993
Villa Mills	8 August 1993
Gil Ontai	23 June 1993
Mary Ann Salaber	20 May 1993
Jesse Santos	28 June 1993
Cesar Solis	8 and 15 July 1993

Mits Tomita	1 July 1993
Yen Tu	25 June 1993
Edward Wong	10 June 1993
Karbeck Wong	14 and 17 June 1993
Simon Wong	5 August 1993
Calvin Woo	14 June 1993
Vernon Yoshioka	12 July 1993

Note: All interviews were completed by the author in person in San Diego.

Notes

Chapter One

1. Based on the labels generally employed in San Diego, I use the terms "Asian" and "Asian American" interchangeably throughout this text to refer to individuals whose ancestry can be traced to Asia who are living in the United States, regardless of their citizenship status. When referring to Asians who live in Asia, I often use "Asian" or "Asian national."

2. The individuals interviewed were chosen precisely because of their involvement in organizations, and because of the information they could provide me concerning community history, events, and organizations. I determined who the main actors in the community were through direct contact during my fieldwork, or indirectly through their reputation and through recommendations by others. Interviews lasted two to three hours and were conducted throughout San Diego County at interviewees' offices, businesses, and homes, as well as at my residence, restaurants, and other public spaces. I asked questions concerning their personal history, which included information on immigration, education, occupation, and family; their involvement in nonethnic and ethnic-based organizations; their political opinions; and the extent of their involvement in political activities. Many told me about the history of the Asian community in San Diego and detailed the development of its activities, although I also relied on primary and secondary documents for much of the earlier history. I asked follow-up questions based on the respondent's answers and based on my knowledge of the community from my ethnographic fieldwork. I transcribed six interviews, and I paid a professional transcriber to transcribe the rest of the recorded interviews verbatim. I listened to all the interviews a second time to correct any errors in the transcriptions. The interviewees and dates of interviews appear on pages 243–244.

3. For classic discussions of communities see Emile Durkheim (1947), who discusses the processes of mechanical and organic solidarity, and Ferdinand Tonnies (1955 [1887]), who discusses the transition from gemeinschaft to gesselschaft principles.

Chapter Two

1. The eighteen incorporated cities are Carlsbad, Chula Vista, Coronado, Del Mar, El Cajon, Encinitas, Escondido, Imperial Beach, La Mesa, Lemon Grove, National City, Oceanside, Poway, San Diego, San Marcos, Santee, Solano Beach, and Vista.

2. There are approximately eighteen Native American reservations in San Diego County.

3. Within the city limits live approximately half the Thai, Korean, and Japanese population; more than 60 percent of the Filipino, Chinese, and Asian Indian population; and approximately 90 percent of the Southeast Asian population.

4. The areas with a high percentage of Asian Americans included: National City, 17 percent; southeast San Diego, 22 percent; Mid City, 13 percent; Kearny Mesa, 11 percent; University City, 12 percent; Del Mar–Mira Mesa, 22 percent; north San Diego, 13 percent; Sweetwater, 14 percent; and South Bay, 14 percent (San Diego Association of Governments 1991).

Chapter Three

1. I used the unprocessed UPAC archival collection (hereafter, UPAC Archives) stored at the San Diego State University Library, personal collections of interviewees, and information from interviews for historical material. See also Võ 2000.

2. In the past, the Chinese Community Church and the Oceanview United Church of Christ (Japanese) belonged to the same religious association and held joint youth tournament basketball games and a few other social events. Leaders of the Chinese Community Church were also leaders of the Chinese Social Service Center, and about half of the Japanese American Citizens League board belonged to the Oceanview Church.

3. From its inception, UPAC included Pacific Islanders, integrated them with UPAC's general programs, and developed specific programs to meet their needs. Pacific Islander American and Asian American scholars have argued for both the inclusion and exclusion of Pacific Islanders in the Asian American grouping. Nonprofit organizations, local and national, have been on the frontlines of these debates, with some taking UPAC's path and others opting not to include Pacific Islanders.

4. A participant explained that they recognized that Asian American Vietnam veterans were suffering from alcohol and drug addiction problems and that ethnic-specific mental health services for them were few. He felt these problems resulted from the racism they experienced as "Asians" who looked like the "enemy" and from the fear of being killed by fellow U.S. soldiers who might mistake them for the "enemy."

5. Started in 1972, the San Diego Chinese Center provides for the needs of seniors and new immigrants; the organization was sponsored by the Chinese Consolidated Benevolent Association in conjunction with San Diego State University School of Social Work, Center on Aging. There were three Guamanian organizations: Sons and Daughters of Guam, whose main purpose was social and cultural; the Guamanian Alliance, which was interested in improving educational and social welfare opportunities; and Chamorro Nation, which wanted to establish a communications network among the Guamanian people. The San Diego Chapter of

the Japanese American Citizens League has been active since 13 August 1933, although inactive from 1942 through 1946.

6. Minutes of COPAO monthly meeting, 20 February 1975.

7. "UPAC Recommendations on the Allocation of Revenue Sharing Funding," 5 April 1973.

8. Bok Lim C. Kim, PAC National Issues Task Force representative. Statement recorded on video about San Diego Asian community, 1974.

9. Vernon Yoshioka, "UPAC Statement on the Immigrants from Viet Nam and Cambodia," 7 May 1975.

10. Resolution passed by San Diego County Human Relations Commission, 7 May 1975.

11. Letter from James S. Fukumoto, Executive Director, San Diego County Human Relations Commission to Senator Alan Cranston, 30 April 1975.

12. Proposed Asian American Resource Center for Vietnamese Refugees in Camp Pendleton, California, submitted by Grace Blaszkowski, Asian American Affairs Officer; Kathy Tsund, Director, Chinese Social Service Center; Marjorie Lee, Social Worker, Korean Social Service Center; and Beverley Yip, Project Director, UPAC: Special Services.

13. In the early 1980s, the U.S. Office of Refugee Resettlement cut funding for social adjustment services such as mental health services and began funding employment-related programs. As a result, many of the current programs and services UPAC created specifically for the Vietnamese, Laotian, and Cambodian populations emphasize economic self-sufficiency. For example, the Family Day-Care Training Program teaches eligible participants how to establish and run their own licensed day-care centers from their homes. The Refugee Service Cooperative provides hands-on bilingual training in gardening, landscape maintenance, and janitorial services.

14. At first, UPAC encouraged Southeast Asians to form autonomous organizations so they could officially become member organizations of UPAC. The Vietnamese Alliance Association and the Vietnamese Community Foundation both joined UPAC in 1976; the Cambodian Association of San Diego joined in 1977; and the Laotian Friendship Association joined soon after.

15. Indochinese Mutual Assistance Associations were formed in areas across the country where refugees settled to provide them a sense of autonomy in controlling the decisions made regarding their communities. It is a controversial organization in that it often duplicates the hierarchical power structure of the homeland.

16. Bounhong Khommarath, "Message from the Chair," Special Report, San Diego Refugee Coalition, March 1993. The coalition's objective was to share information, to recommend and advise public officials regarding refugee policies, and to assist in problem solving. While the wave of Southeast Asian refugees triggered the inception of the organization, it includes all refugee groups in the San Diego area. According to a comparative study of Refugee Data Center Statistics and local health program statistics, San Diego County in federal fiscal year 1991–1992 resettled approximately 2,907 refugees; about 36 percent were Vietnamese, and the rest were Russians, Somalis, Iraqis, and Kurds, and much smaller numbers of Ethiopians, Cambodians, Hmong, Laotians, Ugandans, Zairians, and Armenians.

17. Minutes of COPAO monthly meeting, 20 February 1975.

18. Minutes of Special Meeting of the COPAO Board of Directors and Delegates, 11 March 1975. For two years, there was no Filipino organization affiliated with UPAC, although there were still programs that included the Filipino population, and there were Filipinos still active on the staff and board. In 1977, the Philippine American Community of San Diego, an organization formed in 1959 to promote social, economic, educational, and cultural interests, became part of the UPAC Board of Directors.

19. In the late 1880s, Margaret Iwanaga-Penrose's grandfather came to America as a merchant marine and became a Baptist minister. He went back to Japan and was disowned by his Buddhist parents, so he returned to America with his wife and children, where he preached among coethnics in logging camps and farms in Tacoma, Washington. His son (Margaret's father) worked in the Alaskan salmon industry and on Washington berry farms to support himself through architectural school at the University of Washington, and then went to Japan to further his education in architecture. During World War II, he was drafted into the Japanese army (naturalization restrictions did not allow him to become a U.S. citizen, so he was still a citizen of Japan), while his natal family was forced into internment camps. After the war, he brought his Japanese wife and children, including Margaret, to the United States, where they have remained.

20. Bok-Lim C. Kim video.

21. Letter from Marjorie Lee, Chair of UPAC, to Housing and Community Services Department, 20 April 1977.

22. In the 1970s, they had a diversity of contracts: Pan Asian Senior Services, Emergency Shelter and Support Services, Indochinese Assistance Project, the Role of Cultural Heritage in Public Policy, Pan Asian Culture and Education, Indochinese Health and Education Project, and Salad Bowl (summer recreational education activities for youth).

23. The Pan Asian Senior Nutrition Program, which delivers nutritious ethnic meals to seniors, was funded by the County of San Diego Area Agency on Aging and operated on alternate days at the (Japanese) Kiku Gardens Retirement Home, Japanese Christian Church, Samoan Congregational Church, Sons and Daughters of Guam Club, and (Southeast Asian) Linda Vista Recreation Center. Another program for seniors, the Home Help services program, allows UPAC staff to visit and care for Japanese, Chinese, Samoan, Guamanian, and Filipino seniors. Ethnic-specific projects included the Korean Outreach Project, Filipino Juvenile Delinquency Prevention Project, Samoan Community Exercise for Better Health Project, and Lao and Hmong Information and Referral Program.

24. In 1987, the organization reported delivering nearly 25,000 meals to seniors, both homebound and at neighborhood churches and apartment complexes.

25. A representative from UPAC complained that although cities like San Francisco and Los Angeles have had substance-abuse programs since the 1970s, UPAC was given funding for the first drug-prevention program only in 1990 and for the first alcohol-prevention program in 1991.

26. A Filipino sergeant, the Asian American liaison for the San Diego Police Department, informed me that the police received their first official Filipino gang case in 1987 and that Asian gang cases have increased rapidly since then.

27. Iwanaga-Penrose had previously been in charge of mainstream public and private social service agencies in Austin, Texas, some of which worked with minority populations, particularly African Americans, Latinos, and Asian Americans.

28. The main groups included are Korean, Vietnamese, Cambodian, Lao, Hmong, Japanese, Thai, Chinese, Filipino, Samoan, and Guamanian.

29. UPAC also delivers health and human care services to other minority groups in current programs that include Latinos and Ethiopian Americans. The Family Counseling and Community Education Program in which the organization subcontracts with Jewish Family Services provides crisis intervention and counseling to Soviet and Iranian refugees.

30. For example, the 1990 per capita income for Asian Americans was quite modest at $13,806, with vast differences among ethnic groups (U.S. Bureau of the Census 1993: 7): Japanese, $19,373; Asian Indian, $17,777; Chinese, $14,876; Filipino, $13,616; Thai, $11,970; Korean, $11,177; Vietnamese, $9,032; Laotian, $5,597; Cambodian, $5,120; Hmong, $2,692; and other Asian, $11,000.

31. Although UPAC activists also worked on K–12 education discrimination in hiring of teachers and administrators, multicultural curriculum development, more accurate U.S. census counts, supporting court nominations, and other seemingly "non–social service" work, this section focuses on indirect services performed in alliance with other communities of color.

32. UPAC Statement of Purpose, adopted 12 July 1973.

33. Ramon Valle and Charles Martinez, "Evaluation of UPAC Indirect Services," prepared for UPAC on a Volunteer Community Consultant Basis, 12 June 1978.

34. CRG was funded by revenue-sharing monies through the Department of Human Services of the Human Resources Agency. The report was submitted on 31 March 1977.

35. Letter from Minority Coalition signed by Margaret Castro, Chicano Federation; Vernon Sukumu, Black Federation; and Beverly Yip, UPAC, to Board of Supervisors, 10 June 1976.

36. Vernon Yoshioka, UPAC Acting Chair, presentation to San Diego City Council, 5 April 1973.

37. Vernon Yoshioka, Chair of UPAC and President of JACL, to State Advisory Committee, U.S. Commission on Civil Rights, 1 December 1973. Yoshioka stated that the only pan-Asians employed in administration, personnel, or affirmative action were a few secretaries or clerks.

38. In the U.S. District Court for the Southern District of California, Civil Action No. 76-1094-S: *United States of America; Chicano Federation of San Diego County, Inc.; Union of Pan Asian Communities; and Council of Pilipino American Organizations, Plaintiffs, v. San Diego County (a public corporation); David K. Speer, Chief Administrative Officer of San Diego County; William D. Winterbourne, Director of the Department of Civil Service and Personnel for San Diego County; C. Hugh Friedman, Troy M. Moore, Veryl J. Mortenson, King O. Taylor, Timothy M. Considine, Members, San Diego County Civil Service Commission; John P. Williamson, Acting Marshal, San Diego Marshal's Office; San Diego County Marshals Office, Defendants*, filed 5 May 1977.

39. The conference was organized by a handful of Asian American social workers in Los Angeles who came together as a group in 1968. This first conference of its kind was attended by approximately 700 Asian American mental health workers, community groups, and National Institute of Mental Health officials. A post-planning committee of fourteen Asian American delegates from various regions and ethnicities met to discuss how to implement the recommendations and resolutions.

40. Minutes from PAC San Diego Ad Hoc Committee, National Federation for Asian American Mental Health, 19 October 1973.

41. "San Diego Holds Mini Conference," *Asian/Pacific Summarizer* (Asian American Mental Health Federation) 1, 3 (March 1974). In addition to UPAC, other ethnic organizations were active in these conferences, such as the Chinese Social Service, Korean Outreach Project, Operation Samahan, SDSU School of Social Work, COPAO, Sons and Daughters of Guam, Asian Pacific Congress, and Japanese American Citizens League.

42. The organizers originally received a $130,000 grant for three years to establish a National Federation for Asian American Mental Health and later would obtain additional funding. It was funded as a project of the Center for Minority Group Mental Health Programs of the National Institute of Mental Health of the U.S. Department of Health, Education, and Welfare.

43. Letter from Vernon Yoshioka, UPAC Chair, to Paige Barber, Chair of Asian American Mental Health Federation, 25 January 1974.

Chapter Four

1. The Buddhist Church of San Diego (29 March 1971) and Ocean View United Church of Christ (16 April 1971), both Japanese American, sent letters to the principal of San Diego High School protesting the play.

2. APAC Region I—News Release, 9 February 1987.

3. Letter from Mary Ann Salaber to KFMB TV, July 18, 1986. Salaber sent a copy of the letter to Asian American lawyers, UPAC, the Japanese American Citizens League, the Chinese Social Service Center, Asian Pacific American Coalition (APAC), and the three Asian Pacific college students' associations in San Diego.

4. Letter from UPAC to Larry Himmel, "San Diego at Large," KFMB TV, 22 July 1986.

5. APAC then consisted of 650 organizations in California alone, with 150 members in San Diego. Their stationery lists five regions in California and one on the East Coast: San Diego, Los Angeles, Central Valley, Sacramento, San Francisco, and Washington, D.C. According to the list of officers, committee chairs, regional boards of governors, and at-large state delegates, there were Asian Indian, Chinese, Japanese, Filipino, Korean, Cambodian, Laotian, and Vietnamese involved in the organization.

6. Articles of Incorporation of the Asian Pacific American Advocates Coalition (APAAC), also known as Asian Pacific American Coalition (APAC), 7 August 1981.

7. Letter from APAC to Larry Himmel, "San Diego at Large," KFMB TV, 14 August 1986.

8. Letter from Mingyew Leung to Community Relations Task Force, 30 November 1986.

9. According to its Mission Statement, HRC was formed "to promote and foster mutual respect and understanding, examine the causes of tension, discrimination and intolerance between various groups and to provide assistance in fostering intergroup understanding and civic peace." Similar committees have been formed in other cities with the intent of appeasing voters, particularly minority constituents, and in some cases, they can be rather ineffective and powerless.

10. Letter from the HRC Media/Community Relations Task Force Subcommittee to President and General Manager of KFMB TV, 24 February 1987.

11. Information on this meeting is from Mary Ann Salaber's notes, 25 February 1987; Mary Ann Salaber, interview by author, 20 May 1993; and various newspaper articles.

12. Letter from Dan Arden, producer of *San Diego at Large*, to UPAC, 3 March 1987. Arden uses the term "Asian" here, so the reference is not only to the Chinese.

13. Larry Himmel's show was eventually cancelled. At the time my research was concluding, he worked as a local television weather reporter and a DJ for a jazz radio station.

14. APAC's written interpretation of Randy Miller's statement, 27 February 1987.

15. *APAC Alert*, Year, Vol. 6, No. 3, March 1987.

16. The Pan Asian Lawyers Association is a local nonprofit organization founded in 1978 and formally incorporated in 1985, part of the Asian Pacific Bar Association (APBA), the statewide bar association for the twelve major local Asian and Pacific Islander bar associations throughout California; APBA belongs to the National Asian Pacific American Bar Association. PALS stated in its information brochure that the organization "has continued to be a place where Asian lawyers can socialize with one another, but it has also developed into an organization that has sought to serve the legal needs of the Asian community." Lawyers involved with PALS have contributed legal services to UPAC, and some were on the board of this pan-Asian social service organization.

17. Letter from Asian Pacific American Law Students Association, University of San Diego, to KS-103, 8 March 1987.

18. Letter from JACL to KS-103, 4 March 1987

19. Statement by Dennis S. Kobata, Asian/Pacific Islander Media Responsibility Coalition, to the County of San Diego Human Relations Commission Community Media Task Force, 9 April 1987. Address for the coalition is listed as c/o *Pan Asian Express*, a local Asian newspaper.

20. San Diego County Human Relations Commission Media/Community Relations Subcommittee Public Statement, March 1987.

21. Letter from KS-103 President/General Manager to Human Relations Commission, 13 March 1987.

22. Letter from Chris Conway, KS-103, to Congressman Jim Bates, 27 March 1987.

23. Report from the California Attorney General's Commission on Racial, Ethnic, Religious, and Minority Violence, April 1986.

24. Letter from Mingyew Leung to KS-103, March 3, 1987. He sent copies of this letter to local, California, and national pan-Asian organizations; Chinese, Japanese, and Filipino organizations; student organizations; the FCC; and local politicians to solicit their support.

25. Statement by Dennis S. Kobata, Asian/Pacific Islander Media Responsibility Coalition, to the County of San Diego Human Relations Commission Community Media Task Force, 9 April 1987.

26. Letter from COPAO to KSDO Radio, 27 April 1987.

27. Memo from Bonnie Feinman and Andy Thompson, Co-chairs, to Community Media Task Force Members, inviting organizations to their April "Public Hearing on the Media," 4 March 1987.

28. Portillo also represented a new locally formed group, Coalition of Hispanic Professionals, which included the Society of Hispanic Engineers, the Labor Council for Latin American Advancement, the Association of Mexican American Educators, the Mexican American Business and Professional Association, La Raza Lawyers Association, the Personnel Management Association of Aztlan, and the Hispanic Bankers Association.

29. For further information, see the Asian American Journalist Association website, http://www.aaja.org/index.html.

30. The consortium is composed of the Asian Law Caucus, the Asian American Legal Defense and Education Fund in New York, and the Asian Pacific American Legal Center in Los Angeles. According to the report, Asians were the target of 3.4 percent of hate crimes, but comprised only 2.9 percent of the population.

31. After the protest was underway, Disguise, the company that created the costumes, stopped manufacturing them, recalled those already in stores, and issued a public apology.

32. This British-based show is supposed to be a parody of Japanese-style game shows and includes a Japanese narrator with a thick accent and other Asian actors making bizarre noises and contorted faces; it also mocks martial arts poses and Asian businessmen, and displays nonsensical writing that is supposed to be Japanese-like throughout the segments (Lowry 2003).

33. UPAC statement at HRC media hearing, 9 April 1987.

Chapter Five

1. The ABA Mission Statement in 1995 was "to unite and empower the Asian Pacific American business community by providing leadership and promoting economic growth in San Diego."

2. Asian Pacific American Chamber of Commerce brochure, n.d., and APACC bylaws, 25 August 1984.

3. Even though they attracted sponsors from diverse ethnic groups for this event, the organization had a problem maintaining this ethnic balance. An organizer comments: "That group was trying to get more Asians involved, but it was predominantly founded and made up of Filipino business people; . . . but it could never attract the Chinese and the Japanese and Southeast Asians no matter how much we tried. Couldn't do it. . . . Because it was looked at and perceived as a Filipino organization."

4. Letter from Lynne Choy Uyeda, Chair of ABA/LA Corporate Advisory Council, 13 July 1990.

5. The mission statement of this nonprofit organization spelled out the general goals: "1) to promote the growth of Asian-owned businesses and the unity of the Asian Business Community: 2) to provide educational opportunities for the betterment of its members and other interested individuals; and 3) to contribute to the welfare and progress of the Asian Community." Asian Business Association, San Diego, Articles of Incorporation, September 12, 1990.

6. ABA claimed that, "state-wide, our membership is over 3,500 Asian-owned business members ranging from professional services to small shop keepers." Only a few officers and board members had any contact with members from the ABA organizations in Los Angeles, San Francisco, or Orange County. ABA was also part of a larger network called the Council of Asian American Business Associations of California (CAABA-CAL), an umbrella organization started in 1988 to develop a cohesive, unitary statewide presence by bringing together groups from the state to pursue state and national procurement programs. The founding members were Asian American Architects and Engineers (San Francisco and Los Angeles); Asian Business Association (Northern and Southern California); Associated Asian Certified Public Accountants (San Francisco); and United Asian Contractors Association (San Francisco). Bylaws of the Council of Asian American Business Associations of California, Inc., 1988.

7. U.S. Bureau of Census, *Statistics for Metropolitan Statistical Areas with 1,000 or More Minority-Owned Firms, "Asians in America 1990 Census"* (Washington, D.C.: U.S. Government Printing Office, 1992), 60.

8. According to county records, in each fiscal year from 1989 to 1992, the county awarded about 20 percent of its contracts to minorities and women, over $20 million. The County of San Diego Minority and Women Business Enterprise Directory for June 1993 listed the following ethnic codes: Hispanic, Black, Native American, Asian/Pacific Islander, and Caucasian.

9. Brochure created by Equal Opportunity Contracting Program Publications, February 1993. This resolution included the city's Independent Corporations: San Diego Convention Center Corporation, Centre City Development Corporation, San Diego Housing Commission, San Diego Data Processing Corporation, and Southeast Economic Development Corporation and Redevelopment Agency. The goals were: construction, 20 percent Minority Business Enterprise (MBE) and 7 percent Women Business Enterprise (WBE); professional services, 12 percent MBE and 3 percent WBE; and vendor, 10 percent MBE and 10 percent WBE. These businesses can include consultants, vendors, architects, developers, construction, and banking. Each year a directory was created to be used as a resource by city buyers, department personnel, prime contractors, and other agencies and organizations throughout San Diego. In order for a business to qualify, it must be certified by the City of San Diego or the California State Department of Transportation (CAL-TRANS), or hold interim certifications (good for ninety days) with any of the member agencies of San Diego Joint Agency Contracting Opportunities Task Force (JACOTF). Since 27 February 1991, JACOTF includes the County of San Diego, S.D. County Water Authority, S.D. Unified Port District, S.D. Unified School District, S.D. Association of Governments, Metropolitan Transit Development

Board, City of San Diego, and CALTRANS, which is designated as the central certification agency. At least 51 percent of the business must be owned and controlled by one or more socially and economically disadvantaged individuals.

10. Quoted in "Pooling Asian Resources," *San Diego Executive*, May 1993.

11. Stated by Jack McGrory, city manager, at ABA meeting, 5 March 1991.

12. Richmond, Virginia, had a Black population of just over 50 percent and had set a goal of 30 percent in awarding city construction contracts to minority-owned businesses. At that time, only 0.67 percent of municipal contacts had been awarded to minorities (see Williams 1989).

13. Federal courts struck down public sector minority business programs in Georgia, Wisconsin, Florida, and Illinois. Other cities dropped or modified their minority contracting programs as a result of the 1989 decision.

14. Letter from John Witt, San Diego City Attorney, to James Smith, Contract Compliance Officer, via Severo Esquivel, Deputy City Manager, 7 December 1989.

15. The legal suit was brought against the city by the local Associated General Contractors, a trade group representing 328 construction companies, most owned by White male engineers.

16. In the first half of 1994, construction contracts to minorities were 6.7 percent compared to 21.3 percent the previous year when the EOCP plan was still in effect.

17. The most common complaints I heard were that large minority firms were unfairly taking advantage of the program, that men were listing their wives as owners to qualify as WBE, that prime contractors were not actually using the minority subcontractors they listed in the proposals, and that the EOCP program was being mismanaged.

18. In June 1991 in San Francisco, Chinese American architects and engineers protested the classifying of Asian Indians as minority business owners on the basis that they had not suffered historical discrimination.

19. *San Diego County Statistical Abstract 1993*, prepared and published by the San Diego Economic Development Corporation. Other large nonmanufacturing employers in the area were the University of California San Diego, the County of San Diego, San Diego Unified School District, and the City of San Diego.

20. Many active in ABA were also active in the San Diego Yantai Friendship Society, part of the sister cities program, which was supposed to foster cultural exchanges, though many of their programs have focused on business opportunities with Yantai, which has a major port for Pacific Rim trade. Along with the San Diego Port Commission, ABA sponsored a delegation from Shanghai. While its efforts have focused mostly on China, ABA was attempting to reach out to other Asian countries as well, for instance, by hosting a meeting on how to do business in Vietnam.

21. In their brochure, the Hispanic Chamber of Commerce states their organization "represents the interest of approximately 10,000 Hispanic firms in San Diego County" and accounts for $560 million in annual sales. In 1992, Al Kercheval was the first Black individual on the board of the 121-year-old San Diego Chamber of Commerce.

22. Letter from ABA to David Nuffer, Chair-Elect, Greater San Diego Chamber of Commerce, 2 November 1992. The newly appointed president of the Cham-

ber, Gilbert Partida, an international trade lawyer who founded the Hispanic Chamber of Commerce in 1988, was the first minority president in the Chamber's history (Gembrowski 1993), and the new chair, David Nuffer, an Anglo who owned a public relations firm, made the controversial decision to have cosponsors for the event and to form a reciprocal board membership with the Black, Hispanic, and Asian Chambers.

23. Letter from statewide ABA leaders to Members of the Council on California Competitiveness commissioned by Governor Pete Wilson, 27 March 1992.

24. For example, at an event on doing business in Vietnam, many of the questions focused on corruption in the Vietnamese government and the lack of economic regulations or protections. At another luncheon I attended for a delegation of business leaders from Shanghai, the question was about human rights violations in China and the kinds of economic sanctions the United States could levy against China, jeopardizing economic investments.

25. In San Diego, a 1.5-generation Vietnamese American employed by San Diego County was the main organizer, and his primary difficulty was not the ethnic barriers, but the apprehension among Asians toward unions and their historical connection to socialism and communism.

26. "Staged for Success: A Commentary on the Realities of An Association," *Asian Business Association News* (Los Angeles) 7, 4 (October 1991).

27. "Pan Asian Business Association Formed," *Asian Business Association News* (San Diego), September/October 1990.

28. During the early 1990s, economic alliances among "disadvantaged" groups for economic resources often meant an alliance between people of color and White women (and sometimes veterans, mainly white males, and the disabled), an often uncomfortable alliance.

29. Participating organizations were Alba "80," American Indian Business Association, ABA, Black Economic Development Task Force, Filipino-American Chamber of Commerce, Indian Human Resource Center, Mexican American Business and Professional Association, San Diego Hispanic Chamber of Commerce, and the San Diego Urban League.

30. Minutes of the Communities United for Economic Justice meeting, 22 September 1992.

31. On 30 May 1988, the California Public Utilities Commission (CPUC) issued General Order 156 providing all utility companies with gross annual revenues in excess of $25 million and their regulated subsidiaries and affiliates with uniform rules and guidelines to develop and implement Women- and Minority-Owned Business Enterprises. Each utility (electric, gas, and telephone) company agreed to procure at least 15 percent from minority and 5 percent from women by 1993. There was disagreement by some that this would be difficult to achieve and should be based on availability, so many suggested the figure should be raised or lowered accordingly.

32. SDG&E employed over 4,000 workers in the area and had over one million customers. The company stipulated it would work to diversify in the areas of service, procurement, banking, insurance, advertising, professional services, employment and employee development, governance, and corporate contributions, though minorities complained that the company's progress was "slow."

33. Hal Brown was the past president of the Black Economic Development Task Force, Inc., of San Diego County, a cocreator of the Afro-American Association and the San Diego chapter of the Congress of Racial Equality in 1961, and a business professor at San Diego State University.

34. Minutes of the CUEJ meeting, 22 September 1992.

Chapter Six

1. Parrillo 1982 and Wilke and Mohan 1984 fall into the first group; in the second are Erie and Brackman 1993; Chang 2001; Espiritu 1992; Fong 1994; Horton 1995; Y. Jo 1980; Lien 2001; Nakanishi 1991; Saito 1998; and Zia 2000.

2. These estimates were for the 1990 primary elections. This compares to Anglos, who make up 58 percent of the state's population, 71 percent of eligible voters, 79 percent of registered voters, and 83 percent of voters. Immigrants without citizenship are ineligible to vote, but even those who become citizens or residents are not registering to vote nor are they voting (Din 1984; Ulhaner, Cain, and Kiewiet 1989). While a fair number of Asians become naturalized quickly, perhaps because citizenship allows them to take advantage of the reunification provisions of the immigration policy and sponsor relatives for immigration, they have been slow to acclimate themselves to the political process (Erie and Brackman 1993).

3. Minutes of meeting held 22 December 1991. An invitation to the Voters League meeting on 25 January 1992 stated: "The purpose of the ALFA Voters League is to promote active, well informed citizenship, to educate and activate the County's electorate and to develop and tap candidates coming from the ALFA groups to run for Elective public office in the County and City."

4. Judging from my discussion with Asian American leaders, her reception at mayoral forums held by Asian Americans, and the number of Asian American community fund-raisers given for her, Golding was clearly the favorite candidate. She was pro-business and pro-growth, whereas her major opponent, Peter Navarro, an economics professor at the University of California, Irvine, was president of Prevent Los Angeles Now (PLAN), an organization opposed to growth. A Filipino who volunteered to work on Navarro's campaign, especially with Asian voters, explained to me that "unfortunately he [Navarro] only attended a few Asian events and just gave up on the Asian community."

5. In July 1991, when Golding was a county supervisor, the title of her talk at the ABA dinner was "Utilizing Asians and Other Minority Communities as Resources to Develop the Future of San Diego."

6. Several individuals were also officers in the Filipino-American Democratic Club, which provided them with a model for organizing. An officer with this club suggested to Filipinos that they expand their organization to include all Asians, but Filipino Democrats wanted the Asian organization to establish itself first, before discussing the possibility of a joint endeavor.

7. See "1992 Asian Pacific American Democratic Platform," prepared by the Democratic National Committee's Asian Pacific American Advisory Council, May 1992. The council was appointed in 1990 to represent the concerns of the Asian Pacific American community.

8. Although the San Diego County Democratic Party's endorsements were a technical violation of a state law barring party involvement in nonpartisan races, the law was not being enforced by the attorney general's office.

9. In 1993, of the 1,342,494 registered voters in San Diego, 504,694 were registered Democrats and 606,516 were registered Republicans.

10. With the addition of another congressional seat through reapportionment in 1992, two of the five-member delegation to the U.S. House of Representatives were liberal Democrats, whereas previously there were four conservative Republicans (Smolens 1992). This changing of the guard was brought about by larger political transformations as well, such as the recession and the anti-incumbency sentiment that negatively affected Republican candidates.

11. The Chinese Community Action Committee (CCAC) that briefly existed in the 1990s raised money for Secretary of State March Fong Eu and for Lieutenant Governor of Delaware S. B. Woo, and Filipinos raised $17,000 for Gloria Ochoa for Congress. According to some Chinese I talked to, the PAC used Mandarin Chinese, which excluded a number of Cantonese-speaking Chinese, and there were conflicts about its relationship with mainland China and Taiwan, in addition to debates about whether or not to support Chinese candidates from other states. Some have complained that ethnicity is not the problem, but that San Diego Asians were spending money on Asian candidates from other areas and instead needed to consider encouraging and giving money to local Asian candidates, since they would have a direct impact on the community.

12. When I was doing my fieldwork, the ABA political action education council issued a statement clarifying its nonprofit status, recognizing it needed to educate members when some questioned the organization's "political" involvement: "It [ABA] is a nonprofit, 502 (c)6, Business Education organization, it can take official positions on events, resolutions, propositions, ballot issues, and such, as it relates to economic and business ramifications affecting the community at large, but it cannot support individual candidates running for public office. Individuals acting as private citizens, not as ABA members, can endorse candidates for public office." ABA can educate its members to support candidates through educational forums, although it must remain legally nonpartisan.

13. On 4 June 1991, in their talk titled "Redistricting and Its Implications," City Council members Wes Pratt of the Fourth District and Tom Behr of the Fifth District discussed their views on the redistricting plan that was passed by the city and its future implications for the Asian community in their districts. City Council member Ron Roberts spoke on "What Is the Proposed Twin-Airport and What Effect Will It Have on International Trade" in August 1991.

14. ABA memo regarding the Asian Business Leaders Ad Hoc Political Caucus, n.d.

15. For example, they held a fund-raiser on 21 March 1992 for Councilman Bob Filner, a candidate for U.S. Congress, District 50, which had a 15 percent Asian American population. They supported Filner because he had nominated Asian Americans for major city boards and commissions, and he voted in their favor on several occasions. His district was one of the fastest-growing Asian American communities in the county, encompassing Southeast Asian communities along the

University–El Cajon corridor and the large Filipino American communities of South Bay.

16. The adjacent restaurants, located on the edge of downtown in the waterfront area, were sold to Taiwanese owners and converted to a Denny's restaurant. At the time I was conducting my research, many of the meetings for Asians were held in the Kearny Mesa area, north of downtown, in newer and larger Asian, primarily Chinese, restaurants.

17. Charter members of PAVE included Dr. George Yee, president of Miramar College, and Dennis Kobata, a Jesse Jackson delegate at the 1984 Democratic National Convention, along with members of UPAC, Chinese Social Service Center, and Pacific Asians for the Rainbow.

18. Filipinos were the only subgroup to sponsor a separate forum, and this was only for the mayoral candidates in the 1992 primary election.

19. Questions asked of various candidates included: "The population of San Diego County is approximately 10 percent Asian American, yet there are only 3 [Asian American] lawyers out of 240 lawyers working at the District Attorney's office. Two out of 68 lawyers work at the County counsel. There is [sic] a total of 9 Pan Asian lawyers out of 525 lawyers working for the city and county of San Diego, representing only 1.7 percent of the total. Do you view this underrepresentation as a problem, how will you rectify this problem? Would you support the Coalition Redistricting Map for the County, which was submitted by the ABA, the Asian American Political Coalition, Camino Real Group, and the Harbor Community Council when redistricting is revisited in mid-1990s? Will you support the appointment of Asian Americans to key County and/or City boards and commissions? In law enforcement, the San Diego City Police has only 5 percent Pan Asian and not a single Pan Asian Officer in upper management. The Sheriff's Department is worse with only 3.4 percent Pan Asians in its general ranks. In view of our increasing population, and the growing concern over Asian youth gangs, do you view these percentages as a problem? If so, what do you propose to do to resolve this problem?"

20. Letter from ABA Executive Committee to mayoral candidate, City Councilman Ron Roberts, 5 April 1992.

21. Some of the appointments ABA supported were to the City of San Diego's Professional Selection Committee, Southeast Economic Development Corporation's Loan Committee, Bankers Small Business Community Development Corporation, Agents Advisory Council for San Diego Foundation for Medical Care, Centre City's Asian Thematic Advisory Committee, Public Utilities Commission Minority Advisory Commission San Diego Representative, and the Centre City Development Corporation Board of Directors. "Message from the President," *Asian Business Association News* (San Diego) 1, 3 (January 1992).

22. The San Diego Police Department created the African American and Latino community liaison position in the early 1990s, later followed by liaison positions for the Asian American community and for the gay and lesbian community.

23. While many of the political aides have been Filipinos, there have been Chinese and Korean aides as well.

24. When City Council member Tom Behr wanted to hire a liaison to work with the Asian community, he contacted the ABA president at the time, who recommended a Filipina, a Laotian, and a Vietnamese Chinese, the last of whom was hired.

25. The San Diego Unified Port District is a special-purpose unit of the government created in 1962 to manage the harbor, operate the international airport at Lindbergh Field, and administer the public tidelands surrounding San Diego Bay. The Port District encompasses the cities of San Diego, National City, Chula Vista, Imperial Beach, and Coronado (information from the San Diego Unified Port District brochure, May 1991). Two other major appointments were made at the same time. One was the appointment of Joe Wong, a U.S.-born Chinese whose family has an extensive history in San Diego, to the Centre City Development Corporation. The other was Su-Mei Yu, a local Chinese entrepreneur born and raised in Thailand who also runs an agency that provides support services to Southeast Asian refugee women, and who has been extensively involved in mainstream Democratic politics, to the San Diego Convention and Visitors Bureau. Both were involved in mainstream organizations, but they were also involved with Asian American organizations, and they solicited endorsements from Asian leaders and organizations, even though credit cannot solely be given to these organizations for their placements.

26. In redrawing the districts, planners can consider "(a) topography; (b) geography; (c) cohesiveness, contiguity, integrity, and compactness of territory; and (d) community of interests of the districts" (*State Elections Code*, Section 35000).

27. While reapportionment and redistricting affects local representatives at the state and national level, the focus of minority groups in San Diego at this time was at the city and county levels.

28. Previously, council candidates were nominated by the district; the top two choices in each district ran in an at-large runoff, which made it difficult for minority candidates to win. Efforts to change this system got under way in the 1970s, and the reform was defeated twice in San Diego before being approved in 1988.

29. In 1991, the statewide Coalition of Asian Pacific Americans for Fair Reapportionment (CAPAFR), a nonpartisan coalition with local affiliates, formed to prevent racial gerrymandering that split its population into separate districts and to ensure that Asian Pacific communities were fairly represented in the redistricting and reapportionment process.

30. Some of the areas include Linda Vista, which has a large Southeast Asian population; Mira Mesa, where many Filipinos live; Scripps Ranch, where more Chinese are moving; and Kearny Mesa, which has a mixture of Asians.

31. In 1990, the Chicano Federation sued the city council, charging it with intentionally diluting the voting strength of Latinos in District 8, located in the southern portion of the city near the Mexican-U.S. border. The federation won the legal struggle when a compromise was reached under U.S. district court supervision, giving San Diego its first Latino-majority city council district, with 61.5 percent Latino and 80 percent minority population. The main areas of the district cover Barrio Logan, Logan Heights, southwest Golden Hills, San Ysidro, and Otay Mesa. Two previous Latino representatives of District 8, Jess Haro and Uvaldo Martinez, were the first elected, after being appointed by the council to fill unexpired terms and then resigning due to legal troubles. When the seat was vacated by Bob Filner, who was elected to the U.S. Congress, seven of the ten candidates who ran in the special election were Latino. Juan Vargas, a Latino, won and ran uncontested shortly afterward in the regular election period.

32. During the 1980 reapportionment, each district had about 370,000 residents, and in the 1990 reapportionment, each district would have about 500,000, indicating the population increase within the ten-year period.

33. Memo from Norman w. Hickey, Chief Administrative Officer to Board of Supervisors, 31 July 1991.

34. The Chicano Federation stated that the county's proposal violated the federal Voting Rights Act by failing to maximize the voting strength of minorities. In the Chicano Federation plan, White residents would comprise almost 25 percent; Hispanics, 43 percent; Blacks, 16 percent; and Asians, 15 percent. This plan included redrawing the Fourth District to include San Diego City Council Fourth and Eighth Districts.

35. The last time a Latino was elected to the county board was in 1973.

36. In its proposal dated 28 August 1991, the four-organization coalition's alternative proposal stated District 1 would be at least 45 percent Hispanics, 8 percent Black, and 10 percent Asian, and District 4 would be 17 percent Asian, 13 percent Black, and 16 percent Latino. Before the redistricting, the districts had 35 percent and 27 percent Hispanic populations, respectively.

37. The federation also wanted the county to increase the number of districts from five to seven, to allow for the creation of more minority districts, but this request was denied.

38. The cochairs of the event were three Filipinos, three Chinese, one Laotian, one Japanese, and one person of mixed Asian ancestry, with more than half of them not born in this country. Listed below the cochairs were four subgroups, with nineteen from the Pilipino community, thirteen Chinese, seven Japanese, and four from the Southeast Asian community. In addition, even on Colby's mainstream fund-raising committee, of his four campaign chairs, one was Japanese and one was of mixed Asian ancestry.

39. Other areas in the district include Linda Vista, Kearny Mesa, Mira Mesa, Scripps Ranch, Sabre Springs, Carmel Mountain Ranch, and Rancho Bernardo.

Chapter Seven

1. Mike Stepner, Acting Planning Director, City of San Diego Planning Department, memorandum to CCDC regarding the Chinese/Asian Thematic Historic District, 17 July 1987, 12.

2. See Linda Trinh Võ, "The Chinese/Asian Thematic Historic District," *Asian Business Association News* (San Diego) 1, 4 (April 1992).

3. *Chinese/Asian Thematic Historic District Report*, prepared by the City of San Diego Planning Department/Urban Conservation Section, April 1987.

4. Ibid.

5. The regulations passed by the city council stipulated that approval of the projects would be carried out by mainstream organizations, such as the Historical Site Board, City of San Diego Planning Department and Planning Commission, and Redevelopment Agency. Marina, Urban Design Plan Development Guidelines Planned District Ordinance, Adopted by Redevelopment Agency Resolution R 1626, 1 August 1988, 45–46 and 72–73.

6. Letter from Gerald M. Trimble, Executive Vice President of CCDC, to CCDC regarding recommendations for the Chinese/Asian Thematic Historic District, 9 July 1987. They hired anthropologist Ray Brandes, architect Wayne Donaldson, and attorney Marie Lia to assist in the project.

7. The author determined the ethnicity of the Advisory Committee based on the names listed in the *Chinese/Asian Thematic Historic District Report*, April 1987.

8. In the *Chinese/Asian Thematic Historic District Report*, December 1991, from CCDC, there are descriptions of twenty Japanese and Chinese buildings, with no mention of Filipino ones (although a former restaurant was called the Manila).

9. House of China is a sixty-year-old nonprofit cultural/educational organization located in Balboa Park to preserve, present, and promote Chinese culture. House of China letter to San Diego Historical Site Board, 29 April 1987.

10. Letter from Tom Hom, Church Moderator, to San Diego Historical Site Board, 25 April 1987.

11. Letter from Chinese Historical Society to San Diego Historical Site Board, 28 April 1987.

12. City Planning Department Report to the Honorable Mayor and City Council, City of San Diego, Report No. 87-502, Subject: Chinese/Asian Thematic Historic District, 5 October 1987, 4.

13. *Chinese/Asian Thematic District Report*, 1991, 1.

14. The owners of the Regal and Anita Hotels fought the city council to have the building demolished and agreed to salvage some portions for incorporation into the replacement high-rise building. The structures in the Gaslamp Quarter are the Callan Hotel, Manila Café, Lincoln Hotel, Stingaree Building, Kabazon (Nanking) Café, Island Hotel, Tai Sing Building, Quin Building, Sun Café, Manos Market, Tool Sales/Laundry Building, Montijo Building, and Lowenstein Building. The seven buildings in the Marina District are Plants and Fireproofing Building, Ying-On Merchants and Labor Association Building and its annex, Chinese Consolidated Benevolent Association Building, Quin Residence, Quong Building, and Chinese Mission Building. The Chinese Mission began in 1885 and the school opened under the sponsorship of the California Chinese Auxiliary of the Congregational American Missionary Association and moved to the site in 1907. The landowners wanted to rebuild on this site, so the building was moved several blocks before being converted to a Chinese museum. The Ying-On Merchant and Labor Benevolent Association Building, in operation since 1927, is still a business and social gathering place for local merchants and residents. The owners originally objected to having their building designated for the local and National Register of Historic Places, since this meant that they could not, at a future date, destroy the building and replace it as they wished. The main streets of the Asian District are Third, Fourth, and Fifth Streets and Island Avenue, with several structures located on Sixth and Market Streets.

15. The Woo Chee Chong Building housed a grocery business from 1898 to 1964 and expanded to three locations in San Diego (Clifford 1990c), but closed in 1995.

16. A city planner expresses this view: "From the long term planning 'Urban Development' perspective, preservation of special communities provides cities with

variety, context, history, and roots. Preservation of these does not always mean pre-serving monumental architecture. The Chinese/Asian District would provide the City of San Diego with a contextual base of a series of 'ethnic communities' which made up what our City is today, and an architectural base of small wooden build-ings which are important to our understanding to [sic] how our urban center began." Mike Stepner, Acting Planning Director, City of San Diego Planning Department Memorandum to CCDC regarding the Chinese/Asian Thematic Historic District, 17 July 1987.

17. City Planning Department Report to the Centre City Development Cor-poration Board of Directors, 14 July 1987, Report No. 87-383; City Planning Department Report 87-502, 5. See also the City of San Diego Historical Site Board Report, Issue/Project: Chinese/Asian Thematic Historic District, 17 April 1987.

18. National Register of Historic Places Inventory Nomination Form for Chinese/Asian Thematic Historic District, 29 April 1987.

19. Stepner memo, 17 July 1987.

20. Proposal by the San Diego Chinese Center to CCDC for the Lincoln Build-ing, 8 July 1991.

21. Brochure on San Diego Chinese Center, n.d. The center offers translation, job referral, immigration information, housing assistance, escort services, and other social welfare services. The center, formerly the Chinese Social Service Center, changed its name when it began to include some cultural programs, such as spon-soring the Chinese New Year Food and Cultural Faire, the Chinese Theater, Man-darin Affair, and the Chinese New Year Dinner, all mainly fund-raising events.

22. SDCC News, the Newsletter of the San Diego Chinese Center 2, 5 (Septem-ber/October 1990).

23. Personal memo sent to Mayor Maureen O'Conner regarding the Recom-mendation by the Centre City Development Corporation to enter a negotiation agreement with Vista Hills Foundation for the Lincoln Hotel, 18 February 1992.

24. Memo from the Executive Vice President of CCDC to Property Owners, Gaslamp Quarter Planning Board Members, and Other Interested Parties, 30 August 1991.

25. Apparently, they had been given inaccurate estimates of the cost. Since the hotel is a historic building, the redevelopment plans must maintain as much of the existing structure as possible. The building is long and narrow, so much of the work must be done by hand, making it an extremely expensive project.

26. Letter, unsigned, to CCDC, 2 July 1991.

27. Letter from Rom Sarno, Chair, Mayor's Asian Advisory Board, to CCDC, July 12, 1991.

28. Centre City Development Corporation Chinese/Asian Thematic Historic District Advisory Committee Mission Statement passed on 25 March 1993.

29. The official states he actually said: "Let's face it, this opposition is really about prejudice. The mentally ill are one of the few groups its [sic] still socially acceptable to put down. They're the 'niggers' of the 90's."

30. Memo from VM to Mayor Maureen O'Conner regarding the Recommen-dation by The Centre City Development Corporation to enter a Negotiation Agree-ment with Vista Hills Foundation for the Lincoln Hotel, February 18, 1992.

31. San Diego Daily Transcript, 20 February 1992, Local Scene section, 3A.

32. Vista Hills letter, 27 February 1992.

33. Vista Hills, Proposal to Develop the Lincoln Hotel Summary, n.d.

34. CAT meeting at CCDC, 3 March 1992.

35. It would have been difficult for IMAA to fund such as massive project, and UPAC already had another low-income housing project in the works, which was primarily for the Southeast Asian population. Additionally, giving the Southeast Asian population the housing project in the district would be quite controversial, considering that they were not one of the Asian subgroups with a history there. Clearly, this suggestion was made to influence the vote and was never a serious consideration.

36. "'Asiatown,' 23 September General Meeting," *FACC News Notes* 1, 4 (September 1991).

37. Letter from the San Diego Filipino-American Foundation, Inc., to CAT, 2 March 1992.

38. Letter from Romulo Sarno Jr., Chair of the Asian Advisory Board, to Wilson Hom, President of the San Diego Chinese Center, 11 September 1991.

39. Both ABA and UPAC officially endorsed Wong for the position. Wong's vision for the Chinese/Asian Thematic Area was for public/private cooperation to transform the area to a mixed-use residential and commercial development that included museums, art galleries, shops, restaurants, outdoor markets, and cafés, with an area to accommodate ethnic parades, festivals, fairs, and celebrations. Joseph Wong, Asian Business News, *Asian Business Association News* 2, (October 1993), 7.

40. Position paper on CCDC and Asian Thematic District by the Asian Business Association, San Diego, 1 January 1992.

41. For example, at the Filipino Forum for Mayoral Candidates held in March 1992, candidates were asked: "The recent controversy regarding the Lincoln Hotel in the Chinese/Asian Thematic Historic District resonates of racial dissonance historically confronted by minority peoples. 1. Are you committed to the official mission of the Chinese/Asian Historic Thematic District? If so would you support a strong economic action plan for the district, one that emphasizes Asian Heritage and Culture as well as promotes Pacific Rim Trade and commerce? 2. What specifically would you do to ensure equal and viable participation by the Asian-American Communities who have historical roots downtown?"

42. Although they had more than just the Lincoln Hotel issue in mind, members of ABA, along with others in the Asian American community, later held fundraisers for two of the city council members who voted in favor of giving the hotel to the Asian American community. One council member, Ron Roberts, went on to run for mayor unsuccessfully; another, Bob Filner, ran for U.S. Representative successfully. City Council members Valerie Stallings and especially Tom Behr were instrumental in convincing their colleagues to vote in favor of the Asian American community.

43. Position paper on CCDC and Asian Thematic District by ABA, San Diego, 1 January 1992.

44. The committee consists of seven individuals appointed for a two-year term; members can be reappointed once. Selection of applicants was made by CCDC's Executive Board, not CAT.

45. It is located in the Kabazon Café Building. Chinese/Asian Thematic Historic District Report by CCDC, December 1991, 11.

46. Chinese/Asian Thematic Historic District Advisory Committee meeting, 15 December 1994.

47. Letter from ABA to CAT regarding the Lincoln Hotel, 25 February 1992.

48. CAT Meeting at CCDC, 19 March 1992.

49. Invitation from the Chinese/Asian Thematic Historic District Advisory Committee, 26 May 1994. The event was presented in cooperation with the Chinese Historical Society, Japanese American Historical Society of San Diego, Chinese Consolidated Benevolent Society, Operation Samahan Clinic, San Diego Filipino-American Humanitarian Foundation, and Centre City Development Corporation.

Chapter Eight

1. Edison Uno was Assistant Dean of Students at the University of California, San Francisco from 1969 to 1974. In the late 1960s, he was one of the leaders to establish Ethnic Studies at San Francisco State University. Starting in the early 1970s, he was one of the initial activists in the struggle to repeal the law that permitted the incarceration of Japanese Americans in detention camps.

2. "Gook" was an epithet used during the Philippine-American War (1899–1902) to refer to the native Filipino population, during the Korean War to refer to Koreans, and particularly during the Vietnam War to refer to the Vietnamese (Wei 1993: 38).

3. Suzie Wong is a character from the 1960s Paramount Studio movie *The World of Suzie Wong*, starring William Holden and Nancy Kwan, who played a prostitute in Hong Kong.

References

Abelmann, Nancy, and John Lie. 1995. *Blue Dreams: Korean Americans and the Los Angeles Riots.* Cambridge: Harvard University Press.

Abraham, Margaret. 2000. *Speaking the Unspeakable: Marital Violence among South Asian Immigrants in the United States.* New Brunswick, N.J.: Rutgers University Press.

Almaguer, Tomás. 1994. *Racial Fault Lines: The Historical Origins of White Supremacy in California.* Berkeley: University of California Press.

Anderson, Benedict. 1983. *Imagined Communities: Reflections on the Origin and Spread of Nationalism.* London: Verso.

Anderson, Susan. 1991. "Rivers of Water in a Dry Place—Early Black Participation in California Politics." Pp. 55–69 in *Racial and Ethnic Politics in California,* ed. Byran O. Jackson and Michael B. Preston. Berkeley: Institute for Governmental Studies Press.

Arnold, Thomas K. 1987. "Miller to Leave Spot at KSDO-FM." *Los Angeles Times* (8 April).

———. 1993. "Power Grab Stirs Strife in San Diego Asian Community." *San Diego Reader* (1 July), 5.

Barkan, Elliott Robert. 1992. *Asian and Pacific Islander Migration to the United States: A Model of New Global Patterns.* Westport, Conn.: Greenwood Press.

Barringer, Herbert, Robert W. Gardner, and Michael J. Levin. 1993. *Asian and Pacific Islanders in the United States.* New York: Russell Sage Foundation.

Barth, Fredrik. 1969. "Introduction." Pp. 9–38 in *Ethnic Groups and Boundaries: The Social Organization of Culture Difference,* ed. Fredrik Barth. Boston, Mass.: Little, Brown.

Basch, Linda, Nina Glick Schiller, and Cristina Szanton Blanc. 1995. *Nations Unbound: Transnational Projects, Postcolonial Predicaments and Deterritorialized Nation-States.* Australia: Gordon and Breach.

Bates, Jim. 1975. "Jim Bates Reports, Supervisor 4th District, County of San Diego." *Voice News & Viewpoint* (14 May), A-4.

Bellah, Robert N., Richard Madsen, William M. Sullivan, Ann Swidler, and Steven M. Tipton. 1985. *Habits of the Heart: Individualism and Commitment in American Life.* Berkeley: University of California Press.

Bernstein, Leonard. 1992. "Voting-Bias Suit against County Killed," *Los Angeles Times* (12 May).

Blumberg, Rhoda Lois. 1991. *Civil Rights: The 1960's Freedom Struggle*. Revised Edition. Boston: Twayne.

Bonacich, Edna, and John Modell. 1980. *The Economic Basis of Ethnic Solidarity: A Study of Japanese Americans*. Berkeley: University of California Press.

Bonus, Rick. 2000. *Locating Filipino Americans: Ethnicity and the Cultural Politics of Space*. Philadelphia: Temple University Press.

Brandes, Ray, Susan Carrico, and Toni Nagel. N.d. "San Diego's Chinatown and Stingeree District."

Braun, Gerry. 1993a. "Democrats Endorse 2 in Non-Partisan Council Races." *San Diego Union-Tribune* (10 June), B-1.

———. 1993b. "6 Candidates Compete to Succeed Tom Behr." *San Diego Union-Tribune* (29 August), B-1.

Braun, Gerry, and Ruth L. McKinnie. 1997. "Do We All Get Along? San Diego's Race Relations Contend with a Few Sour Notes." *San Diego Union-Tribune* (12 June), A-1.

Browning, Rufus P., Dale Rogers Marshall, and David H. Tabb. 1984. *Protest Is Not Enough: The Struggle of Blacks and Hispanics for Equality in Urban Politics*. Berkeley: University of California Press.

Cain, Bruce. 1991. "The Contemporary Context of Ethnic and Racial Politics." Pp. 9–24 in *Racial and Ethnic Politics in California*, ed. Byran O. Jackson and Michael B. Preston. Berkeley: Institute for Governmental Studies Press.

Cain, Bruce E., and D. Roderick Kiewiet. 1986. *Minorities in California*. Pasadena: California Institute of Technology.

Cain, Bruce E., D. Roderick Kiewiet, and Carole J. Uhlaner. 1991. "The Acquisition of Partisanship by Latinos and Asian Americans." *American Journal of Political Science* 35 (2) (May): 390–422.

Camoroff, Jean. 1985. *Body of Power, Spirit of Resistance: The Culture and History of a South African People*. Chicago: University of Chicago Press.

Cantlupe, Joe. 1994a. "City OKs Bias Study at Cost of $500,000," *San Diego Union-Tribune* (9 March).

———. 1994b. "Minority Building Firms Losing Millions," *San Diego Union-Tribune* (4 June), A-1 ff.

———. 1994c. "Minority-contractors Program Altered," *San Diego Union-Tribune* (10 August), B-1 ff.

Cariño, Benjamin V. 1987. "The Philippines and Southeast Asia: Historical Roots and Contemporary Linkage." Pp. 305–326 in *Pacific Bridges: The New Immigration from Asia and the Pacific Islands*, ed. James T. Fawcett and Benjamin V. Cariño. Staten Island, N.Y.: Center for Migration Studies.

Carrier, Lynne. 1992a. "City Council OKs Major Centre City Expansion Program." *San Diego Daily Transcript* (29 April).

———. 1992b. "Council Still in Dispute over Fate of Lincoln Hotel." *San Diego Daily Transcript* (4 March), 1-A.

Castillo, Adelaida. 1976. "Filipino Migrants in San Diego, 1900–1946." *Journal of San Diego History* 12: 27–35.

Chan, Kenyon. 1984. "Moving beyond Ethnic Stereotypes: Asian and Pacific Americans." *Television and Children* 4 (1): 12–15.

Chan, Sucheng. 1991. *Asian Americans: An Interpretive History.* Boston: Twayne.

———. 2003. "Politics and the Indochinese Refugee Exodus, 1975–1997." Pp. 171–222 in *Remapping Asian American History,* ed. Sucheng Chan. Walnut Creek, Calif.: AltaMira Press.

Chang, Gordon H., ed. 2001. *Asian Americans and Politics: Perspectives, Experiences, Prospects.* Washington, D.C.: Woodrow Wilson Center Press, and Stanford, Calif.: Stanford University Press.

Chao, Julie. 1997. "Head of the Class? Asian Americans Aren't All Geniuses." *San Francisco Examiner* (10 October).

Chin, Steven A. 1994. "Hate Crimes That Target Asians Are Underreported, Study Finds." *San Diego Union-Tribune* (25 April), A-5.

Christensen, Terry, and Larry N. Gerston. 1984. *Politics in the Golden State: The California Connection.* Boston: Little, Brown.

Chu, Amy. 1982. "The Climb to Gold Mountain." *San Diego Reader* (8 April).

Clifford, Jane. 1990a. "Echoes of Hostile Times." *San Diego Tribune* (23 February).

———. 1990b. "Tom Hom's Life Best of Old, New." *San Diego Tribune* (14 August).

———. 1990c. "Woo Chee Chong Stores Almost a Century of History." *San Diego Tribune* (14 August).

Collins, Patricia Hill. 1991. *Black Feminist Thought: Knowledge, Consciousness, and the Politics of Empowerment.* New York: Routledge.

Comaroff, Jean. 1985. *Body of Power, Spirit of Resistance: The Culture and History of a South African People.* Chicago: The University of Chicago Press.

Core, Richard. 1987. "KSDO's Offer to Apologize for Jokes Doesn't Suit Affronted Asian Groups." *San Diego Tribune* (27 March), B-4.

Cornacchia, Eugene J., and Dale C. Nelson. 1992. "Historical Differences in the Political Experiences of American Blacks and White Ethnics: Revisiting an Unresolved Controversy." *Ethnic and Racial Studies* 15 (1) (January): 102–124.

Cornelius, Wayne A. 1982. "America in the Era of Limits: Nativist Reactions to the 'New' Immigration." *Working Papers in US-Mexican Studies* 3. San Diego: University of California, San Diego, 1–31.

Cornell, Stephen. 1988. *The Return of the Native: American Indian Political Resurgence.* New York: Oxford University Press.

Cox, Oliver C. 1948. *Caste, Class, and Race.* New York: Doubleday.

Cronin, Matthew. 1992. "Asians Demand More Than Token Influence Downtown: The Lincoln Hotel Project Turns into a Battleground." *Uptown,* March 1992, 5.

Curran-Downey, Mary. 1987a. "Pan Asian Group Upset by TV 'Acupuncturist.'" *San Diego Union* (26 February).

———. 1987b. "Rights Agency Wants an Apology from DJ." *San Diego Union* (March 3), B-3.

Dahl, Robert. 1961. *Who Governs? Democracy and Power in the American City.* New Haven: Yale University Press.

Daniels, Dwight. 1997. "Election Shows How Far Enclave Has Come: Rancho Santa Fe, Which Once Barred Nonwhites, Taps Asians." *San Diego Union-Tribune* (14 June), B-3.

Daniels, Roger. 1988. *Asian America: Chinese and Japanese in the United States since 1850.* Seattle: University of Washington Press.

Davis, F. James. 1991. *Who Is Black? One Nation's Definition.* University Park: Pennsylvania State University Press.

Der, Henry. 1993. "Asian Pacific Islanders and the 'Glass Ceiling'—New Era of Civil Rights Activism? Affirmative Action Policy." Pp. 215–231 in *The State of Asian Pacific America: Policy Issues to the Year 2020.* Los Angeles: LEAP Asian Pacific American Public Policy Institute and UCLA Asian American Studies Center.

de Tocqueville, Alexis. 1969. *Democracy in America.* Trans. George Lawrence, ed. J. P. Mayer. New York: Anchor.

Dhingra, Pawan. 2003. "The Second Generation in "Big D": Korean American and Indian American Organizations in Dallas, Texas." *Sociological Spectrum* 23: 247–278.

Din, Grant. 1984. "An Analysis of Asian/Pacific American Registration and Voting Patterns in San Francisco." M.A. thesis, Claremont Graduate School.

Dirlik, Arif. 1996. "Asians on the Rim: Transnational Capital and Local Community in the Making of Contemporary Asian America." *Amerasia Journal* 22 (3): 1–24.

Du Bois, W.E.B. 1990 [1986]. *The Souls of Black Folks.* New York: Vintage Books.

Dunn, Ashley. 1994. "Asian American Study Reveals Hidden Poverty." *San Diego Union Tribune* (19 May), A-1.

Durkheim, Emile. 1947. *The Division of Labor in Society.* [Trans. George Simpson]. Glencoe, Ill.: Free Press.

Enloe, Cynthia. 1981. "The Growth of the State and Ethnic Mobilization: The American Experience." *Ethnic and Racial Studies* 4 (2): 123–136.

Erie, Steven P., and Harold Brackman. 1993. *Paths to Political Incorporation for Latinos and Asians Pacifics in California.* Berkeley: California Policy Seminar, University of California.

Espiritu, Yen Le. 1992. *Asian American Panethnicity: Bridging Institutions and Identities.* Philadelphia: Temple University Press.

———. 1995. *Filipino American Lives.* Philadelphia: Temple University Press.

———. 2003. *Home Bound: Filipino American Lives across Cultures, Communities, and Countries.* Berkeley and Los Angeles: University of California Press.

Espiritu, Yen, and Paul Ong. 1994. "Class Constraints on Racial Solidarity among Asian Americans." Pp. 295–322 in *The New Asian Immigration in Los Angeles and Global Restructuring,* ed. Paul Ong, Edna Bonacich, and Lucie Cheng. Philadelphia: Temple University Press.

Estes, Donald H. 1978. "Before the War: The Japanese in San Diego." *Journal of San Diego History* 24 (4) (Fall), 425–455.

Flacks, Richard. 1994. "The Party's Over—So What Is to Be Done?" Pp. 330–352 in *New Social Movements: From Ideology to Identity,* ed. Enrique Laraña, Hank Johnston, and Joseph R. Gusfield. Philadelphia: Temple University Press.

Flynn, Pat. 1991. "County Gets Minority Voting Plan." *San Diego Union* (24 August), B-1.

———. 1992. "Singed Council Passes Remap Hot Potato to Voters." *San Diego Union* (14 January), B-1.

Fong, Timothy P. 1994. *The First Suburban Chinatown: The Remaking of Monterey Park, California*. Philadelphia: Temple University Press.

Fugita, Stephen S., and David J. O'Brien. 1985. "Structural Assimilation, Ethnic Group Membership, and Political Participation among Japanese Americans: A Research Note." *Social Forces* 63 (4) (June): 986–995.

Gall, Susan B., and Timothy L. Gall, eds. 1993. *Statistical Record of Asian Americans*. Washington, D.C.: Gale Group.

Gamson, William A. 1975. *The Strategy of Social Protest*. Homewood, Ill.: Dorsey Press.

Gans, Herbert J. 1962. *The Urban Villagers: Group and Class in the Life of Italian-Americans*. New York: Free Press.

———. 1979. "Symbolic Ethnicity: The Future of Ethnic Groups and Cultures in America." *Ethnic and Racial Studies* 2: 1–20.

Gembrowski, Susan. 1993. "Our Civil and Civic-Minded New President." *Metropolitan*, February.

Gim, Ruth H. Chung. 1995. "The Sites of Race and Ethnicity in Psychological Research on Asian Americans." Pp. 413–420 in *Privileging Positions: The Sites of Asian American Studies*, ed. Gary Y. Okihiro, Marilyn Alquizola, Dorothy Fujita-Rony, and K. Scott Wong. Pullman: Washington State University Press.

Glazer, Nathan, and Daniel Patrick Moynihan. 1963. *Beyond the Melting Pot: The Negroes, Puerto Ricans, Jews, Italians, and Irish of New York City*. Cambridge: MIT Press.

Gold, Steven J. 1992. *Refugee Communities: A Comparative Field Study*. Newbury Park: Sage.

Gordon, Linda. 1987. "Southeast Asian Refugee Migration to the United States." Pp. 153–173 in *Pacific Bridges: The New Immigration from Asia and the Pacific Islands*, ed. James T. Fawcett and Benjamin V. Carino. Staten Island, N.Y.: Center for Migration Studies.

Gordon, Milton. 1964. *Assimilation in American Life*. New York: Oxford University Press.

Graham, Hugh Davis. 1990. *The Civil Rights Era*. New York: Oxford University Press.

Granberry, Michael. 1990. "Judge Delays Verdict on Redistricting Battle." *Los Angeles Times* (7 November), B-2.

Guerra, Fernando J. 1991. "The Emergence of Ethnic Officeholders in California." Pp. 157–192 in *Racial and Ethnic Politics in California*, ed. Bryan O. Jackson and Michael B. Preston. Berkeley: Institute for Governmental Studies Press.

Gutiérrez, David G. 1995. *Walls and Mirrors: Mexican Americans, Mexican Immigrants, and the Politics of Ethnicity*. Berkeley: University of California Press.

Hamamoto, Darrell Y. 1992. *Monitored Peril: Asian Americans and the Politics of Representation*. Minneapolis: University of Minnesota Press.

———. 1994. *Monitored Peril: Asian Americans and the Politics of TV Representation*. Minneapolis: University of Minnesota Press.

Hamilton, Charles V. 1982. "Foreword." Pp. xvii–xx in *The New Black Politics: The Search for Political Power*, ed. Michael B. Preston, Lenneal J. Henderson Jr., and Paul Puryear. New York: Longman.

Harrison, Laird. 1987. "Chinese Jokes Ire TV, Radio Fans in San Diego." *Asian Week* (20 March).

Hayano, David. 1981. "Ethnic Identification and Disidentification: Japanese-American Views of Chinese-Americans." *Ethnic Groups* 3: 157–171.

Hein, Jeremy. 1989. "States and Political Migrants: The Incorporation of Indochinese Refugees in France and the United States." Ph.D. dissertation, Northwestern University.

Heizer, Robert F., and Alan F. Almquist. 1971. *The Other Californians: Prejudice and Discrimination under Spain, Mexico, and the United States to 1920*. Berkeley: University of California Press.

Hing, Bill Ong. 1993. *Making and Remaking Asian America through Immigration Policy, 1850–1990*. Stanford, Calif.: Stanford University Press.

Hirahara, Naomi. 1987. "Controversial Media Portrayal of Asians Awakens the 'Sleeping Giant' of San Diego." *Rafu Shrimpo, Los Angeles Japanese Daily News* (6 April).

Ho, Fred, ed., with Carolyn Antonio, Diane Fujino, and Steve Yip. 2000. *Legacy to Liberation: Politics and Culture of Revolutionary Asian Pacific America*. Brooklyn: Big Red Media; San Francisco: AK Press.

Ho, Pensri. 2002. "Young Asian American Professionals in Los Angeles: A Community in Transition." Pp. 134–146 in *Intersections and Divergences: Contemporary Asian American Communities*, ed. Linda Trinh Võ and Rick Bonus. Philadelphia: Temple University Press.

Hornor, Edith R. 1994. *California Cities, Towns, and Counties*. Palo Alto: Information Publication.

Horstman, Barry M. 1991. "County's Hispanic Population Up 86%." *Los Angeles Times* (San Diego) (28 February), B-1 ff.

———. 1992. "It Was Year of the Political Upset in San Diego." *Los Angeles Times* (29 November), B-1 ff.

Horton, John. 1995. *The Politics of Diversity: Immigration, Resistance, and Change in Monterey Park, California*. Philadelphia: Temple University Press.

Houston, Velina Hasu, and Teresa K. Williams, guest coeditors. 1997. "No Passing Zone: The Artistic and Discursive Voices of Asian-Descent Multiracials." *Amerasia Journal* 23: 1.

Huard, Ray. 1991a. "Asian-Americans' Political Clout Here Growing Slowly," *San Diego Tribune* (13 August), A-1.

———. 1991b. "Asians Latching onto Power of Politics." *San Diego Tribune* (27 July), A-1.

Hu-DeHart, Evelyn, ed. 1999. *Across the Pacific: Asian Americans and Globalization*. Philadelphia: Temple University Press.

Hurh, Won Moo, and Kwang Chung Kim. 1989. "The 'Success' Image of Asian Americans: Its Validity, and Its Practical and Theoretical Implications." *Ethnic and Racial Studies* 2(4) (October): 512–538.

Ichioka, Yuji. 1988. *The Issei: The World of the First Generation Japanese Immigrants, 1885–1924*. New York: Free Press.

Ignacio, Lemuel F. 1976. "The Pacific/Asian Coalition: Origin, Structure, and Program." *Social Casework* 57 (3) (Mar.): 131–135.

Jenkins, J. Craig. 1983. "Resource Mobilization Theory and the Study of Social Movements." *Annual Review of Sociology* 9: 527–553.

Jewell, K. Sue. 1993. *From Mammy to Miss America and Beyond: Cultural Images and the Shaping of U.S. Social Policy*. London: Routledge.

Jo, Moon J., and Daniel D. Mas. 1993. "Changing Images of Asian Americans." *International Journal of Politics, Culture, and Society* 6 (3) (Spring): 417–442.

Jo, Yung-Hwan, ed. 1980. *Political Participation of Asian Americans: Problems and Strategies*. Chicago: Pacific/Asian American Mental Health Research Center.

Jones, James E., Jr. 1988. "The Origins of Affirmative Action." *University of California-Davis Law Review* 21: 383–419.

Kasfir, Nelson. 1979. "Explaining Ethnic Political Participation." *World Politics* 31 (3) (April): 365–388.

Kasinitz, Philip. 1992. *Caribbean New York: Black Immigrants and the Politics of Race*. Ithaca: Cornell University Press.

Keely, Charles B. 1973. "Philippine Migration: Internal Movements and Emigration to the United States." *International Migration Review* 7 (Summer): 177–187.

Kelley, Robin D. G. 1994. *Race Rebels: Culture, Politics, and the Black Working Class*. New York: Free Press.

Kibria, Nazli. 2002. *Becoming Asian American: Second Generation Chinese and Korean American Identities*. Baltimore: Johns Hopkins University Press.

Kim, Bok-Lim C. 1973. "Asian-Americans: No Model Minority." *Social Work* (May): 44–53.

———. 1978. *The Asian Americans: Changing Patterns, Changing Needs*. Montclair, N.J.: Association of Korean Christian Scholars in North America.

Kim, Illsoo. 1981. *New Urban Immigrants: The Korean Community in New York*. Princeton: Princeton University Press.

Kitano, Harry H. L. 1969. *Japanese Americans: The Evolution of a Subculture*. Englewood Cliffs, N.J.: Prentice-Hall.

Kitano, Harry H. L., and Roger Daniels. 1988. *Asian Americans: Emerging Minorities*. Englewood Cliffs, N.J.: Prentice-Hall.

Kraul, Chris. 1992. "Chamber Picks Latino as Its New President." *Los Angeles Times* (11 November), B-1 ff.

Kuramoto, Ford H. 1976. "Lessons Learned from the Federal Funding Game." *Social Casework* 57 (3) (Mar.): 208–218.

Kwong, Peter. 1987. *The New Chinatown*. New York: Hill and Wang.

LaNoue, George R. 1991. *Minority Business Programs and Disparity Studies: Responding to the Supreme Court's Mandate in* Richmond v. Croson. Washington, D.C.: National League of Cities.

Lau, Angela. 1990a. "Asian Leaders Lobby for Children." *San Diego Union* (19 June), B-3.

———. 1990b. "Asians Tackle Growing Drug Problem: Need Seen to Debunk Popular Myth of 'Model Minorities.'" *San Diego Union* (8 October), B-1.

———. 1990c. "An Epidemic of Hate Crimes against Asians is Reported." *San Diego Union* (24 June), B-3.

———. 1991a. "Competition Fierce for Downtown Hotel Lease." *San Diego Union* (9 September), B-1.

———. 1991b. "Downtown Sites Ok'd for Both Chinese Center and Vista Hill." *San Diego Union* (11 September), B-1.

———. 1992. "Oriental Gangs: Rise in Numbers, Fears." *San Diego Union-Tribune* (9 February), A-1.

———. 1993a. "Cambodians Still Fear Violence." *San Diego Union-Tribune* (17 August), B-1 ff.

———. 1993b. "Suicide Spurs Asian Cops to Organize." *San Diego Union-Tribune* (22 February), B-1.

———. 1994. "San Diego Asians Plan Revival of Historic Chinatown." *San Diego Union-Tribune* (20 August), B-1.

———. 1996. "Chinese Museum Dedicated Today." *San Diego Union-Tribune* (13 January), B-1.

———. 1997. "Senior-Housing Project Designed with Chinese Style: Downtown Building to Blend with Historic Third Avenue District." *San Diego Union-Tribune* (5 May), B-2.

Lee, Murray. 2002. "Ah Quin: One of San Diego's Founding Fathers." Pp. 308–328 in *The Chinese in America: A History from Gold Mountain to the New Millennium*, ed. Susie Lan Cassel. Walnut Creek, Calif.: AltaMira.

Lee, Stacy J. 1996. *Unraveling the Model Minority Stereotype: Listening to Asian American Youth*. New York: Teachers College Press.

Lee, Wen Ho, with Helen Zia. 2002. *My Country versus Me: The First-Hand Account by the Los Alamos Scientist Who Was Falsely Accused of Being a Spy*. New York: Hyperion.

Leonard, Karen Isaksen. 1992. *Making Ethnic Choices: California's Punjabi Mexican Americans*. Philadelphia: Temple University Press.

Levy, Mark R., and Michael S. Kramer. 1972. *The Ethnic Factor: How America's Minorities Decide Elections*. New York: Simon and Schuster.

Lien, Pei-te. 2001. *The Making of Asian America through Political Participation*. Philadelphia: Temple University Press.

Light, Ivan. 1972. *Ethnic Enterprise in America: Business and Welfare among Chinese, Japanese, and Blacks*. Berkeley: University of California Press.

Light, Ivan, and Edna Bonacich. 1988. *Immigrant Entrepreneurs: Koreans in Los Angeles, 1965–1982*. Berkeley: University of California Press.

Lipsitz, George. 1988. *A Life in the Struggle: Ivory Perry and the Culture of Opposition*. Philadelphia: Temple University Press.

Liu, John M., and Lucie Cheng. 1994. "Pacific Rim Development and the Duality of Post-1965 Asian Immigration to the United States." Pp. 74–99 in *The New Asian Immigration in Los Angeles and Global Restructuring*, ed. Paul Ong, Edna Bonacich, and Lucie Cheng. Philadelphia: Temple University Press.

Liu, Judith. 1977. "Celestials in Golden Mountain: The Chinese in One California City, San Diego, 1870–1900." M.A. thesis, San Diego State University.

Loewen, James. 1971. *The Mississippi Chinese: Between Black and White*. Cambridge: Harvard University Press.

Lopez, Alejandra. 2002. "Demographics of California Counties: A Comparison of 1980, 1990, and 2000 Census Data." *CCSRE Race and Ethnicity in California: Demographics Report Series*, No. 9 (June). Stanford, Calif.: Center for Comparative Studies in Race and Ethnicity.

Lopez, Graziano. 1975. "Refugee Counseling Offered—Government Declines Asian Community Help." *Voice News & Viewpoint* (14 May), A-6.

Lott, Juanita Tamayo. 1976. "The Asian American Concept: In Quest of Identity." *Bridge, An Asian American Perspective* (November): 30–34.

Louie, Miriam Ching Yoon. 2001. *Sweatshop Warriors: Immigrant Women Workers Take on the Global Factory.* Cambridge, Mass.: South End Press.

Louie, Steve, and Glenn Omatsu. 2001. *Asian Americans: The Movement and the Moment.* Los Angeles: UCLA Asian American Studies Center Press.

Lowe, Lisa. 1991. "Heterogeneity, Hybridity, Multiplicity: Marking Asian American Differences." *Diaspora: A Journal of Transnational Studies* 1 (Spring): 24–44.

———. 1996. *Immigrant Acts: On Asian American Cultural Politics.* Durham: Duke University Press.

Lowry, Brian. 2003. "'Banzai'—A Controversy by Fox." *Los Angeles Times* (11 July), E-34.

Maira, Sunaina Marr. 2002. *Desis in the House: Indian American Youth Culture in New York City.* Philadelphia: Temple University Press.

Marchetti, Gina. 1993. *Romance and the "Yellow Peril": Race, Sex, and Discursive Strategies in Hollywood Fiction.* Berkeley: University of California Press.

Marx, Karl. 1987 [1852]. *The 18th Brumaire of Louis Bonaparte.* New York: International.

Mazumdar, Sucheta. 1989. "Race and Racism: South Asians in the United States." Pp. 25–35 in *Frontiers of Asian American Studies: Writing, Research, and Commentary,* ed. Gail Nomura, Russell Endo, Stephen H. Sumida, and Russell C. Leong. Pullman: Washington State University Press.

McAdam, Doug. 1982. *Political Processes and the Development of Black Insurgency, 1930–1970.* Chicago: University of Chicago Press.

McCarthy, John, and Mayer Zald. 1977. "Resource Mobilization and Social Movements: A Partial Theory." *American Journal of Sociology* 82: 1212–1241.

McClain, Tim. 1992. "Passions Stirred over Hotel's Fate: Allegations of Racism Surface in Meeting over Gaslamp Bldg." *San Diego Daily Transcript* (10 February).

McDonnell, Anita. 1989. "American Culture No Shock to Filipino Immigrants." *San Diego Union* (11 December), B-1.

Melendy, Brett H. 1977. *Asians in America: Filipinos, Koreans, and East Indians.* Boston: Twayne.

Mendel, Ed. 1994. "GOP Candidates Try to Mobilize the Asian-American Community." *San Diego Union-Tribune* (20 June), A-3.

Miller, Matt. 1993. "Japanese Portrayal in Movie under Fire." *San Diego Union-Tribune* (30 July), F-1.

Min, Pyong Gap. 1988. *Ethnic Business Enterprise: Korean Small Business in Atlanta.* Staten Island: Centre for Migration Studies.

Mineta, Norman. 1994. "Preface: Beyond 'Black, White, and Other.'" Pp. vii–viii in *Confronting Critical Health Issues of Asian and Pacific Islander Americans,* ed. Nolan W. S. Zane, David T. Takeuchi, and Kathleen N. J. Young. Thousand Oaks, Calif.: Sage.

Minocha, Urmil. 1987. "South Asian Immigrants: Trends and Impacts on the Sending and Receiving Societies." Pp. 347–373 in *Pacific Bridges: The New*

Immigration from Asia and the Pacific Islands, ed. James T. Fawcett and Benjamin V. Carino. Staten Island: Center for Migration Studies.

Morris, Aldon D. 1984. *The Origins of the Civil Rights Movement: Black Communities Organizing for Change*. New York: Free Press.

Mura, David. 1994. "A Shift in Power, a Sea Change in the Arts: Asian American Constructions." Pp. 183–204 in *The State of Asian America: Activism and Resistance in the 1990s*, ed. Karin Aguilar-San Juan. Boston: South End Press.

Nagel, Joane. 1996. *American Indian Renewal: Red Power and the Resurgence of Identity and Culture*. New York: Oxford University Press.

Nagel, Joane, and Susan Olzak. 1982. "Ethnic Mobilization in New and Old States: An Extension of the Competition Model." *Social Problems* 30 (2) (December): 127–143.

Nakanishi, Don T. 1985–1986. "Asian American Politics: An Agenda for Research." *Amerasia* 12 (2): 1–27.

———. 1986. *The UCLA Asian Pacific American Voter Registration Project*. Los Angeles: Asian Pacific American Legal Center.

———. 1991. "The Next Swing Vote? Asian Pacific Americans and California Politics." Pp. 25–54 in *Racial and Ethnic Politics in California*, ed. Byran O. Jackson and Michael B. Preston. Berkeley: Institute of Governmental Studies, University of California.

Nakao, Annie. 1996. "Asians Have Large Share of Poverty: Report Aims to Shatter Stereotype of Rich, Educated 'Model Minority.'" *San Francisco Examiner* (1 October), A-1.

Nelson, Dale C. 1979. "Ethnicity and Socioeconomic Status as Sources of Participation: The Case for Ethnic Political Culture." *American Political Science Review* 73: 1024–1038.

Novarro, Leonard. 1986. "Chinatown Museum Will Preserve Past." *San Diego Tribune* (24 March), C-1.

———. 1993. "Fortune and Fame? Commissioner Susan Lew's Success and Contacts May Help Develop More Trade with Asia." *San Diego Union-Tribune* (21 March), J-1 ff.

Ogawa, Dennis. 1971. *From Japs to Japanese: The Evolution of Japanese-American Stereotypes*. Berkeley: McCutchan.

O'Hare, William P., and Judy C. Felt. 1991. *Asian Americans: America's Fastest Growing Minority Group*. Number 19 (February). Washington, D.C.: Population Reference Bureau.

Okamura, Johnathan Y. 1981. "Situational Ethnicity." *Ethnic and Racial Studies* 4 (4) (October): 425–465.

Okihiro, Gary. 1994. *Margins and Mainstreams: Asians in American History and Culture*. Seattle: University of Washington Press.

———. 2001. *Common Ground: Reimagining American History*. Princeton: Princeton University Press.

Olzak, Susan. 1983. "Contemporary Ethnic Mobilization." *Annual Review of Sociology* 9: 355–374.

Omatsu, Glenn. 1994. "The 'Four Prisons' and the Movement of Liberation: Asian American Activism from the 1960s to the 1990s." Pp. 19–70 in *The State of Asian*

America: Activism and Resistance in the 1990s, ed. Karin Aguilar-San Juan. Boston: South End Press.

Omi, Michael. 1993. "Out of the Melting Pot and into the Fire: Race Relations Policy." Pp. 199–214 in *The State of Asian Pacific America: Policy Issues to the Year 2020.* Los Angeles: LEAP Asian Pacific American Public Policy Institute and UCLA Asian American Studies Center.

Omi, Michael, and Howard Winant. 1986. *Racial Formation in the United States: From the 1960s to the 1980s.* New York: Routledge and Kegan Paul.

Ong, Aihwa. 1999. *Flexible Citizenship: The Cultural Logics of Transnationality.* London: Duke University Press.

Ong, Paul. 1990. "California's Asian Population." In *California's Asian Population: Looking Toward the Year 2000,* ed. Lucie Cheng and Paul Ong. Pacific Rim Emerging Issues Series, #1. Los Angeles: Center for Pacific Rim Studies.

Ong, Paul, and John M. Liu. 1994. "U.S. Immigration Policies and Asian Migration." Pp. 45–73 in *The New Asian Immigration in Los Angeles and Global Restructuring,* ed. Paul Ong, Edna Bonacich, and Lucie Cheng. Philadelphia: Temple University Press.

Ortiz, Isidro D., and Marguerite V. Marin. 1989. "Reaganomics and Latino Organizational Strategies." Pp. 245–270 in *Social and Gender Boundaries in the United States,* ed. Sucheng Chan. Lewiston, Maine: Edwin Mellen Press.

Osajima, Keith. 1988. "Asian Americans as the Model Minority: An Analysis of the Popular Press Image in the 1960s and 1980s." Pp. 165–174 in *Reflections on Shattered Windows: Promises and Prospects for Asian American Studies,* ed. Gary Y. Okihiro, Shirley Hune, Arthur A. Hansen, and John M. Liu. Pullman: Washington State University Press.

Osborne, Lawrence. 1994. "Passage From India: San Diego's Quietly Prosperous Minority." *San Diego Reader* (13 January).

Padilla, Felix. 1985. *Latino Ethnic Consciousness: The Case of Mexican Americans and Puerto Ricans in Chicago.* Notre Dame, Ind.: University of Notre Dame Press.

Parenti, Michael. 1967. "Ethnic Politics and the Persistence of Ethnic Identification." *American Political Science Review* 61 (September): 717–726.

Park, Robert. 1950. *Race and Culture.* New York: Free Press.

Parrillo, Vincent N. 1982. "Asian Americans in American Politics." In *America's Ethnic Politics,* ed. Joseph S. Roucek and Bernard Eisenberg. Westport, Conn.: Greenwood Press.

Petersen, William. 1966. "Success Story, Japanese American Style." *New York Times Magazine* (9 January), 20–21, 33, 36, 38, 40–41, 43.

Peterson, Roberta. 1976. [No title.] *The Pan Asian Bulletin* (November), 2.

Pierce, Emmet. 1991a. "Board Must Figure Out Crazy Quilt." *San Diego Union* (16 September), B-1.

———. 1991b. "Increased Minority Clout Sought via Remap of Mid-City." *San Diego Union* (31 August), B-2.

———. 1991c. "Minority Leaders Spurn 2 Plans for Supervisor Remap." *San Diego Union* (31 July), B-3.

———. 1991d. "Minority-race Supervisorial District Sought." *San Diego Union* (10 August), B-1.

————. 1991e. "Rival Minority Vote Plans Eyed." *San Diego Union* (3 November), B-2.

————. 1991f. "Storm Clouds Appear over County Redistricting Plan." *San Diego Union* (30 September), B-3.

————. 1991g. "Supervisors Sued over Redistricting Plan." *San Diego Union* (17 September), B-1.

Pinderhughes, Dianne M. 1987. *Race and Ethnicity in Chicago Politics: A Reexamination of Pluralist Theory.* Urbana and Chicago: University of Chicago Press.

Piven, Frances Fox, and Richard A. Cloward. 1979. *Poor People's Movements: Why They Succeed, How They Fail.* New York: Vintage Books.

Polner, Murray. 1993. "Asian-Americans Say They Are Treated Like Foreigners." *New York Times* (7 March), B-1.

Ponce, Ninez, and Tessie Guillermo. 1994. "Health Policy Framework." Pp. 397–425 in *Confronting Critical Health Issues of Asian and Pacific Islander Americans,* ed. Nolan W. S. Zane, David T. Takeuchi, and Kathleen N. J. Young. Thousand Oaks, Calif.: Sage.

Portes, Alejandro. 1984. "The Rise of Ethnicity: Determinants of Ethnic Perceptions among Cuban Exiles in Miami." *American Sociological Review* 49 (June): 383–397.

Portes, Alejandro, and Robert D. Manning. 1986. "The Immigrant Enclave: Theory and Empirical Examples." Pp. 47–68 in *Competitive Ethnic Relations,* ed. Susan Olzak and Joane Nagel. New York: Academic Press.

Powell, Ronald W. 1994. "Hacienda Project Is Both a Dream—and a Gamble." *San Diego Union-Tribune* (10 July), B-1.

Reimers, David M. 1985. *Still the Golden Door: The Third World Comes to America.* New York: Columbia University Press.

Richardson, Bruce. 1987. "Himmel TV Show Sparks Complaints." *East San Diego County Daily Californian* (16 January), 3-A.

Rodgers, Terry. 1992a. "City Council Again Rejects Plan for a Center for the Mentally Ill." *San Diego Union-Tribune* (5 March), B-5.

————. 1992b. "New Bids Sought for Hotel." *San Diego Union-Tribune* (19 March), B-8.

Romero, Fernando. 1991. "For Many Here, Power Is Still a Foreign Word." *San Diego Union* (21 November), A-19.

Rouse, Roger. 1991. "Mexican Migration and the Social Space of Postmodernism." *Diaspora* 1 (1) (Spring): 8–23.

Rumbaut, Rubén G. 1995. "Vietnamese, Laotian, and Cambodian Americans." Pp. 232–270 in *Asian Americans: Contemporary Trends and Issues,* ed. Pyong Gap Min. Thousand Oaks, Calif.: Sage.

————. 1996. "A Legacy of War: Refugees from Vietnam, Laos, and Cambodia." Pp. 315–333 in *Origins and Destinies: Immigration, Race, and Ethnicity in America,* ed. Silvia Pedraza and Rubén G. Rumbaut. Belmont, Calif.: Wadsworth.

Saito, Leland T. 1998. *Race and Politics: Asian Americans, Latinos, and Whites in a Los Angeles Suburb.* Urbana: University of Illinois Press.

Saito, Leland T., and John Horton. 1994. "The New Chinese Immigration and the Rise of Asian American Politics in Monterey Park, California." Pp. 233–263 in *The New Asian Immigration in Los Angeles and Global Restructuring,* ed. Paul Ong, Edna Bonacich, and Lucie Cheng. Philadelphia: Temple University Press.

San Diego Area PAC Report. 1976. June.

San Diego Association of Government Information. 1991. *1990 Census Race and Hispanic Origin: Population Change, 1980–1990.* SANDAG, March–April.

San Diego Association of Governments. 1991. "1990 Census Population by Race by Subregional Area." San Diego: SourcePoint.

San Diego Economic Development Corporation. "San Diego County Statistical Abstract 1993." San Diego: San Diego Economic Development Corporation.

Schoenberger, Karl. 1993. "Breathing Life in Southland." *Los Angeles Times* (4 October).

Scott, George M., Jr. 1990. "A Resynthesis of the Primordial and Circumstantial Approaches to Ethnic Group Solidarity: Towards an Explanatory Model." *Ethnic and Racial Studies* 13 (2) (April): 147–171.

Sethi, Rita Chaudhry. 1994. "Smells Like Racism: A Plan for Mobilizing against Anti-Asian Bias." Pp. 235–250 in *The State of Asian America: Activism and Resistance in the 1990s,* ed. Karin Aguilar-San Juan. Boston: South End Press.

Shaw, Gary. 1992. "Chamber Changes the Guard, Adds Some Diversity." *San Diego Daily Transcript* (18 December).

Sheehan, Margot. 1992. "Streets of Asian Dreams." *San Diego Reader* (4 June).

Shinagawa, Larry Hajime, and Michael Jang. 1998. *Atlas of American Diversity.* Walnut Creek, Calif.: AltaMira Press.

Shiroishi, Julie. 1996. "Return to Little Tokyo." *AsianWeek* (10 May).

Showley, Roger. 1980. "Tom Hom's Vision, Chinese Heritage Bring Success." *San Diego Union* (19 August), B-1 ff.

———. 1992. "98% of Arrivals Here Last Year Were Foreigners." *San Diego Union-Tribune* (6 June), A-1 ff.

Silverio, Simeon G., Jr. 1991. "The Need for an Asian American Candidate." One Man's View. *San Diego Asian Journal* (10–16 January), 5.

Smith, Anthony D. 1981. *The Ethnic Revival in the Modern World.* Cambridge: Cambridge University Press.

Smolens, Michael. 1991. "27% Turnout Seen; Would Be 10-Year High in Such a Vote." *San Diego Union* (16 September), B-1 ff.

———. 1992. "Schenk, Filner to Alter Area's Congress Team." *San Diego Union-Tribune* (5 November), B-1 ff.

Sommers, Terri. 2003. "America's Latest Tech Export: Jobs." *San Diego Union-Tribune* (31 August), A-1.

Stanfield, John H., III. 1993. "Methodological Reflections: An Introduction." Pp. 3–15 in *Race and Ethnicity in Research Methods,* ed. John H. Stanfield III and Rutledge M. Dennis. Newbury Park, Calif.: Sage.

Strand, Paul J. 1989. "The Indochinese Refugee Experience: The Case of San Diego." Pp. 105–120 in *Refugees as Immigrants: Cambodians, Laotians, and Vietnamese in America,* ed. David W. Haines. Totowa, N.J.: Rowman and Littlefield.

"Success Story of One Minority Group in U.S." 1966. *U.S. News & World Report.* 26 December, 73–78.

Sue, Stanley. 1993. "The Changing Asian American Population: Mental Health Policy." Pp. 79–93 in *The State of Asian Pacific America: Policy Issues to the Year 2020.* Los Angeles: LEAP Asian Pacific American Public Policy Institute and UCLA Asian American Studies Center.

Sue, Stanley, and Harry H. L. Kitano. 1973. "Stereotypes as a Measure of Success." *Journal of Social Issues* 29 (2): 83–97.

Sue, Stanley, Derald Wing Sue, and David W. Sue. 1975. "Asian Americans as a Minority Group." *American Psychologist* 30: 906–910.

Sung, Betty Lee. 1967. *The Story of the Chinese in America.* New York: Collier Books.

Suttles, Gerald D. 1972. *The Social Construction of Communities.* Chicago: University of Chicago Press.

Suzuki, Bob H. 1977. "Education and the Socialization of Asian Americans: A Revisionist Analysis of the 'Model Minority' Thesis." *Amerasia Journal* 4 (2): 23–51.

Tachibana, Judy. 1986. "California's Asians: Power from a Growing Population." *California Journal* (November): 535–543.

Takagi, Dana Y. 1992. *The Retreat from Race: Asian-American Admissions and Racial Politics.* New Brunswick, N.J.: Rutgers University Press, 1993

Takahashi, Jere. 1997. *Nisei/Sansei: Shifting Japanese Identities and Politics.* Philadelphia: Temple University Press.

Takaki, Ronald. 1989a. *Strangers from a Different Shore: A History of Asian Americans.* New York: Penguin Books.

———. 1989b. "Who Killed Vincent Chin?" Pp. 23–29 in *A Look Beyond the Model Minority Image: Critical Issues in Asian America,* ed. Grace Yun. New York: Minority Rights Group.

Tchen, John Kuo Wei. 1999. *New York before Chinatown: Orientalism and the Shaping of American Culture, 1776–1882.* Baltimore: Johns Hopkins University Press.

Telles, Paul. 1991. "Linda Vista Couple's Stores a Boon to Asians." *San Diego Union* (6 December), B-3.

Thornton, Michael C., and Robert J. Taylor. 1988. "Intergroup Attitudes: Black American Perceptions of Asian Americans." *Ethnic and Racial Studies* 11 (4) (November): 474–488.

Tilly, Charles. 1973. "Do Communities Act?" *Sociological Inquiry* 43 (3–4): 209–240.

———. 1978. *From Mobilization to Revolution.* Cambridge: Harvard University Press.

Tonnies, Ferdinand. 1955 [1887]. *Community and Association.* Translated by C. P. Loomis. London: Routledge and Kegan Paul.

Traitel, Dee Anne, and Joe Cantlupe. 1992. "Disadvantaged or Unduly Privileged?" *San Diego Union-Tribune* (24 May), B-1.

———. 1993. "Consultants' Costs Mount for Studies to Improve Agency." *San Diego Union-Tribune* (4 July), B-4.

Trueba, Henry T., Lilly Cheng, and Kenji Ima. 1993. *Myth or Reality: Adaptive Strategies of Asian Americans in California.* Washington, D.C.: Falmer Press.

Tuan, Mia. 1998. *Forever Foreigners or Honorary Whites? The Asian Ethnic Experience Today.* New Brunswick, N.J.: Rutgers University Press.

Uhlaner, Carole J., Bruce E. Cain, and D. Roderick Kiewiet. 1989. "Political Participation of Ethnic Minorities in the 1980s." *Political Behavior* 11 (3) (September): 195–231.

Union of Pan Asian Communities. 1978. *Understanding the Pan Asian Client: A Handbook for Helping Professionals.* San Diego: Union of Pan Asian Communities.

UPAC Union. 1997. "UPAC's Multi-Cultural Economic Development Project Supports Self-Sufficiency." *Union of Pan Asian Communities Newsletter* 2, no. 1 (February): 5.

U.S. Bureau of Census. 1963a. *Census of Population: 1960*, Vol. 1: *Characteristics of the Population*, Part 6: *California*. Table 79. Washington, D.C.: U.S. Government Printing Office.

———. 1963b. *Census of Population: 1960*, Vol. 1: *General Characteristics of the Population, United States Summary*, Table 28. Washington, D.C.: U.S. Government Printing Office.

———. 1973a. *Census of Population: 1970*, Vol. 1: *Characteristics of the Population*, Part 6: *California*, Table 67. Washington, D.C.: U.S. Government Printing Office.

———. 1973b. *Census of Population: 1970*, Vol. 1: *Characteristics of the Population*, Part 6: *California*, Section 1, Table 81. Washington, D.C.: U.S. Government Printing Office.

———. 1983a. *Census of Population: 1980*, Vol. 1: *General Population Characteristics*, Part 6: *California*, Table 15. Washington, D.C.: U.S. Government Printing Office.

———. 1983b. *Census of Population and Housing: 1980, Census Tracts, San Diego, California*, Table P-18. Washington, D.C.: U.S. Government Printing Office.

———. 1983c. *1980 Census of Population and Housing: Population and Housing Characteristics for Census Tracts, and Block Numbering Areas, San Diego, California, MSA*, Section 2, Table 26. Washington, D.C.: U.S. Government Printing Office.

———. 1990a. *Census of Population and Housing*, Summary Tape File 1C, 040 California.

———. 1990b. *Census, Population by Race and Ethnicity*, Summary Tape File 1A.

———. 1990c. *Census*, Summary Tape File 1A.

———. 1993. *We the Americans: Asians*. U.S. Department of Commerce, Economics and Statistics Administration. (September) Washington D.C.: U.S. Government Printing Office.

U.S. Commission on Civil Rights. 1988. *The Economic Status of Americans of Asian Descent*. Publication No. 95. Washington, D.C.: Clearinghouse.

———. 1992. *Civil Rights Issues Facing Asian Americans in the 1990s*. (February). Washington D.C.: U.S. Government Printing Office.

Vartabedian, Ralph. 1992. "Aerospace Careers in Low Orbit." *Los Angeles Times* (16 November), A-1.

Vigil, James Diego, and Steve Chong Yun. 1990. "Vietnamese Youth Gangs in Southern California." Pp. 146–162 in *Gangs in America*, ed. C. Ronald Huff. Newbury Park, Calif.: Sage.

Võ, Linda Trinh. 1995. "Paths to Empowerment: Panethnic Mobilization in San Diego's Asian American Community." Ph.D. dissertation, University of California, San Diego.

———. 1996. "Asian Immigrants, Asian Americans, and the Politics of Economic Mobilization in San Diego." *Amerasia Journal* 22 (2): 89–108.

———. 2000. "Performing Ethnography in Asian American Communities: Beyond the Insider-versus-Outsider Perspective." Pp. 17–37 in *Cultural Compass: Ethnographic Explorations of Asian America*, ed. Martin F. Manalansan. Philadelphia: Temple University Press.

———. 2001. "The Politics of Social Services for a 'Model Minority': The Union of Pan Asian Communities." Pp. 241–272 in *Asian and Latino Immigrants in a Restructuring Economy: The Metamorphosis of Southern California*, ed. Marta López-Garza and David R. Diaz. Stanford, Calif.: Stanford University Press.

Võ, Linda Trinh, and Rick Bonus. 2002. *Contemporary Asian American Communities: Divergences and Intersections.* Philadelphia: Temple University Press.

Vu, Thanh Thuy. 1995. "A Taste of Vietnam: East of San Diego's Vietnamese Fare." *San Diego Union-Tribune* (10 August), F-1.

Wallerstein, Immanuel. 1974. *The Modern World System.* New York: Academic Press.

Wang, L. Ling-chi. 1991. "The Politics of Ethnic Identity and Empowerment: The Asian American Community Since the 1960s." *Asian American Policy Review* 2 (Spring): 43–56.

Warner, W. Lloyd, and Leo Srole. 1945. *The Social Systems of American Ethnic Groups.* New Haven: Yale University Press.

Waters, Mary C. 1990. *Ethnic Options: Choosing Identities in America.* Berkeley: University of California Press.

Wei, William. 1993. *The Asian American Movement.* Philadelphia: Temple University Press.

Wellman, Barry. 1979. "The Community Question: The Intimate Networks of East Yorkers." *American Journal of Sociology* 84 (5) (March): 1201–1231.

Wilke, Arthur S., and Raj P. Mohan. 1984. "The Politics of Asian Americans: An Assessment." *International Journal of Contemporary Sociology* 21 (3 and 4) (July and October): 29–71.

Wilkens, John. 1991. "Asian Community Transformed: Population in U.S., County Grows Diverse while Doubling." *San Diego Union* (12 June).

Williams, Patricia. 1989. "The Obliging Shell: An Informal Essay on Formal Equal Opportunity." *Michigan Law Review* 87 (August): 2128.

Williams-León, Teresa, and Cynthia L. Nakashima. 2001. *The Sum of Our Parts: Mixed Heritage Asian Americans.* Philadelphia: Temple University Press.

Wilson, William J., and Robert Aponte. 1985. "Urban Poverty." *Annual Review of Sociology* 11: 231–258.

Woldemikael, Tekle M. 1989. *Becoming Black Americans: Haitians and American Institutions in Evanston, Illinois.* New York: AMS Press.

Wolf, Leslie. 1991. "Minority Coalition Draws District Map." *San Diego Tribune* (24 August), B-1.

Wolfinger, Raymond E. 1965. "The Development and Persistence of Ethnic Voting." *American Political Science Review* 59 (December): 896–908.

Wong, Bernard. 1977. "Elites and Ethnic Boundary Maintenance: A Study of the Roles of Elites in Chinatown, New York City. *Urban Anthropology* 6 (1): 1–22.

———. 1982. *Chinatown: Economic Adaptation and Ethnic Identity of the Chinese.* New York: Holt, Rinehart and Winston.

Wong, Kent. 1994. "Building an Asian Pacific Labor Alliance." Pp. 335–349 in *The State of Asian America: Activism and Resistance in the 1990s*, ed. Karin Aguilar-San Juan. Boston: South End Press.

Wong, Sau-ling C. 1995. "Denationalization Reconsidered: Asian American Cultural Criticism at a Theoretical Crossroads." *Amerasia Journal* 21 (1 and 2): 1–28.

Xiang, Shaokun. 1991. "Convoy Street Increasingly Is Where East, West Meet." *San Diego Union-Tribune* (19 May), A-6.

Yancey, William, Eugene Ericksen, and Richard Juliani. 1976. "Emergent Ethnicity: A Review and Reformulation." *American Sociological Review* 41 (June): 391–403.

Yip, Beverley. 1976. "UPAC News." *Pan Asian Bulletin* (December).

Yoon, In-Jin. 1991. "The Changing Significance of Ethnic and Class Resources in Immigrant Businesses: The Case of Korean Immigrant Businesses in Chicago." *International Migration Review* 25 (2): 303–332.

Young, Crawford. 1976. *The Politics of Cultural Pluralism.* Madison: University of Wisconsin Press.

Yu, Elena S. H. 1980. "Filipino Migration and Community Organizations in the United States." *California Sociologist* 3 (2) (Summer): 76–102.

Yuh, Ji-Yeon. 2002. *Beyond the Shadow of Camptown: Korean Military Brides in America.* New York: New York University Press.

Yung, Judy. 1999. *Unbound Voices: A Documentary History of Chinese Women in San Francisco.* Berkeley: University of California Press.

Zald, Mayer, and John McCarthy, eds. 1979. *The Dynamics of Social Movements: Resource Mobilization, Social Control, and Tactics.* Cambridge, Mass.: Winthrop.

Zane, Nolan, and David T. Takeuchi. 1994. "Introduction." Pp. ix–xv in *Confronting Critical Health Issues of Asian and Pacific Islander Americans,* ed. Nolan W. S. Zane, David T. Takeuchi, and Kathleen N. J. Young. Thousand Oaks, Calif.: Sage.

Zhou, Min. 1992. *Chinatown: The Socioeconomic Potential of an Urban Enclave.* Philadelphia: Temple University Press.

Zia, Helen. 2000. *Asian American Dreams: The Emergence of An American People.* New York: Farrar, Straus and Giroux.

Index

Linda Trinh Võ is Associate Professor of Asian American Studies at the University of California, Irvine; she is the co-editor with Rick Bonus of *Contemporary Asian American Communities: Intersections and Divergences* (Temple). She also co-edited, with Marian Sciachitano, *Asian American Women: The "Frontiers" Reader* and, with Gilbert Gonzalez, Raul Fernandez, Vivian Price, and David Smith, *Labor Versus Empire: Race, Gender, and Migration.*

Also in the **Asian American History and Culture** series: